MUSIC, SPACE AND PLACE

Music, Space and Place

Popular Music and Cultural Identity

Edited by
SHEILA WHITELEY, ANDY BENNETT and STAN HAWKINS

ASHGATE

Published by
Ashgate Publishing Limited
Gower House
Croft Road
Aldershot
Hants GU11 3HR
England

Ashgate Publishing Company
Suite 420
101 Cherry Street
Burlington, VT05401-4405
USA

Ashgate website: http://www.ashgate.com

British Library Cataloguing in Publication Data
Music, space and place : popular music and cultural
    identity. – (Ashgate popular and folk music series)
    1. Popular music – History and criticism 2. World music –
    History and criticism 3. Music – Social aspects
    4. Nationalism in music 5. Sound recordings – Production and
    direction
    I. Whiteley, Sheila II. Bennett, Andy, 1963– III. Hawkins,
    Stan
    781.6'3

Library of Congress Cataloging-in-Publication Data
Music, space and place : popular music and cultural identity / edited by Sheila Whiteley,
    Andy Bennett, and Stan Hawkins.
        p. cm. – (Ashgate popular and folk music series)
    Includes bibliographical references and index.
        Contents: Music, space and place – Rap and hip hop : community and cultural identity –
    Musical production/politics of desire.
    ISBN 0-7546-3737-9 (alk. paper)
        1. Popular music–Social aspects. 2. Rap (Music)–Social aspects. 3. Popular
    music–History and criticism. 4. Popular culture. I. Whiteley, Sheila, 1941– II. Bennett,
    Andy, 1963– III. Hawkins, Stan. IV. Series.

ML3470.M896 2004
781.64'09–dc221
                                                                            2003052342
ISBN 0 7546 3737 9

Typeset in Times New Roman by IML Typographers, Birkenhead and printed in Great
Britain by T.J. International Ltd, Padstow

Contents

List of Figures and Music Examples

Figures

Music Examples

List of Contributors

Editors

Sheila Whiteley is Professor of Popular Music at the University of Salford, Greater Manchester, the first such appointment in the UK. She was General Secretary (1999–2001) of the International Association for the Study of Popular Music (IASPM) and is now Publications Officer. Her publications include *The Space Between the Notes: Rock and the Counter Culture* (Routledge, 1992); *Women and Popular Music: Sexuality, Identity and Subjectivity* (Routledge, 1998) and *Too Much Too Young. Popular Music, Age and Gender* (Routledge, 2003). She was editor of *Sexing the Groove: Popular Music and Gender* (Routledge, 1998), and contributed chapters to *Reading Pop: Approaches to Textual Analysis in Popular Music*, ed. Richard Middleton (Oxford University Press, 2000) and *'Every Sound There Is': The Beatles' Revolver and the Transformation of Rock and Roll*, ed. Russell Reising (Ashgate, 2002).

Andy Bennett is Senior Lecturer in Sociology at the University of Surrey. Prior to studying for his Ph.D. at Durham University he spent two years in Germany working as a music teacher with the Frankfurt Rockmobil project. He has published articles on aspects of youth culture, popular music and local identity in a number of journals including *Sociology*, *Sociological Review*, *Media Culture and Society* and *Popular Music*. He is author of *Popular Music and Youth Culture: Music, Identity and Place* (Macmillan, 2000) and *Cultures of Popular Music* (Open University Press, 2001) and co-editor of *Guitar Cultures* (Berg, 2001). Andy is Chair of the UK and Ireland branch of the International Association for the Study of Popular Music (IASPM) and co-convenor of the British Sociological Association Youth Study Group.

Stan Hawkins is Professor of Musicology at the Department of Music and Theatre, Oslo University. He is author of *Settling the Pop Score: Pop Texts and Identity Politics* (Ashgate, 2002). In addition to publishing many articles on popular musicology, he has contributed chapters to *Reading Pop: Approaches to Textual Analysis in Popular Music*, ed. Richard Middleton (Oxford University Press, 2000); *Sexing the Groove: Popular Music and Gender*, ed. Sheila Whiteley (Routledge, 1998); *Analyzing Pop*, ed. Allan Moore (Cambridge University Press, 2003), and *Madonna's Drowned Worlds*, ed. Santiago Fouz-Hernández and Freya Jarman-Ivens (Ashgate, 2004). Hawkins is the Norwegian representative for the IASPM-Nordic branch and editor-in-chief for *Popular Musicology Online*.

Contributors

Kevin Dawe is Lecturer in Ethnomusicology at the University of Leeds. A music and science graduate, he has an M.Sc. in anthropology (London) and a Ph.D. in ethnomusicology (The Queen's University of Belfast). Kevin has recently co-edited the book *Guitar Cultures* (Berg, 2001) and made TV and video programmes with the BBC on the music and cultures of Papua New Guinea and heavy-metal guitar music. He is currently editing a book called *Island Musics* and completing a single-authored book on the music of Crete. He is reviews editor of the *British Journal of Ethnomusicology*.

Sarah Daynes is a sociologist (Ph.D., Ecole des Hautes Etudes en Sciences Sociales, Paris, 2001) whose work concerns the intersections between music, race, diaspora and identity. A post-doctoral scholar at the Center for the Study of Ethnicity and Race, Columbia University, she teaches in the Sociology departments of Columbia University and the New School University / Graduate Faculty. Her Ph.D. dissertation, 'The Rastafari movement: collective memory, music and religion', is being published in France and Great Britain.

Kay Dickinson lectures in Film Studies at King's College, University of London. She is the editor of *Movie Music: The Film Reader* (Routledge, 2003) and *Teen TV: Genre, Consumption and Identity* (bfi, 2004).

Reebee Garofalo, a professor at Umass Boston, is affiliated with the College of Public and Community Service and the American Studies Program. Garofalo's most recent books are *Policing Pop* (Temple, 2003) and *Rockin' Out: Popular Music in the USA* (2nd edn, Prentice-Hall, 2002). He is Treasurer of the International Association for the Study of Popular Music/USA, and an editor for several popular music journals, and is a member of the Editorial Collective of the *Journal of Popular Music Studies*.

Claire Levy is Associate Professor of Music and Head of Music History in the Institute of Art Studies at the Bulgarian Academy of Sciences. She was awarded a senior Fulbright scholarship held at the Department of African-American Studies, Indiana University (1994–95). Publishing extensively (in Bulgarian and English) on a variety of popular music topics in both academic and popular publications, including *Bulgarsko Musikoznanie, Kultura, European Meetings in Ethnomusicology, New Sound and Popular Music*, she is also the author of a number of book chapters, and editor of the text book *Popular Music Today: Practices, Approaches* (Bulgarian Musicology, 2001) and *Music and Cultural Identity* (Bulgarian Musicology 4/2003). Her book *From Blues to Pop* is forthcoming. From 2001 to 2003 she served as General Secretary of IASPM, and from 2003 as Chair of IASPM.

Emma Mayhew has completed a Ph.D. entitled *The Representation of Women in Popular Music: The Feminist, Feminine and Musical Subject*. She has taught

Cultural Studies, Gender Studies, and Sociology at the University of Wollongong from 1992 to 2002. She currently works for the Federal Department of Communications, IT and the Arts. Her research interests include the music press, fan cultures, and the repesentation of the singer's voice in popular culture.

Tony Mitchell is a senior lecturer in Cultural Studies at the University of Technology, Sydney. He was chairperson of IASPM from 1997 to 1999. He is the author of *Popular Music and Local Identity: Pop and Rap in Europe and Oceana* (University of Leicester Press, 1996), and editor of *Global Noise: Rap and Hip Hop Outside the USA* (Wesleyan University Press, 2001). He is currently editing *Liminal Sounds and Images: Transnational Chinese Popular Music* for Hong Kong University Press.

Deborah Pacini Hernandez, Associate Professor of Anthropology at Tufts University, is a specialist on Caribbean and US Latino popular music and culture. She has conducted fieldwork in the Dominican Republic, Colombia, Cuba and among US Latinos, and is the author of *Bachata: A Social History of a Dominican Popular Music* (Temple University Press, 1995), co-editor of *Rockin' Las Americas: Rock Music Cultures in Latin and Latino America* (University of Pittsburgh Press, forthcoming), and numerous articles on Spanish Caribbean and US Latino popular music. She is a member of the editorial collective of the *Journal of Popular Music Studies* (IASPM-USA).

Jacqueline Warwick is Assistant Professor of Music at Dalhousie University, Canada. She completed a Ph.D. in Musicology at UCLA, where she was the founding editor of the online journal *ECHO: a music-centred journal*. Her scholarship addresses popular music and youth culture, particularly the kinds of music that are important to teenage girls. Her publications include articles on the Beatles and on Toronto's bhangra subculture of the mid-90s, and liner notes for a compilation CD of girl group music. Her book *Girl Groups, Girl Culture: Popular Music and Identity in the 1960s* is forthcoming from Routledge.

Lee Watkins has taught class and instrumental music in state schools in Cape Town and worked in community arts organizations. He has written scores for musicals and plays. His graduate studies focused on commercial radio and local music content in Durban, and on hip hop in Cape Town. He completed an M.A. in ethnomusicology at the University of Natal, in Durban, South Africa and is presently reading for a Ph.D. in ethnomusicology at the University of Hong Kong. The subject focuses on Filipino musicians in Hong Kong and south-east Asia.

Peter Webb is a researcher and lecturer in Media Studies at the University of Birmingham based in the Department of Sociology. He has published a variety of work on popular music and the internet. His research interests are in popular music and the music industry, globalization, social theory and the internet. He is also a musician who has released a number of albums and singles under the name of 'Statik Sound System' and is currently with the independent label Remote Records (see www.statiksoundsystem.tv).

Acknowledgements

Claire Levy's chapter, 'Who is the "other" in the Balkans? Local ethnic music as a *different* source of identities in Bulgaria', originally appeared in a slightly different form in *Music, Popular Culture, Identities*, ed. Richard Young, Critical Studies series (General Editor Myriam Diaz-Diocaretz), vol. 19, 215–29, Amsterdam and New York: Editions Rodopi, 2002.

Kay Dickinson's chapter, 'Believe': vocoders, digital female identity and camp', was first published in *Popular Music*, **20**(3), Cambridge University Press, 2001, 333–47.

Tony Mitchell's chapter, 'Doin' damage in my native language', first appeared in a slightly different form in *Popular Music and Society*, **24**(3), Routledge, 2000, pp. 45–58, www3.niu.edu/popms/. He would like to dedicate it to André Prévos, who died in 2002, and who will be remembered particularly for his work on French hip hop.

Every effort has been made to trace all the copyright holders, but some have proved untraceable. The publishers will be pleased to make the necessary arrangements at the first opportunity.

General Editor's Preface

The upheaval that occurred in musicology during the last two decades of the twentieth century has created a new urgency for the study of popular music alongside the development of new critical and theoretical models. A relativistic outlook has replaced the universal perspective of modernism (the international ambitions of the 12-note style); the grand narrative of the evolution and dissolution of tonality has been challenged, and emphasis has shifted to cultural context, reception and subject position. Together, these have conspired to eat away at the status of canonical composers and categories of high and low in music. A need has arisen, also, to recognize and address the emergence of crossovers, mixed and new genres, to engage in debates concerning the vexed problem of what constitutes authenticity in music and to offer a critique of musical practice as the product of free, individual expression.

Popular musicology is now a vital and exciting area of scholarship, and the Ashgate Popular and Folk Music series aims to present the best research in the field. Authors will be concerned with locating musical practices, values and meanings in cultural context, and may draw upon methodologies and theories developed in cultural studies, semiotics, poststructuralism, psychology and sociology. The series will focus on popular musics of the twentieth and twenty-first centuries. It is designed to embrace the world's popular musics from Acid Jazz to Zydeco, whether high tech or low tech, commercial or non-commercial, contemporary or traditional.

Professor Derek B. Scott
Chair of Music
University of Salford, UK

Introduction

For any student of popular music, and I would include here performers, practitioners, and researchers, the biennial conferences of the International Association for the Study of Popular Music (IASPM) highlight the advances made in scholarship over the last decade. Now in its 24th year, the association has nourished its members worldwide with a forum for debate and networking, and is thus the most important source of communication for those with a real interest in contemporary research into popular music. While the international reputation of many of its members is evidenced by the number of books that dominate library shelves and catalogues devoted to popular music, its very real strengths lie equally in recognizing the research abilities of its younger members, those who are working on their Ph.D.s, or who have recently become university lecturers. It is this vitality that continually challenges outdated concepts and which demands a fresh appraisal of debates that seemed, somehow, settled and part of the commonsense of popular music discourse.

It is curious, then, that IASPM has produced no series of books to draw on the expertise of its members and front those debates that characterize the cutting edge of popular music research. We are thus grateful to Professor Derek Scott, General Editor, Ashgate, and himself a member of IASPM, for encouraging us to produce our first book – one that explores contemporary debates on music, space and place; rap and hip hop: community and cultural identity; and musical production and the politics of desire. The editors, Sheila Whiteley (Publications Officer, IASPM), Andy Bennett (Chair of the UK and Ireland Branch of IASPM) and Stan Hawkins (Chair of the Norwegian Branch of IASPM) have been responsible for framing the debates, and the chapters are written by colleagues from IASPM whose research interests largely reflect their own 'space and place' across the globe.

To an extent, their respective chapters point to the authors' position as interpreters of popular music, constructing historical significance for a cultural form that is everyday, ubiquitous, recent and personal. Significant moments are shaped through personal experience as well as by an awareness of broader changes, in the organization of leisure, in commercial production, and in changing media technologies. Not least, the more recent insistence on excavating the 'discursive architecture of the text in search of the ideological interests behind the natural-seeming assumptions which support dominant interpretations'[1] has provided new insights into the socially marginalized – whether defined in terms of race or sexuality – not least in the sonic and heavily gendered space of the studio.

What draws the debates together is the recognition that musical processes take place within a particular space and place, one which is inflected by the imaginative and the sociological, and which is shaped both by specific musical practices and by the pressures and dynamics of political and economic circumstances.

Part 1: Music, Space and Place

This debate is concerned with exploring discourses concerning national culture and identity. As an increasing number of popular music researchers now acknowledge, the search for social and cultural meanings in popular music texts inevitably involves an examination of the urban and rural spaces in which music is experienced on a day-to-day basis. As well as providing the socio-cultural backdrop for distinctive musical practices and innovations, urban and rural spaces also provide the rich experiential settings in which music is consumed. In each case, music becomes a key resource for different cultural groups in terms of the ways in which they make sense of and negotiate the 'everyday' (DeNora, 2000). Both as a creative practice and as a form of consumption, music plays an important role in the narrativization of place, that is, in the way in which people define their relationship to local, everyday surroundings. Such is the story of contemporary western popular musics, such as punk (Shank, 1994), metal (Harris, 2000) and hip hop (Mitchell, 1996; Bennett, 2000), but it is also true of many non-western popular music forms which do not enjoy the same level of global circulation and popularity, notably Papua New Guinean Stringband music (Crowdy, 2001) and Algerian Raï (Schade-Poulson, 1999).

The significance of space and place in relation to the musicalization of everyday life (Shank, 1994) has been dramatically illustrated in relation to issues as varied as the construction of national identity (Bailey, 1994), the development of local cultural industries (Wallis and Malm, 1984), the trans-local cultural exchanges occurring between displaced peoples of the world's many diasporas (Lipsitz, 1994; Slobin,1993) and the gendering of space and place (Cohen, 1991). Moreover, as existing research illustrates, the mapping of the relationship between music, space and place demands an understanding of the ways in which the various component aspects of this relationship overlap and intertwine. Thus, for example, work on local music-making processes has demonstrated how the act of music-making becomes invested with a series of rich discourses concerning the impact of local cultures on collective creativity, even to the point that the actual sounds and timbres produced by musicians in given local settings are deemed to result from their sharing of particular forms of local knowledge and experience. This point is illustrated in Cohen's description of the way in which Liverpool musicians attempted to account for the style and sound of locally produced music:

> Some attributed it to the influence of the Beatles or to the absence of students from the music scene, who tended to favour more 'alternative' types of music. Some suggested that the lack of 'angry' music or music of a more overtly political nature

reflected the escapist tendency of the bands that produced instead music of a 'dreamy' and 'wistful' style. Others pointed out that Merseysiders had understandably grown cynical about politics and therefore avoided writing about it.[2]

Such observations begin to demonstrate how locally produced music interacts with the 'local structure of feeling' (Bennett, 1997). The anecdotes and commentaries offered by individuals in relation to music emanate from a common stock of understandings concerning music's relationship to the local. Such understandings, in turn, crucially inform notions of collective identity and community in given regions and localities. As Lewis observes: 'People look to specific musics as symbolic anchors in regions, as signs of community, belonging, and a shared past.'[3]

Music, then, plays a significant part in the way that individuals author space, musical texts being creatively combined with local knowledges and sensibilities in ways that tell particular stories about the local, and impose collectively defined meanings and significance on space. At the same time, however, it is important to note that such authorings of space produce not one, but a series of competing local narratives (Bennett, 2000). The contested nature of space and place in late modernity has been accentuated in recent decades by increasing global mobility. According to Appadurai, such are the global flows of people and 'culture' that contemporary urban spaces are most effectively conceptualized as ethnoscapes, that is 'landscape[s] of persons who constitute the shifting world in which we live: tourists, immigrants, refugees, exiles, guestworkers and other moving groups and persons.'[4] As Smart observes, the concept of ethnoscapes 'allow[s] us to recognise that our notions of space, place and community have become more complex'.[5] Indeed, during recent decades, urban spaces in different parts of the world have become increasingly contested terrains, the contestation of space and marking out of cultural territory being facilitated considerably through musical innovations and practices. Notable examples of this include local variations in rap music (Mitchell, 1996; Bennett, 2000) and the increasing significance of bhangra and post-bhangra styles for the youth of the south Asian diaspora (Banerji and Baumann, 1990; Huq, 1999; Bennett, 2000).

The significance of music in relation to the articulation of notions of community and collective identity, grounded in physically demarcated urban and rural spaces, is matched by its role in the articulation of symbolic notions of community, which transgress both place and time. This quality of popular music genres and texts has been extensively examined in relation to diasporas, forged communities of displaced people forced to leave their countries and regions of origin through a variety of factors, including slavery or, more recently, economic motivation or the need to escape persecution. The world's major diasporas originate from Africa and the Indian sub-continent, although recent socio-political developments have given rise to new diasporic trends, notably in the 'new Europe', which has seen an increasing number of people from former

Eastern bloc countries seeking new lives in the economically more secure countries of the European Community.

Research on the role of music in relation to notions of collective identity and community among different diaspora populations has revealed much about the connective properties of music. Music, it has been illustrated, can bond displaced peoples, effectively bridging the geographic distance between them and providing a shared a sense of collective identity articulated by a symbolic sense of community. This view is supported by Lipsitz's assertion that music functions 'as a device for building unity between and across immigrant communities.'[6] Lipsitz goes on to suggest that, because of its status 'as a highly visible (and audible) commodity, [music] comes to stand for the specificity of social experience in identifiable communities when it captures the attention, and, even allegiance of people from many different locations.'[7] According to Gilroy, much of music's effectiveness in this respect relates to its utility in the complex synthesizing of locally acquired experiences with commonly shared memories and/or collectively held views, opinions and images relating to traditional culture, heritage and, ultimately, a shared point of origin. The ability of music to [encapsulate and] organize memories and experiences in this way is effectively captured in Gilroy's observations concerning the role and significance of reggae in articulating a shared sense of community among the globally dispersed peoples of the African diaspora. According to Gilroy, the appeal of reggae music

> ... was facilitated by a common fund of urban experiences, by the effect of similar but by no means identical forms of racial segregation, as well as by the memory of slavery, a legacy of Africanisms, and a stock of religious experiences defined by them both.[8]

As the above observation illustrates, part of music's role in facilitating such a collective sense of identity and feeling of community among dispersed diasporic populations is achieved by spiritually transporting them to a common place – an imagined 'spiritual' homeland. This point is made very effectively by Hebdige in his seminal work on the meaning and significance of dub reggae for British youth of African-Caribbean origin during the late 1970s. According to Hebdige, dub provided a powerful means of 'communication with the past, with Jamaica, and hence Africa [that was] considered vital for the maintenance of black identity.'[9]

In this section of the present book, the issue of reggae and its symbolic significance for the African diaspora is further investigated by Daynes. In a critical examination of the work of Gilroy and Hebdige, Daynes argues that descendants of African peoples around the world can no longer be accurately described as existing in a state of diaspora. Rather, she suggests, such peoples are now in 'quasi-diaspora'. The 'Africa' which links globally dispersed African peoples, observes Daynes, exists not as a homogeneous centre but rather as a series of ideal constructs, a utopia which serves as the symbolic anchoring of a shared past and an imagined future. Daynes then goes on to consider the cultural process through which the symbolism or 'idea' of African becomes a cultural frame of reference for peoples of African origin as they negotiate issues of identity, place and belonging in different urban and socio-political contexts around the world. Centrally important here, argues Daynes, is the symbolic transformation of the reggae text. Focusing on the rhetoric of oppression central to reggae lyrics, Daynes suggests that this is re-read in ways that make sense in particular local contexts. Thus, she argues, while reggae music *talks* it is also *talked to*: audiences for reggae actively work on the text, taking the key themes and issues explored in reggae songs and symbolically transforming their meanings in ways that make sense in the context of their own everyday lives.

Inevitably perhaps, the power that can be invested in music as a statement of identity has also led to music becoming an instrument and expression of nationalism. The most obvious example of music being used in this way are national anthems which, in combination with flags and emblems, 'serve as an identification of states and state representatives at political meetings, sports competitions and other international gatherings.'[10] Similarly, music can become a strong marker of national pride and identity during times of war and internal socio-economic crisis.[11] Popular music forms have also become the voice of nationalistic concerns. For example, across western Europe, the punk-derived 'OI' music of far-right skinhead bands is used as a musical platform for neo-Nazism and its radical views on contemporary socio-political issues such as asylum seekers and the use of foreign labour (guestworkers) (Funk-Hennings, 1995). A parallel trend can be seen in contemporary dance music, the hardcore techno-based style known as GABBA attracting similar support from neo-Nazi and other far-right factions.

If certain popular music styles have become aligned with extreme forms of nationalism, others have been criticized for their alleged undermining of the national culture. At its most extreme, such criticism has assumed the form of officially authorized censorship and sanctions against musicians and their supporters. An example of this is provided in Willet's study of the *Swing Jugend* (Swing Kids) of Hitler's Germany who rebelled against Nazi attempts to curb the influence of 'undesirable' foreign cultural influences by listening and dancing to banned American jazz and swing records at illegally organized events. As Willet observes, the *Swing Jugend* met with a hostile reaction from the German authorities, for whom swing music was symptomatic of the alleged ' "degenerate" culture and sleaziness [engendered by] American casualness.'[12] A similar example is seen in Easton's account of the attempts made in the former Soviet Union to officially censor music by the Beatles and other western rock groups. As Easton notes, this was done partly on the pretence of maintaining public order but also in the interests of keeping Soviet society free of any potentially corrupting influences from the west. Rock music 'was seen as a bourgeois, decadent genre that represented the decay in capitalist countries.'[13]

This 'fear of the other' and the cultural élitism that it often incorporates need not necessarily be directed against the threat of corrupting influences from the 'outside'. On the contrary, similar forms of cultural élitism are often used within national and regional populations where tensions exist due to the presence of different ethnic groups and/or religious faiths. Again cultural associations built around music often serve as a barometer for more widely pronounced socio-cultural relationships. A case in point is Regev's study of Israeli rock and *Musica mizrakit*. As Regev points out, these distinctive musical styles embody competing notions of Israeli identity. Those who follow Israeli rock perceive it 'as a sign of being progressive and cosmopolitan' and thus cast it in a discourse of 'national achievement' which has a *bona fide* place in the national culture of Israel.[14] By contrast *Musica mizrakit* is excluded 'from the dominant "Israeliness"' due to the fact that it incorporates elements from traditional Middle Eastern and Mediterranean musics and is performed by native Israelis.[15]

Levy's featured chapter on *chalga*, a Bulgarian popular music that draws on the traditional Gypsy music *chalgija*, provides a further illustration of the way in which music can be exploited as a means of rehearsing ideologues of cultural élitism. As Levy observes in her discussion of contemporary Bulgaria, expressions of cultural élitism are centred around the need to adhere to and copy the cultural conventions of the European west, the latter becoming 'a rose coloured icon of progress.' However, in a similar fashion to the scenario described by Regev in relation to Israel, such ideological work can be achieved only by effectively 'bracketing out' the multi-ethnic historical influences which have forged Bulgaria's past and remain a centrally defining aspect of its present. Thus, as Levy observes, instead of trying to build a future in which elements of east and west – Orient and Europe – can exist simultaneously, cultural élites insist on equating the 'national "self"' with an imagined "pure Bulgarian identity"', this in turn relying on an ideological airbrushing of the 'multi-ethnic traces' of Bulgaria's past. Given its national profile, *chalga* music has become a central target for the rehearsing of such cultural élitist discourse, and, thus, a key site of struggle over the issue of Bulgarian identity. While local Gypsies and Turks embrace *chalga* as an expression of their cultural heritage and place in contemporary Bulgarian society, cultural elites refuse to acknowledge *chalga*. Despite the wide popularity of *chalga* in Bulgaria, dominant cultural discourses continue to refer to the music as 'vulgar' and 'uncivilised' and it has been sidelined by the national Bulgarian media who refuse to feature *chalga* on national TV and radio.

If popular music has become a central means for the framing of discourses concerning national culture and identity, then it carries a similar currency in relation to the construction of gender identities and the gendering of place. In his study of the music scene in Austin, Texas, Shank notes how Cowboy Song, an established music genre in Texas dating back to the 1800s, draws on aspects of folklore tradition and popular discourse in its portrayal of the cowboy as 'a strong masculine hero' whose character traits continue to inform the Texan male identity.[16] Similarly, Evans (2001) notes how the acoustic blues of African-American bluesmen communicated a series of messages concerning the ruggedness and independence of the authentic 'bluesman', a discourse which was often emphasized in the lyrics of African-American blues artists, such as Robert Johnson and John Lee Hooker. Songs by these artists often equate the value or necessity of such character traits with the demands of the physical environment, the hardship and brutality of life in the Deep South of the USA being a continual point of reference in song lyrics.

The role of music in the gendering of place is also the subject of Dawe's chapter in this book on the significance of *lyra* music on the Greek island of Crete. The *lyra*, a three-stringed bowed 'fiddle', was traditionally played by shepherds. In contemporary Cretan society it retains this association with the rugged masculinity of the shepherd, whose deemed affinity with the purity and isolation of Crete's remote mountain and valley areas is said to manifest itself in the music produced on the *lyra*. This, in turn, has a considerable bearing on the way that gender relations are understood and enacted in the context of Cretan society. Indeed, according to Dawe, *lyra* music symbolizes the gendered space of the Cretan mountain village, its musical timbres resonating with the processes of gendered domination and subordination that underpin everyday life in these remote rural communities.

A further way in which music maps onto and becomes a medium for the articulation of particular discourse of space and place relates to its function as a creative resource in the context of urban and regional spaces. As Finnegan notes, at the local level music functions as one of a series of 'pathways' via which individuals negotiate the 'impersonal wilderness of urban life.'[17] Although instances of local music-making vary, both in size and productivity, in every city and many provincial towns around the globe there are identifiable music 'scenes'. Straw suggests that music scenes 'actualize a particular state of relations between various populations and social groups, as these coalesce around specific coalitions of musical style.'[18] However, scene also has a deeply symbolic value, denoting a process through which places become globally acknowledged centres for particular musical styles. This is most typically seen in relation to urban locations, as in Merseybeat or the Nashville sound. However, it may also apply to a whole region, as observed, for example, in the ready associations made between blues music and the 'deep south' of the USA (Evans, 2001).

While a comprehensive literature exists on local music scenes, little attempt has been made to focus on the way in which scenes are conceptually constructed and rationalized by those musicians and artists who belong to them. This is the subject of Webb's chapter on the development of the 'Bristol sound'. The principal city in the south-west of England, Bristol first came to musical prominence during the early 1990s following the international success of several locally-formed groups, most notably Massive Attack, Portishead, and Reprazent. Similarly, Bristol rapper Tricky also received huge critical acclaim and is accredited with the creation of trip hop, a style which many consider synonymous with the Bristol sound. Using extensive data drawn from interviews with Bristol musicians, including members of Massive Attack and Portishead, Webb examines the discursive practices through which these musicians conceptualize the Bristol music scene and their relationship to it. Drawing on Bourdieu's notion of cultural capital and Schutz's concepts of 'relevance' and 'typification', Webb considers how those local musicians with acknowledged cultural capital are able to create dominant discourses of Bristol music through their acquired power to determine and communicate conceptual frameworks of relevance and typification.

Part 2: Rap and Hip Hop: Community and Cultural Identity

The relationship between popular music, space and place assumes a more specific focus in this debate, which explores the ways in which rap has contributed towards a particular sense of identity, fostering indigenous resistance vernaculars for otherwise socially marginalized minorities in Cuba, France, Italy, New Zealand and South Africa. As Tricia Rose wrote in her ground-breaking book *Black Noise: Rap Music and Black Culture in Contemporary America*, 'relationships between black cultural practice, social and economic conditions, technology, sexual and racial politics and the institutional policing of the popular terrain are complex and in constant motion.'[19] Today, this complexity is complicated further by rap's shifting relationship to dominant culture and its impact on the public domain of popular music. Yet, 'such is the form in which a great many people know it and make it part of their lives: as recorded (and only occasionally live), mass-produced and distributed popular culture.'[20]

As a form of popular resistance, rap thus appears contradictory, due largely to its heavily mediated commercial presence worldwide. Artists such as Eminem are afforded a more glaringly public profile; Black American artists continue to be significant and constitute authenticity. However, while many principal trends and styles of global hip hop culture and rap continue to reflect the ongoing influence of its African-American roots, rap music has itself forged specific identities within different societies worldwide. For the politically oppressed, it has retained its original focus, operating as a form of cultural resistance, challenging oppressive regimes, and thus serving to establish and contribute towards the formation of ethnic and geographic identities, while carving out 'spaces of freedom'.

It is within this context that hip hop reflects its African-American precedents where rap, as originating in rhythmic patois interlocked with a continuous breakbeat, both emerged from, and fused with hip hop culture, itself a response to the impoverished conditions experienced by poor Blacks and Hispanics after the creation of the Cross-Bronx Express in the late 1960s and early 1970s, and the demolishing of 60,000 homes in predominantly marginalized ethnic communities. Because of this, it is recognized that hip hop is, in effect, a resistant lifestyle that includes not simply rap, but also sound, break dancing, graffiti, attitude and language (including patois). Frustrations and tensions can thus be channelled into active expression, empowering the hip hop community and facilitating a 'coming to voice'[21] – a term used to represent an act of resistance, finding a voice that can be heard from the margins where groups and individuals are removed from power. Hip hop is about being a spokesperson and representative for those without power, a political voice, with rap providing a focus for symbolic resistance and symbolic power for alienated minorities, such as those in Cuba and South Africa, where Public Enemy's 'Fight the Power' retains the sense of ethnic-based action which infuses their own struggle for recognition.

> Got to give us what we want
> Gotta give us what we need
> Our freedom of speech is freedom or death
> We got to fight the powers that be
> Let me hear you say
> Fight the power.

It is also the case that hip hop's philosophy embodies the need not only to fight the power, but also to reclaim power, and the power to acquire admission to public space remains a main focus of rap and Black cultural expression where music is the central voice rather than the individual. Above all, rap is about history, symbols or statements of realism, marginalization and social situations, geography, youth and ethnicity. Geography, as Krims points out, is significant in creating its own separate coding of authenticity: 'the rhythm, instrumentation and vocal style may be accepted in one genre but not in another.'[22] This in turn relates to the concept of community and its relationship to cultural identity, the expression of, for example, racial tension and the sense of confusion surrounding national identity. Thus, the sense of rebellion that characterized the early years of American hip hop remains important for many, providing a specific sense of identity for other alienated minorities. However, as Gates[23] observes, 'Identities are things we make up, but not just out of any old things … Identities are the names we give to the different ways we are positioned by, and position ourselves in, the narratives of the past.'

Rap, then, can be considered as both an embedded African-American culture and a mobile culture which has become re-rooted in diverse locations, so retaining a double identity as both a vernacular (see Rose, 1994; Potter, 1995; Keyes, 1996) and a mass culture that continues to imply 'the pliability of capital and the extent to which a politically engaged culture such as hip hop can most easily be put to the service of dominant ideologies'.[24] However, while rap has been assimilated into a diversity of musical genres, so generating a commercial viability worldwide, hip hop itself (sound, rhythm, poetics, dress, attitude) remains embedded within cultures that are largely depoliticized and/or alienated from the dominant culture, so providing a sense of personal and group empowerment.

It is this distinction that informs the writings on rap and hip hop by Tony Mitchell, Lee Watkins, Deborah Pacini Hernandez and Reebee Garofalo. Not least, all four writers identify language as significant. As Forman argues, 'The transformation of silence into language and action involves also defining a cultural standpoint and articulating this perspective not only as speech art but speech leading to action, change, and liberation.'[25] The active use of language thus allows individuals to present themselves in and from a cultural standpoint, and reinforcing this standpoint can itself facilitate change. The contributors here are therefore principally concerned with hip hop culture, underground, and 'authentic' or 'resistant' scenes, examining the ways in which rap music has been deployed within a local and often racially-oppressive context. Rap here has become central to identity formation within a context of social resistance, as part of a process of collective self-definition. It is this association of rap music with marginalized and aggrieved groups that informs the following chapters. The debate is partly concerned with the extent to which, from its origins as an African-American vernacular practice (Rose, 1994), rap has been transformed into a range of relocalized cultural inflections. This also takes into account the ways in which rap's sounds figure in identities and how it has become relocalized as an inscribed moral geography (Kong, 1995).

It is also evident that locally inflected hip hop scenes and rap music have sometimes been in place for well over a decade and are continuing to develop. The problems involved here concern how rap music works socially, what it is and what it does, not least because of the ways in which racial dynamics are fronted in different contexts, and hence the cultural value of rap across the countries under discussion – France, Italy, New Zealand, South Africa, Cuba. The debate situates rap music within distinctive cultural and social realities, and explores its placement in different societies related to the 'design' of the music, its role in forming cultural identities and, indeed, how identity can be formed at the level of the song through word, sound and image. The various geographic locations are foregrounded in the communal activity at the level of resistance politics, and the contributors show how the musical poetics change according to the local requirements, interacting with race, language and musical style while mediating the specifics of locality. This, in turn, opens out the debates surrounding the ways in which the global and the local intersect in the sounds of rap music in vastly separated parts of the globe. What emerges are glimpses of the ways in which locality and place intersect in the developing history of rap and hip hop.

Deborah Pacini Hernandez and Reebee Garofalo's chapter, 'The emergence of *rap Cubano*: an historical perspective', picks up on many of the points raised above, not least questions concerning globalization. Cuba, as one of the few surviving socialist societies, provides a particularly interesting case study in that it offers a unique insight into how 'dissent' is imagined and articulated 'within the context of a socially and ideologically progressive yet economically and politically besieged, tightly controlled revolutionary society.' As Pacini

Hernandez and Garofalo point out, the rap phenomenon in Cuba demands a more nuanced analysis of facile homologies such as rap, oppression and social protest, not least because rap's clear and unambiguous origins in the United States – the country most responsible for Cuba's economic hardships – are reconciled with Cuban rappers' strong sense of national identity.

Clearly race is significant within this context. As the authors observe, Cuban rappers are dark-skinned and would be identified as Black in the United States. As such, they relate to rap as a particular creation of the oppressed African-American minority in the USA. The focus on racism, however, presents problems. Within the context of a country where the official discourse asserts racism was dismantled by the Revolution, drawing attention to racial difference can be interpreted as a threat to the integrity and unity of Cuban national identity – not least when the country remains under political and economic siege. It thus becomes apparent that young Cuban rappers' conceptions of racial identity and its relationship to their own musical practices can be expected to be quite different from that of their African-American counterparts.

Pacini Hernandez and Garofalo's essay addresses the circulation and meaning of both US rap within Cuba and *rap Cubano*. Their research is based primarily on the city of Havana, rap's most important nexus of activity. They begin with a discussion of the broader historical context of other styles of US popular music – particularly rock – that have circulated within Cuba for decades. As they observe, the establishment of Cuba as a Communist state, resulted in the blockade of all music from the USA – but especially rock. Although the 1970s reflected a more tolerant attitude, the primary mechanisms for the diffusion of US music were via informal networks rather than Cuba's official cultural apparatus or the organized efforts of the international music industry and rap, like rock before it, became an underground (i.e. marginal, not forbidden) phenomenon. The dissolution of the Soviet Union produced a further crisis in Cuba, not least in terms of access to the global market economy and international investment. The worsening economic situation set in motion profound transformations and, for the younger generation, improved access to forms of popular music that had previously conflicted with the goals of the Revolution. Havana's rock fans and bands who had been active, if underground, since the 1960s benefited most from the changes and moved quickly into the newly accessible public spaces. Rap became popular among Habaneros of all colours and was seen as a youthful rather than racial phenomenon. However, as Pacini Hernandez and Garofalo observe, the development of Havana's rap scene has had clear and significant racial dimensions, and these are explored in their discussion of *bonces*, *la moña* and the making of a Cuban rap community.

A principal focus of their ethnographic study concerns DJ Adalberto, an enterprising rap entrepreneur and would-be DJ who obtained a public space for hip hop gatherings where young Habaneros could listen to, dance to, and talk about rap; referred to informally as *el local de la Moña* (the *moña* venue), rap enthusiasts became known as *moñeros*. (In Cuba, *moña* is a generic term for rap and is also the generic Cuban street term for Black musics, particularly those from the USA, including older African-American styles such as soul or funk which had long been popular in Cuba.) All the venues for La Moña have been in old Havana, a traditionally Black and infrastructurally poor neighbourhood, whose central location has made it accessible for *moñeros* across the City.

While Havana's rap scene developed initially around imported recordings, the first Festival de Rap Cubano offered young would-be rappers a socially-sanctioned public venue for displaying their talents, thereby stimulating the creation of 'professional' groups. The festival took place in Alamar, a huge housing project in East Havana constructed by workers' brigades after the Revolution to house Havana's poorest families, most of whom were Black. Organized by Rodolfo Rensoli, a university-trained cultural worker, the festival attracted hundreds of young *moñeros* from all over the city who, for the first time, got to see and hear rap in their language, with texts reflecting local realities. The 1995 Alamar festival was seen as a crystallizing moment in Cuban rap and has stimulated rap festivals and concerts in other parts of Havana, as well as encouraging youngsters of all colours to form rap groups of their own. It has also attracted attention from the international rap community, including US rappers and journalists. Even so, in January 1999, the Cuban label EGREM remained uninterested in Cuban rap and fewer than a handful of Cuban rap groups had managed to obtain a contract either with one of Cuba's jointly owned labels, or other foreign labels willing to invest in production costs.

As the writers observe, 'Given such trying conditions [in a country with such an extraordinarily rich musical culture of its own], what could have accounted for rap's appeal to young *moñeros*?' The answer, it seems, lies in rap's energetic, compelling beats, the rhythmic cadence of its lyrics, and hip hop style – its assertiveness. There was also the belief that rap lyrics should be socially relevant and constructive, that they should communicate, and Cuban rappers have commented on a variety of issues, from the particularities of daily life in Cuba to broader social issues such as AIDS, and to such globally-relevant themes as the destructiveness of war. Rap's connections to the street (defined as a space unmediated by outside influences such as the state cultural apparatus and foreign commercial interests) are also significant, and the themes of Havana rappers also include personal boasting and the pleasures of partying. While Cuban *temas sociales* are often sophisticated rhymes that incorporate an analysis and critique of complex issues, they are not oppositional in the sense that the term is understood in the USA. Cuban rappers are aware that their government has provided free education and healthcare, and a more equitable distribution of resources, and most rappers interviewed by Hernandez and Garofalo were intensely proud of their country and of its accomplishments. They constituted, in effect, a loyal opposition; American rappers have a very different relationship to their government and the police, the 'enemy' characteristic of contemporary gangsta rap. There is in Cuba, then, a sense of optimism that relates more to the street culture of the 1970s South Bronx (Rose, 1994).

It is also interesting to read of Havana's attitude towards women and women rappers. Here, despite the machismo stance of male Cubans, women are valued. Nor do Cuban rappers perceive themselves as victims of institutional racism, which they interpret as vestiges of past structures carried over from pre-Revolutionary times. However, as Pacini Hernandez and Garofalo observe, 'as Cuba becomes less isolated and Cuban rap finds a voice on the international stage, it is inevitable that Cuban conceptions of identity and racial unity will be put to the test.' Significantly, older, more cosmopolitan individuals are encouraging Havana's young rappers not only musically, but also intellectually, developing their skills in social analysis and criticism, particularly in terms of understanding the importance of race.

The importance of race is central to Tony Mitchell's chapter, 'Doin' damage in my native language: the use of "resistance vernaculars" in hip hop in Europe and Aotearoa/New Zealand'. He explores the use of languages other than English in rap music as examples of 'resistance vernaculars' which re-territorialize not only major Anglophone rules of intelligibility but also those of other 'standard' languages, such as French and Italian. Starting with an example from Zimbabwe Legit, he reflects on the linguistic damage directed against the language of the colonizers. The use of such English expressions as 'Power to the People' and 'The ghettos of Soweto', for example, locates rap within the country of origin for the Anglophone listener, so foregrounding what has been termed 'nation conscious rap', while the use of Ndbele as a form of concrete poetry, and Shona, the more 'standard' language of Zimbabwe, and the group's own native dialect, inform the art of rhyming. Multilingual dexterity thus enables rappers to address two major global linguistic groups in the African diaspora while communicating more broadly to the USA and the world at large, so providing specific insights into Deleuze's notion of the rhizomic, diasporic flow of rap music outside the USA and the formation of hybrid 'global' subcultures. This is discussed further with reference to the Swiss rap group, Silent Majority, who rap in a mixture of English, Jamaican patois, French, Spanish and Swahili.

Mitchell also draws attention to the variety of ethnic origins among French rappers and the range of inflections – from hardcore rap to reggae and ragamuffin – that distinguish it from US rap and which provide analogies with British and Italian hip hop. Here, Afrika Bambaataa's Zulu Nation provided one source of inspiration but, for example, the concept of Afrocentrism has been replaced by both a 'Pharaonic' ideology which adapts the Africa of Ancient Egypt into a religious symbology, and the mythologizing of Marseilles, a marginalized city with a high non-European immigrant population. The rich combination of languages – English, Arabic, gypsy expressions, words from African dialects and reverse slang – provides a particular insight into 'resistance vernacular', which is developed in Mitchell's discussion of dialect and local expression in Italian rap. Here, rapping in the dialect of, for example, Messina, provides a way of maintaining contact with the poor and dispossessed who have difficulty in expressing themselves in 'standard' Italian and where the concept of roots indicates a need to establish an exclusively linguistic relationship to one's region. Mitchell ends with a discussion of Maori rappers who adopted the trappings of hip hop culture and explored its affinities with indigenous Maori musical and rhetorical forms. He finds that the African-American rhetoric of hip hop has been replaced by Maori and Polynesian cultural expressions, resulting in a further syncretization of an already syncretic form.

As Mitchell observes, the examples demonstrate the vastly diverse linguistic, political and social dynamics that have developed from Zimbabwe to Greenland to Aotearoa. They demonstrate that the rhizomic globalization of rap has involved modalities of indigenization and syncretism which go far beyond a simple appropriation of a US or African-American musical and cultural idiom. In effect, the global indigenization of rap and hip hop has become a highly adaptable and malleable vehicle for the expression of indigenous resistance vernaculars, their local politics and 'moral geographies' in many different parts of the world.

The final chapter, 'Rapp'in' the Cape: style and memory, power in community', provides a detailed analysis of the emergence of hip hop and its resistance to the apartheid regime of South Africa. As Lee Watkins observes, hip hop remains at the forefront of raising the concerns of those who feel excluded from various domains of power. The focus of his essay is on hip hop and rap among coloured youths in Cape Town, where it first emerged nearly twenty years ago and where, despite the changes in South Africa, there has been no sense of compromise among rappers who continue to strive towards creating a community in which the whole is deemed as important as the individual. In effect, the ideological and performative aspects of hip hop – rap, break-dance and spray-painting – have changed the way in which the disenfranchised feel both about themselves and about the world in which they live; in doing so, they have achieved and maintained a sense of community, albeit on the fringes of society.

Watkins' introduction examines current research into popular music on the South Cape which, he argues, falls short of the wide variety of music scenes that are available for research. As he observes, future research needs to focus on the issues of hip hop in relation to gender, the black diaspora, globalization, the music industry in South Africa, socio-linguistics, the influence of Gangsta-rap on young adults on the Cape Flats and, with greater seriousness, the music style itself. His own discussion is informed by the experiences of three crews and a number of individuals who have been involved in hip hop since its inception: Prophets of Da City (POC), Black Noise, and members of Grave Diggers Productions (GDP). As he observes, most of the hip-hoppers live on the Cape Flats, a desolate area situated far from the city centre, home to the impoverished and unemployed masses of Cape Town, and notorious for its extremely high incidence of violent crimes. The experience of those living in District Six has led to a process of racial identification with oppressed minorities in the USA, and the development of hip hop draws on the demographic history of the Western Cape, the racial policies instituted under British Colonialism, and apartheid. In common with their peers in the rest of the world, hip-hoppers have metamorphosed into global consumers. There is no imposed cultural dominance, however; instead, there is a continual process of negotiation and concensus, which achives participation inside the different spheres of public space and social life. Here, the performative aspects of hip hop and resistance politics have been significant, and hip-hoppers in Cape Town have modelled themselves on organizations in the USA related to hip hop, including the Universal Zulu Hip Hop Nation and the Nation of Islam, so motivating those hip-hoppers who had already forged alliances within the Black Consciousness movement of South Africa. The commitment that rappers displayed in the political arena under apartheid continues, but now criticism is voiced with a view to reconstructing South African society. Today, Cape Town's hip-hoppers are simultaneously engaged in the struggle between resistance and co-optation. Black Noise, for example, spearheads campaigns focused on the AIDS epidemic, crime and unemployment, and there is a new relationship with the outside, one of greater visibility and accessibility – especially to white Afrikaner audiences. For the oppressed youths on the Cape Flats, hip hop and rap have provided an alternative space in which they can develop their own strength, with a view to reclaiming human dignity.

Language, again, remains central to the particular experience of hip hop within Cape Town. As Watkins observes, 'it should be noted that hip-hoppers are not only structured in and through language but that acculturation in language, initiated a few hundred years ago, has resulted in and continues to generate a sense of the past meeting the present, with the inside in dialogue with the outside.' The hip hop language popular in Cape Town is a blend of Afrikaans with other codes such as prison and gangster languages. Modern Cape Afrikaans is traceable to the Creole Dutch formerly spoken in the Western Cape, but contact between settlers and indigenous people such as the Khoi and San provided the grounds for linguistic exchange. Today Afrikaans is a language with rich nuances inspired by location and social status, and the final part of Watkins' essay, explores the lyrics of songs which codify multiple forms of representations, making it difficult for the outsider, even some Afrikaans speakers, to understand, especially when this is combined with ebonics, the ghetto-inspired hip hop language from the USA. Like language itself, rap music has become ideologically loaded because its representational nature legitimizes certain forms of knowledge and certain forms of power through its improvisatory gestures.

The concept of community and cultural identity thus remains integral to the development of hip hop and rap. Not least, the initial appropriation of American hip hop has been superseded by forms of expression that draw on personal and group histories, geography and ideology that resonate with the formation of ethnic and geographic identities. Hip hop culture is, above all, resistant – in the sense of carving out those 'spaces of freedom' which are integral to personal and group consciousness – and, as these localized studies show, marginalized groups continue to explore and claim a collective self-definition within a distinctive musical utterance that connects to the social processes of cultural identity.

Part 3: Musical Production and the Politics of Desire

This debate returns the reader to the way in which music and musical production maps onto and becomes a medium for the articulation of a particular discourse of space and place. Given that pop music is bound up in technology, it seems pertinent to explore a number of questions relating to the identification of authorial presence through production. Indeed, the masculine/feminine binarism continues to underpin much of the discourse surrounding the creative role of the producer in a predominantly male domain. Artistic ideals of originality and romanticism form part of the technological advances in musical production, not least in commercial pop music where sets of values surrounding taste promulgate notions of authenticity. Notably, the centricity of the recording studio in the whole compositional process of pop music blurs the distinction between artist and producer. Control over sound in the studio environment, as Steve Jones (1992) has argued, signifies a site of political power in terms of decision-making. Moreover, the question of performance is often separated from the technological impartiality of the male producer; a positioning that reinforces the gendered binarism of producer/performer.

In all four chapters of this section, the accountability of the producer is measured alongside critiques of women artists within the Anglo-American music industry. The focus falls predominantly on the reference to a catalogue of female artists, whose success has often been attributed to their collaborative associations with male producers/musicians: Alanis Morissette, Madonna, Cher, Björk, Kylie Minogue, Sinéad O'Connor, Courtney Love, Kate Bush, Tori Amos, Carole King, Dusty Springfield, Marianne Faithful, Petula Clarke, Lulu, Victoria Beckham, P.J. Harvey, Laurie Anderson, Annie Lennox. Reponses by each of the authors to performance practices and production processes thus render ideas that are commonly attributed to the constitutive role of the single *auteur*. Implicit in all four debates, albeit from different perspectives, is a Barthesian approach to the subject and their prestige through normalization. This helps situate the critical approaches and textual analyses within the domain of the commercially driven Anglo-American music industry.

An exploration of creativity and authorship is mapped against the patriarchal assumptions that surround the status of the producer, and builds on many of the debates addressed in Sheila Whiteley's *Women and Popular Music* (2000). Emma Mayhew's chapter considers the authorial status of the producer alongside the history and role of women in contemporary popular music. Backed up by examples of female artists, we learn how the male-dominated role of the producer can both authenticate and undermine the creative subjectivity of the artist in question. For the collaborative approach to musical production still frames the long-standing discourse of male genius and rationality. This point is borne out by an examination of Morissette's songwriting partner and producer Glen Ballard. Likewise, in considering Kate Bush's position as producer and music technology expert, Mayhew investigates how Bush's skills as 'creative artist' are measured by fans and the media. Importantly, fans play a major role in positioning the artistic subject, lending credibility to their significance as producers. Here there is a need to measure why different responses by fans to the sound of Tori Amos, for example, demonstrate that the sound of the recording is often separated from the musical expression. Similarly, the issue of creative power relations is a concern for fans in their discussion of Sinéad O'Connor's producers and their role in the recording process. Certainly, the collaborative relations in the studio environment spill into the domain of journalism, fan response, and album reviews.

What emerges in this essay is a need to scrutinize the grand narratives of rock history, which are masterminded by male writers, managers, and producers. To this end, Mayhew's debate draws in the recent re-appropriation of girlhood in the practices of riot grrrl and the provocative term of 'girls' in this context, not least through the inscriptions of jargon in album reviews. Performers such as L7 and even Björk are unable to escape the suspect gaze of males bent on praising and cursing their creative skills at the same time. Mayhew's account concludes that the gender divisions in the creative labours of the producer are about the patriarchal positioning of the producer. This, indeed, illustrates what is still at the core of institutional practices and discourses of creativity. Thus, the ongoing struggles linked to evaluating musical creativity are primarily rooted in the culture/nature dichotomies that emphasize the inequalities which continue to characterize the popular music industry.

A main trajectory in Mayhew's essay signals a move in popular music scholarship towards a more critical evaluation of technology and production. The two middle chapters of Part 3, by Kay Dickinson and Stan Hawkins, extend many of these debates by a close examination of the interpretation of two colossal top hits, respectively, Cher's 'Believe' from 1998, and Madonna's 'Music' from 2000. In both these songs the vocoder is appropriated by both female singers and male producers, providing an opportunity to redefine this gimmicky piece of technology. Notably, there are two male producers behind the processing of these songs: Mark Taylor, the remixer of 'Believe', and Mirwais Ahmadzï, the co-producer of 'Music'. In critical detail, Dickinson sets out to explore the effects of the manipulated voice through a deconstruction of technology and the positioning of the bodily self. Picking up on one of Mayhew's main points, she argues the issue of artistic authenticity through the visceral resonances of the voice and the consequences this has in the political arena of popular music discourse.

Built into this discourse, the concept of cyber identity seems an appropriate platform for investigating the links between sound, musicians, and machines.

Cyber theorists, such as Haraway (1991) and Plant (1997), have examined the question of female control through new technological interactions. Their arguments are introduced in a bid to discover more about the vocoder's flexible cyber-potential. Through an intertextual reading of 'Believe', it is evident how the song embraces a wealth of technologies and genres that evoke a sense of multiplicity (yet incoherence) in the quality of Cher's vocal style. In fact, Cher's constructed identity is so processed through the sound production that it effortlessly fuels the central feminist concerns of cosmetic reconstruction and aesthetic perceptions. However, Cher also warrants serious consideration for what she has signified in terms of representational politics in pop. A critical evaluation of the normalizing power of female construction follows as Dickinson tackles this through a discussion of fetishization which is located in the technological control found in musical production. Although Cher's construction is understandably precarious, at least in terms of the politics and economics of body modification, she does gain currency through a wide audience, not least a large gay following. The full signification of this can be explored through the pervasive discourse of camp. Accordingly, Dickinson's reading of 'Believe' culminates in a political focus on the strategies of camp. As with other camp objects, the vocoder is implicated in the female body, and notwithstanding its 'fakeness', it functions as a formidable instrument of desire. Most of all, the recent popularity of this instrument prompts us to rethink the ever changing representational practices of femininity and homosexuality in commercial pop music, especially with respect to the continual struggles of males for dominance in the recording studio over female artists.

The textual analysis of Cher's 'Believe' raises a wealth of issues linked to personal identity, an issue that surfaces in all chapters in this section. Discussing the production processes in music involves not just considering the realization of the compositional material itself, but also the political positioning of the *author* in the form of the producer, the performer, the engineer or the musician. Technology, indisputably, affects the ways in which we aurally perceive personalities through musical expression. Simon Frith suggests that how performers come across in recordings is all about 'a perception of intimacy',[26] something that ultimately expresses the differences in personality and, hence, preferences in musical taste. Moreover, the ideology of studio production concerns the blurring of technician and musician in the decision-making intentions that characterize the creative process through all the personalities involved. Once again, we return to the tensions that arise from role allocations in the specific space of the recording studio environment, which are often about the privileging of gendered identity.

While on the one hand Madonna might have reversed many of the patriarchal gender roles in the workplace, on the other hand she still predominantly draws in males for sound engineering, production and instrumental performance. Acknowledgement of her creative input by fans, journalists and music critics is invariably afforded to Madonna *and* her teams of musicians, engineers and producers. Stan Hawkins' chapter provides a reading of the recorded score 'Music' in an attempt to debate notions of creativity and pleasure. In this essay, he explores the links between performativity and production within a critical musicological framework. At one level, the production techniques employed in 'Music' are attached to sites of stylistic preference which reaffirm the notions of community that have to do with the enjoyment of commercial pop. Like Cher's 'Believe', Madonna's 'Music' mediates a camp sensibility through a wealth of playful edits and sound processes. Close inspection of some of the techniques employed by Mirwais Ahmadzï and Madonna reveal a digital soundscape that is refreshingly experimental. At the same time, it is powerfully political. In this track, sweeps of electronic gestures and fancy edits disclose a specific aesthetic that denotes a theatricalization of technology. By reference to two specific musical thematic moments in the track that mutate into one idea, the signification of seductiveness alongside notions of *constructed naturalness* is considered within the context of pleasure, fun and enjoyment.

In many ways, 'Music' sets up an imaginary field in which sonic details are extravagantly realized and flaunted. Importantly, Madonna elects to use uncomplicated musical structures: simple tunes, harmonic progressions, and rhythmic riffs. It would seem that the compositional processing of these sounds through elaborate production techniques functions to enhance the simplest musical idea with tremendous audio stimulation. This results in a fetishistic quality that revels in the sheer hyper-artificiality of the mix. The mix therefore becomes a platform for an ideal performance, and offers up a sonic space for the intimacy of Madonna's expression. 'Music' is engineered and edited in a way that strives for perfection through the brilliance of the audio-dynamics of all the countless layers. In this track, the recording-as-performance confirms artistic authority in the voice of the machine. As in Cher's 'Believe', Madonna's voice undergoes a type of morphing through vocoder and filter effects. Such production techniques open up the field for interpreting the implications of vocal embodiment through computerized editing. At the same time, these production techniques bring to the fore the issue of female performativity and all its changes within the domain of automatism and control. Moreover, it could be argued that identity representation through sonic production affects the whole course of our listening experience and the sense of pleasure we derive from the artist.

Theorizing the wider signification of recording technology provides one means to problematize the formative power of gender politics in pop and its historical contingency. This argument can be approached by confronting the significance of the terms 'producer' and 'production'. In Jacqueline Warwick's chapter on production and authorship in girl group music, the employment of such nomenclature is problematized through an intertextual discourse that draws on Marxist feminist analysis, where we learn that the role of singers can swiftly be marginalized to the advantage of instrumentalists and producers who are in control of technology.

In her consideration of girl groups, Warwick makes the crucial point that their songs are solely products of the recording studio. Situated polemically to recording techniques commonly found in rock music, their songs aspire to the aesthetics of a live concert performance. Yet, the high dependency on studio production techniques seems to defy any possibility of an authentic live performance; a point that is implicit in Dickinson's and Hawkins' chapters.

If one tracks the course of female figures with recording careers, the artist Carole King stands out as one of the most important; her famous song from 1960, 'Will You Still Love Me Tomorrow', has had a major influence on pop music. Warwick's contextualization of this song provides an insightful reading of the many layers of mediation that produce the text through discursive relations. Crucially, what emanates from this study is a critique of musical performance and how it is constituted in the intricate politics of recording sessions.

Ellie Greenwich's legendary song from 1964, 'Leader of the Pack', recorded with the group the ShangriLas, provides a compelling model for inspecting the interpersonal sphere of collaboration between women and their husbands or male co-writers. Issues of negotiation, compromise and manipulation characterize the countless narratives that surround the rise and fall of female artists and girl groups. In a detailed investigation of Phil Spector, whose influence on the girl group records cannot be overestimated, a number of issues relating to this megalomaniac producer are uncovered. Through an extraordinarily innovative production style, we learn how the Spector 'wall of sound' on Spector records often obscured the identities of the groups and singers who sang and performed the material. In her analysis of the Ronettes, Warwick highlights the role of the male producer at work, not least through his relationship with his wife, Ronnie Spector, in the song 'Be My Baby'. The musical expression of desire and sexual confidence found in this hit, considered provocative for its time not least through the recording itself, made females more audible and visible in the pop industry. There was (and still is), however, a price for this, as the hierarchy which sets male producers above singers still persists. Turning to feminist standpoint theory, which is grounded in Hegel's work, Warwick unearths the problematics of evaluation and authenticity. Reacting against rock's ideology of the authentic and the assumption of male experience as the norm, she suggests a site of negotiation that is bi-cultural, where girls, in accepting boy culture and inventing ways to find themselves, may indeed devise new forms of empowerment and individualism. Clearly, the struggles within girl music and girl culture are integral to understanding the complex formations and trends of youth culture, especially within the domain of production and recording technology.

Foremost in the essays in this section is an insistence for the interpretation and criticism of production in popular music. As well as working with existing theories and methods, all four authors have felt compelled to devise approaches that identify the intricacies and structures of the recording industry and the roles of producers and songwriters. A central concern is that the issue of authorship and creativity needs to be tackled alongside matters relating to the production of musical texts themselves. Implicit in this approach is a theoretical concern to consider patterns of musical production within an intertextual matrix, where the layers of content and context become integrated into a coherent analysis. Any conception of production relies on historical and social definitions of technological constructs. By working with a variety of tools connected to production, the focus in all the essays rests on the importance and potential of discursive analysis. To a large extent, all authors owe a debt to the pioneering work of feminists, sociologists, cultural theorists, and musicologists working in the field of popular music. This is borne out by the diversity of references that will assist readers in following up many of the debates touched on.

Finally, the full ramifications of recording technology and production represent one way to understand musicians as subjects of historical, social, gendered and political circumstances. The place and the circumstances where an artist produces their creation play a vital part in the way we as fans and listeners receive the ideological meaning in the work created. Undoubtedly, different recording techniques narrate differently the individual tastes of people and the way in which music is experienced. When responding to recorded sound we enter into a world of styles and genres that reflect social structures and musical practices, which ultimately serve as a reminder that the pop track exists as an important artefact of cultural and social history. This makes the consideration of production in pop music and its ensuing politics of desire particularly relevant to popular music scholarship and, as such, an integral ingredient in the debates surrounding music, space and place.

Notes

1. Middleton, R. (ed) (2000), *Reading Pop: Approaches to Textual Analysis in Popular Music*, Oxford: Oxford University Press, p. 12.
2. Cohen, S. (1991), *Rock Culture in Liverpool: Popular Music in the Making*, Oxford: Clarendon Press, p. 15.
3. Lewis, G.H. (1992), 'Who do you love ?: The dimensions of musical taste', in Lull, J. (ed), *Popular Music and Communication*, 2nd edn, London: Sage, p. 144.
4. Appadurai, A. (1990), 'Disjuncture and Difference in the Global Cultural Economy', in Featherstone, M. (ed), *Global Culture: Nationalism, Globalisation and Modernity*, London: Sage, p. 297.
5. Smart, B. (1993), *Postmodernity*, London: Routledge, p. 147.
6. Lipsitz, G. (1994), *Dangerous Crossroads: Popular Music, Postmodernism and the Poetics of Place*, London: Verso, p. 126.
7. Ibid., pp. 126–7.
8. Gilroy, P. (1993), *The Black Atlantic: Modernity and Double Consciousness*, London: Verso, p. 83.
9. Hebdige, D. (1979), *Subculture: The Meaning of Style*, London: Routledge, p. 83.
10. Mach, Z. (1994), 'National Anthems: The Case of Chopin as a National Composer', in Stokes, M. (ed), *Ethnicity, Identity and Music: The Musical Construction of Place*, Oxford: Berg, p. 61.

11.   Warren, R.L. (1972), 'The Nazi Use of Music as an Instrument of Social Control', in Dennisoff, R. Serge, and Peterson, R.A. (eds), *The Sounds of Social Change*, Chicago: Rand McNally and Company, p. 73.
12.   Willett, R. (1989), 'Hot Swing and the Dissolute Life: Style and Popular Music in Europe 1939–49', *Popular Music*, **8** (2), 160.
13.   Easton, P. (1989), 'The Rock Music Community', in Riordan, J. (ed), *Soviet Youth Culture*, Bloomington and Indianapolis: Indiana University Press, p. 49.
14.   Regev, M. (1996), '*Musica mizrakhit,* Israeli rock and national culture in Israel', *Popular Music*, **15** (3), 280.
15.   Ibid., 277.
16.   Shank, B. (1994), *Dissonant Identities: The Rock 'n' Roll Scene in Austin, Texas*, London: Wesleyan University Press, p. 21.
17.   Finnegan, R. (1989), *The Hidden Musicians: Music-Making in an English Town*, Cambridge: Cambridge University Press, p. 306.
18.   Straw, W. (1991), 'Systems of Articulation, Logics of Change: Communities and Scenes in Popular Music', *Cultural Studies*, **5** (3), 368–88.
19.   Rose, T. (1994), *Black Noise: Rap Music and Black Culture in Contemporary America*, Hanover: Wesleyan University Press, p. xv.
20.   Krims, A. (2000), *Rap music and the poetics of identity*, Cambridge: Cambridge University Press, p. 1.
21.   Forman, M. (1994), 'Movin' Closer To An Independent Funk: Black Feminist Theory, Standpoint and Women in Rap', *Women's Studies*, **23** (1), January, 35.
22.   Krims (2000), *Rap music*, p. 151.
23.   Gates, H. (2000), 'A Reporter At Large: Black London', in Owusu, K. (ed), *Black British Culture and Society: A Text Reader*, London: Routledge, p. 178.
24.   Krims (2000), *Rap music*, p. 1.
25.   Forman (1994), 'Movin' Closer To An Independent Funk', p. 35.
26.   Frith, S. (1996), *Performing Rites*, Oxford: Oxford University Press, p. 240.

PART 1
Music, Space and Place

Chapter 1

The musical construction of the diaspora: the case of reggae and Rastafari[1]

Sarah Daynes

Whether they look for remembrance or forgetting, individuals and societies always build a continuity into which they can inscribe themselves, especially when this continuity has been rendered difficult by a historical or geographical rupture, as it has for people said to be 'in diaspora': for them, history is no longer a continuous flow expressed by an uninterrupted transmission, but it becomes a time broken into *before* and *after*; and familiar places, in which history is spontaneously rooted, are not inhabited day after day, but are replaced by an imaginary 'elsewhere' that dwells in memory. The signs that normally surround individuals, continuously reminding them of who they are and where they come from – family, friends, places, objects having a history and a memory[2] –, become scarce in situations of mobility[3]; simultaneously, people have to adapt to a new way of life which may be extremely different from what they knew before. What can they use in order to keep present what is now far from them? Food and music are the easiest tools to transport memories, and they also have an immediate and forceful power of evocation. As Martin Stokes points out, 'the musical event ... evokes and organises collective memories and present experiences of place with an intensity, power and simplicity unmatched by any other social activity'.[4] Many people, when they move, bring their music with them, before anything else; and the most immediate and obvious characteristic of Brixton in London, Belleville in Paris, or Harlem in New York, is indeed a mix of cuisine smells and musical noises. As soon as a community arrives in a foreign country, it organizes networks in order to get food products, cassettes and compact discs. And when this music starts to intermix with the music of the host country, having an influence on it as well as becoming influenced by it, it usually is a good sign of the settlement of the community in the host country. In other words, it means that a collective memory is being built, integrating elements from both 'places' and 'times' in a multiplicity of back and forth symbolic movements between here and there, and giving way to an original and new construct.

   This article focuses on the construction of the African diaspora as a multi-dimensional space of memory made of many places, and the connections between them, and observes the role played by music in this construction. Reggae music emerged in the late 1960s in Jamaica, and quickly spread beyond the island, following the movements of Jamaican migrants who settled abroad. Today, its presence is global and international, so in the case of reggae music, the diasporic experience is multiple, both in terms of space and time. The main question here is how reggae plays a role in the constitution and evolution of the African diaspora as such; I have based my analysis on a corpus of reggae songs from the 1970s and 90s, as well as on fieldwork I conducted in the British West Indies in 1998 and in Great Britain in 1999.[5] While reggae music and Rastafari do not completely coincide, and although reggae music cannot in any way be considered as 'Rastafarian music', they remain linked by a tight relationship; many reggae artists are rastamen, and their faith is hence reflected within the lyrics of their songs. The analysis presented here examines the relationship between reggae music and Rastafari, but is restricted to what is expressed within reggae music itself.

Defining the notion of diaspora within reggae music is complex and a multi-faceted task; there are many issues involved which can be grouped under two main headings: lyrical content, and music diffusion and performance. In terms of content, the idea of diaspora is grounded in the evocation and remembrance of slavery (Gilroy, 1993), extensively present within reggae lyrics; the notions of redemption, resistance and revolution are essentially based on the diasporic experience of the descendants of slavery and on a rhetoric of oppression that was developed in response to domination. At the same time, the notion of diaspora as it appears within reggae music and Rastafari can be considered as having been elaborated from the religious and socio-political dimensions of both movements. In other words, the consciousness of forming a diaspora was not given nor taken for granted, but it emerged progressively within Rastafari as within reggae music, and was literally constructed. In this chapter, I will deliberately leave aside the question of the construction of what I have called a socio-political memory of resistance,[6] although it probably is the most revealing illustration of the progressive emergence of a diasporic consciousness within reggae music; I will focus on two main points: firstly, the relationship to Africa as it appears within reggae lyrics, and the discussion of the theoretical models of diaspora; and secondly, the continuous spatial tracing of the diaspora by reggae music through the medium of sound systems, by focusing on a British sound system.

Africa reinvented: towards a multi-centred model of the diaspora

The African slaves and their descendants faced a double-step geographical dispersal, firstly from Africa to the slave states of the Americas during the Atlantic slave trade, and secondly through ulterior migrations to diverse countries. This dispersal implied a brutal rupture not only with a land but also with traditions, languages, religious practices and kinship systems, which were all deliberately liquidated by the slavery system (Meillassoux, 1986; Patterson, 1967). This rupture, both geographical and socio-cultural, has shaped the progressive construction of the African diaspora since the time of slavery, and strongly influenced the transmission of history and memory, which was rendered difficult and partial. By definition, the slave trade and the slavery systems derived from it imply two fundamental notions, uprooting and domination, and therefore two 'elsewheres', the first being spatial, in reference to a mythical territory of origin, across the ocean (and with it a way of life, a language, a world now out of reach), and the second being temporal, in reference to a sweeter past ('before') and a better future ('after'). This articulation between space and time, by essence rooted in the notion of 'elsewhere', is fundamental within the diaspora, and appears as central within reggae lyrics; for Chude-Sokei, for example, roots reggae is characterized by 'nostalgia and desire for an elsewhere'.[7]

As has already been pointed out by various scholars (Hebdige, 1987; Chude-Sokei, 1994, among others), Africa, as the homeland and place of origin, is omnipresent within reggae lyrics; however, this is but one of the multiple dimensions taken by the relationship to Africa, which also symbolizes another place of spatial and temporal dwelling, an 'elsewhere' with various levels of identification which continuously mix and overlay each other; it is idealized, imagined, fantasized, conceptualized, and intimately experienced; it is a 'reinvented Africa'[8] that confronts three times (past, present and future) and three places (Africa, the West, and the diaspora), through a complex tie that owes as much to reality as to identification and symbolization. Indeed, following scholars like Stuart Hall or Edmund Gordon,[9] the guiding line here is that it is not the 'concrete' symbol in itself that matters, but what people do with it, what meanings they associate with it, how they identify with it, and why. Africa represents what could be called 'an archetypical symbol of elsewhere', grounded in the experience of slavery, and which takes several dimensions, different but simultaneous and entangled.

In the first place, Africa is a spatial 'elsewhere' and a temporal 'before' from which slaves were taken away by force. It is a 'lost paradise' in the sense of Mircea Eliade, elaborated because of the pain of slavery and forced uprooting. Africa is idealized as natural and in conformity to creation; it is a maternal, original and fertile land, source of all life and provider of knowledge on both the roots and the future (as it appears for instance in Buju Banton and Garnett Silk's 'Hello mama Africa', 1999). This maternal figure is associated with Ethiopia, the place of both religious origin and future redemption as mentioned in the Bible, which reinforces its symbolic intensity. As the land of origin and the land of God, Africa is also the place which symbolizes the notions of good, paradise and liberation – in opposition to the West, which represents evil, hell and enslavement. Indeed, Africa also is an archetype of liberty – the only place in which slave descendants can be free.

Secondly, Africa is the original centre from which the diaspora was scattered. It is, in a fundamental way, considered as 'home', the land where ancestors were born, and therefore the only place in which slave descendants do not feel like strangers. This centre, from which the diaspora was scattered, is spatial as well as temporal: it simultaneously represents another time (before the slave trade and exile) and another place (in opposition to the land of bondage). Africa, as the one and only home, is considered within a temporal succession interrupted by slavery: a homeland that was lost but is to be found again. Remembrance of the past of slavery is therefore essential, because of its structural role in the dispersal of the diaspora.[10]

Thirdly, Africa is an alternative to the western world, almost its antithesis: it is both 'civilization' as opposed to barbarism – the real culture of slave descendants – and also a better way to live and 'be in the world'. Being an African and being a European are considered as allegiances that imply essential differences in terms of culture, those differences being transmitted from one generation to the next through what is given at birth as much as through what is acquired after birth; the two ways of life are inherently and diametrically opposed. For example, slavery is considered as 'a white thing' (findings during fieldwork in the UK, 1999) that was exported to Africa by the Europeans. Independently of their place of birth or residence, slave descendants are therefore considered as Africans, and have to remain faithful to their culture (this is, for example, obvious in U Roy and Sister Audrey's 'True born African', 1991). This conception of culture as being given (while simultaneously actively retained and built) is essential to and strongly evident in reggae music; authenticity is an essential issue, in relationship to a European culture considered as imposed, superficial and, above all, 'untrue' and absolutely 'unsuitable' for African people.

Many practices are directly justified by their 'Africanness' (among them, the use of Swahili or Ethiopian languages, for example by Peter Tosh, The Abyssinians, Sizzla or Black Uhuru); what matters is not 'real Africanness', but *attributed* and *recognized* Africanness, such as the fact that a practice symbolizes Africa for the individual. In other words, the symbolic meaning attributed to a practice is more pertinent within identification mechanisms than the 'real' meaning – although it has to remain within some limits. There is a logic of symbolical investment (what makes sense for the people, in relation to their own individual and collective situation; see Gordon, 1998 and Wade, 1999), which can exclude some elements although they are historically 'real', but it always obeys a pertinent logic: although imagined, symbolic ethnicity is not imaginary.[11]

Because reggae music is considered African, in an essentialist view, it is also viewed as a 'cultural recipient' that not only intrinsically holds culture as a whole, but transmits it spontaneously – and this holds true, independently of the lyrical content.[12] In a way, reggae *is* Africa, as many other practices are; as such, it is considered to be powerful in terms of cultural transmission and awareness.

Then, fourthly, as the counterpart of a paradise lost because of slavery, Africa also represents the Promised Land. It is a land of redemption and liberation, a temporal 'elsewhere' that holds the promise of the end of oppression, and to which there will be a return. As Chude-Sokei says: 'For the rastas, Zion, the promised land of Ethiopia, represented both pre-colonial utopia and the imminent future of the black people.'[13] Africa is the place and time of religious redemption and liberation; in reggae music, under this category, it is referred to by using a religious vocabulary extensively borrowed from the Book of Revelation, and is intimately linked to an eschatological future that promises both punishment (of the wicked, the enslavers) and reward (for the righteous, the slaves).[14] It is therefore a 'temporal elsewhere' simultaneously linked to past and future: the place of origin and the place of return, the beginning and the end, a pre-slavery world as well as a better world to come, within a dialectic of expectation and hope,[15] those two 'temporal elsewheres' being tightly entangled.

As an archetypical symbol of 'elsewhere', here both temporal and spatial, Africa therefore represents the place of utopia – the term coming from the Greek *ou*, 'no', and *topos*, 'place', therefore firstly meaning 'in no place' rather than 'in another place'. In no place, or in no time: in the case of Rastafari, Africa is a faraway past and an ideal future still out of reach, as well as a place from which people have been taken away, of which they preserve an 'idea', a memory, and to which they shall return. Therefore, Africa is not exactly a 'no place' or a 'no time', but a place and a time that cannot be reached in the present – or which, as underlined by Henri Desroche (1960), *have to* remain out of reach and within what he calls the category of failure: an elsewhere that must in some way remain a nowhere for the dynamics of the cult. Simultaneously, Africa is also the place of a religious and socio-political utopia that can be (and has been, to some extent) realized through repatriation to Africa; it is therefore a simultaneously unrealized and realized utopia, which conjugates times and articulates places that are both distinct and yet superimposed.

The relationship with Africa is at the heart of the diasporic construction as it appears within reggae music. Not only it is referred to as a centre – since it is the place of origin, to which return is contemplated – but also as a concept that holds ideals, utopia, culture, redemption, revolution, and patterns of survival. Africa is more than a place: it is a 'state of mind' (Majek Fashek, 'Promised Land', 1997), a utopia that is both religious (or celestial) and earthly, a spiritual, social and political quest for a better world in which times and places are superimposed; Africa as a concept can be interpreted as 'a process of building a new, just and free society. Ethiopia becomes a creative social and political symbol'.[16,17]

Finally, the relationship to Africa is both experienced and conceptualized through the essential notion of movement; Africa is the place from which, around which, and to which movements have taken, are taking, and will take place. The present diasporic state is considered as a temporary exile, a short and almost meaningless stopover; the notion of diaspora is conceived within an essential dialectic of movement, whether it is abstract or concrete – from and back to Africa; from cultural alienation to the 'higher grounds' of the original culture; from domination to revolution and liberation; from social death to spiritual awareness and freedom.

    This multi-dimensional, complex concept of Africa as being more than just a
centre of dispersal, is in contradiction with the traditional, centred model of
diaspora. In general, all displaced groups can be described as diasporas – the term
refers to a people without land or a culture without a country.[18] But, as Cohen
points out: 'A member's adherence to a diasporic community is demonstrated by
an acceptance of an inescapable link with their past migration history.'[19] Talking
about diaspora therefore implies an emphasis on the link existing between the
people in exile and their homeland; indeed there is in the use of the term the double
idea of departure and return, an idea that also implies the reconstruction of a
history (or memory?) of the displacement, articulating departure and return, here
and there, before and after.
    According to William Safran, the concept of diaspora should be applied to

> expatriate minority communities whose members share several of the following
> characteristics: 1) they, or their ancestors, have been dispersed from a specific
> original 'center' to two or more 'peripheral', or foreign, regions; 2) they retain a
> collective memory, vision, or myth about their original homeland...; 3) they believe
> that they are not – and perhaps cannot be – fully accepted by their host society and
> therefore feel partly alienated and insulated from it; 4) they regard their ancestral
> homeland as their true, ideal home and as the place to which they or their
> descendants would (or should) eventually return...; 5) they believe that they should,
> collectively, be committed to the maintenance or restoration of their original
> homeland and to its safety and prosperity; and 6) they continue to relate ... to that
> homeland in one way or another, and their ethnocommunal consciousness and
> solidarity are importantly defined by the existence of such a relationship.[20]

    In terms of this definition, slave descendants cannot be considered as being in
diaspora, but in 'quasi-diaspora',[21] some of the points developed by Safran being
absent: (1) the original 'center' is geographically multiple, except if we consider
'Africa' as a homogeneous centre, which is not really accurate although it has been
constructed as such; (3) non-acceptance is not considered as rooted in the group
in exile, but in a racial prejudice that does not apply to slave descendants
only; (4) return is sometimes contemplated (for example in the case of Rastafari),
but not always, indeed rarely. Finally, in most Caribbean countries, slave
descendants are not a minority, but a majority.
    Moreover, Safran's definition emphasizes the unified character of an original
centre, which organizes the community's homogeneity, with which continuous
relationships exist, and to which is expressed a desire of return. But as Clifford
remarks, 'a shared, ongoing history of displacement, suffering, adaptation, or
resistance may be as important as the projection of a specific origin'.[22] Safran's
'center' is not necessarily a territory or a country; in the case of slave descendants,
the centre can indeed be the shared experience of the Atlantic slave trade. What
matters is not the geographical origin, but the idea (that is made, was given and
transmitted) of a 'before' and an 'elsewhere', associated to a shared history, a
common memory, a path of exile characterized by the same pains. Return – like

the relationship maintained with the homeland – does not need to be concrete, nor even really contemplated; and it does not need be the same for everyone. If the notion of diaspora is indeed defined by the inescapable link between the people and their homeland, the homeland itself is characterized by its symbolic distance, and the impossibility of reaching it in the present; the link therefore becomes thought, dreamed, imagined, fantasized, and symbolized. Although this land still exists geographically, it is present only in memory and does not really have a concrete, material existence. For example, rastas who have returned to Ethiopia have not found the Africa that they had imagined, even if they have experienced a justified feeling of return.

In the case of Rastafari and as it is expressed in reggae music, Africa is not only the centre from which the diaspora was scattered through slavery: it is also a spatial elsewhere (beyond an ocean 'reddened by the blood of the trade') and a temporal elsewhere (that calls on both the past and the future). Both Africa and slavery can therefore be considered as symbolic centres; specifically Africa is the central *place*, the land of origin from which was scattered the diaspora, and the slave trade is the central *event* of the diaspora, slavery being the essential collective experience that shaped the shared path of the diaspora; this shared past not only gave birth to the construction of the diaspora as such (since it provoked exile and therefore forced, in a way, the transformation of a disparate people into a diaspora), but also determines the dimensions of diasporic identity by grounding it in an essential opposition between slaves and slave masters.

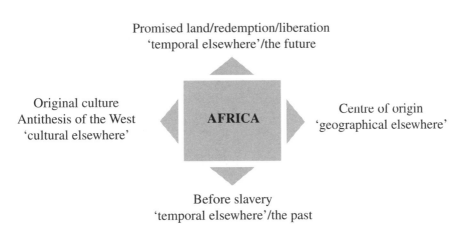

Figure 1.1   Symbolic levels in the representation of Africa

While the model proposed by Safran remains pertinent (see Figure 1.1) – the centre being Africa – it also appears that the prominence given to the notion of centre limits analysis. Africa does not only symbolize a centre; moreover, focusing on the notion of centre implies that the role played by slavery in the construction of the diaspora is neglected. The centrality of Africa is not only due to its homeland character: it also is, and maybe above all, a historical and memorial exigency; the experience of slavery, a history of attempts to erase African origins by the slave masters, and of attempts to preserve their African roots by the slaves and their descendants, have both shaped the relationship with Africa and its essential importance as a centre of origin. As Clifford[23] points out, diaspora is, simultaneously and with equal importance, both a history of dispersion and a memory of the original land. The African diaspora, moreover, is simultaneously rooted in the shared experience of slavery and in the memory of Africa. In other words, it is the history of displacement, traced since the exile, that gives to the homeland its essential importance as a centre; what comes afterwards contributes to the construction of the diaspora and its memory as much as the centre itself – a common origin is therefore not more important that the shared experience that follows it after exile. I have already pointed out that this common origin is not a concrete reality but a social construction: while all the slaves were from Africa, this does not necessarily imply that they shared a common feeling of belonging prior to slavery. The prominence of an 'African identity' over Fon, Ashanti, Yoruba or Bantu, for example, was progressively built through a shared history that starts with the slave trade and within an essential opposition between slaves (Africans) and slave masters (Europeans) that was provoked and even forced by the slavery system.

Therefore, there is a multitude of back and forth movements between an original centre (Africa) and a shared history. There is a paradox between simultaneous unity and diversity, between a centre which has been progressively constructed, because it did not pre-date slavery; and a shared history that is both unique and diversified. The African diaspora was dynamically and progressively built, and still is today, not only in reference to an original centre but also through the movements that pave its history (as expressed by Gilroy, 1993). The 'Black Atlantic' is indeed a multiple and diversified diaspora, which stretches beyond 'nation' and 'ethnicity' and is made of a history of both forced and voluntary movements and crossings between places; it is also an experience of displacement, violence and loss, considered as *structuring* and *constitutive*.[24] So, a diaspora can be understood 'as a practice of dwelling (differently), as an ambivalent refusal or indefinite deferral of return, and as a positive transnationalism'.[25] It is centred around an 'axis of origin and return', but this axis is not necessarily the original homeland: it can be the 'idea' of this land, an experience, or a history. While being based on the idea of return (whether it is possible or impossible, soon to come or very far in the future, towards an existing country or one that has disappeared), diasporas usually indefinitely postpone this same contemplated return, partly because they are rooted in both 'here' and 'there', which are 'vivid, actual, occurring together contrapuntally'.[26] Indeed, what matters is not the centre in itself, but the multifaceted relationship developed with it and conjugated with different times and places, the multiple and contrapuntal tie that exists between the centre of origin and a shared experience – as in music, where superimposed melodic lines have their own independence but give birth to a new dimension when they are combined.

Tracing the space: sound systems and the routes of reggae music

If reggae music evokes the diaspora within its lyrical content, what about the musical performance? The main characteristic of music is indeed to be played and listened to – thus adding to its permanent (and repetitive or, rather, repeatable) character as a recording, a dimension of uniqueness, both in terms of spatiality and temporality. I mentioned briefly, at the beginning of this chapter, that reggae music had spread internationally, primarily by following the movements of Jamaican migrants. This evolution was more than a simple access to new markets; by the end of the 1970s, for instance, 'British reggae' had emerged in Great Britain, with its own artists, recording studios, music shops and, above all, with its specific sound and evolution, distinct from Jamaican reggae. Today, reggae music is listened to and played on the five continents, travelling in a double movement: (1) the international diffusion of Jamaican reggae, through recordings as well as through the concerts given by Jamaican artists; and (2) the emergence of 'local' reggae, as well as the influence reggae can have on other musical styles.[27] The simultaneity of these two movements can be seen as a paradoxical tension between the local and the global: on one hand Jamaican reggae is following the routes of the diaspora – becoming global; on the other hand, reggae music is settling in various places, where it develops its own sound and themes – becoming local. The circulation of reggae music between all the places of the diaspora – and out of the diaspora – is made of these multiple interconnections between the local and the global, and is highly dependent on the various meanings attributed to it by both performers and listeners (the encoding/decoding process stressed by Hall, 1980, or Martin, 1995). The debate about the remembrance of slavery and the relationship to Africa, while remaining essential, takes various modalities, as it is simultaneously perceived as meaningful and attributed new meanings; the socio-political content of the music is actively interpreted, and to a rhetoric of oppression that makes sense beyond Jamaica are added new meanings depending on the geographical locality. In Great Britain, for example, a strong link was made between Rastafari, reggae, and workers' movements; independence and self-determination movements in New Zealand, French Polynesia or Mauritius, have similar links, as do post-colonial issues in Africa.

In other words, music talks, but it is also talked to – reggae is a 'changing same' (Gilroy, 1991) that is continuously being modified and remade. This dynamic relationship between the audience and the music, the local and the global, and the various places of the diaspora, is visible at every level of reggae music. For this discussion, I will take one specific example that shows the modulation of the music and its articulation with space: sound systems, a tradition that is essential to reggae music.

Sound systems can be considered as the heart and soul of reggae music, not only because they have acquired, over time, an essential importance with the success of dance-hall reggae, but also because it has always been through them that songs were primarily released and diffused, and artists discovered. Additionally, they have been central to the evolution of styles and techniques within reggae music, for example when it comes to the emergence and development of dub, in which they played a major role. Sound systems emerged at the end of the 1940s, after the departure of the American troops stationed in Jamaica during the Second World War, who had brought their music recordings with them – and especially New Orleans jazz. To put it very simply, a sound system is organized around a 'selector' who plays records; in the beginning, he was usually accompanied by an 'assistant' in charge of introducing the songs and encouraging the audience by 'scatting' and 'toasting' over the records. Ultimately, the main function of any sound system is very simple: to make people dance – which is why the events are often simply called 'dances'. Over time, with the apparition of ska, rock steady, reggae, and the development of the 'riddims' (the musical versions recorded specifically for sound systems) as well as, in the mid-80s, of digital reggae, 'talk-over' developed to the point of emerging as a specific style within reggae music ('dance-hall reggae'), and the live performances of the 'dee-jays' started being released on records, dance-hall music becoming 'primary to Jamaican music'.[28]

Each sound system has its own sound and therefore its own fans, like any other artist; it is 'just like a mobile club and people follow the sound wherever it is playing'.[29] From Kilimanjaro and Stone Love in Jamaica to Abashanti and Zion Train in the UK or King Shiloh in the Netherlands, sound systems are now present wherever there is a reggae scene. In Great Britain, Jah Shaka is probably the most famous of all, playing at least once a month in London and the surrounding area for the past several years and continuing to expand its nucleus of devoted fans. Jah Shaka has built his reputation on his unique sound as well as his socio-political and religious commitment, largely drawn from Rastafari; he himself asserts that the sound system is an incomparable medium which one can (and should) use as a tool for education and consciousness-raising, and that music is a 'universal language'.[30] Although he plays only British and Jamaican 'cultural' reggae, his dances drive a very mixed crowd (in terms of age, place of origin, nationality, gender, political and religious affiliation, and even musical taste); the variety of the crowd is itself an expression of the diaspora, as well as of the spread of reggae beyond the diaspora as such: a sort of *internationale* of reggae music and of the adherence to the religious and/or socio-political beliefs expressed by Jah Shaka.

For most of his fans, attending his dance is an act of both pleasure and commitment, something that is good for the 'body and soul': they talk of the music, of the dance, of the *ambiance*, and of physical sensations, but always link those to a mental and moral experience expressed in terms of cultural, social and political consciousness and resistance. For them, going to a Shaka dance is equivalent to listening to roots reggae or 'conscious dance-hall' recordings[31] – a musical political act that goes beyond the lyrical content, as the musical sound in itself is considered meaningful.

Jah Shaka would agree with his fans, and this creates a convergence between the goals of the artist, the expectations of the audience, and what happens during the musical performance. Through the sound system, his aim is to educate the people; he considers music to be a language that holds meanings and conveys a message, simultaneously cultural, social, political, religious and historical. This educational character of music is nothing new within reggae music, but an essential component of a general view that considers reggae to be a 'schoolroom' (Anthony B, 'Rastaman school', 1997, or David Jahson, 'Stop, look and listen', 1978) and reggae artists as 'messengers' (Luciano, 'Punch line', 1999). For many artists indeed, as they express it in their songs as well as in interviews, reggae has a mission to educate and to transmit knowledge concerning a broad range of topics (historical, social, cultural, political, religious, and so on), to counterbalance traditional institutions that are thought to be deliberately avoiding the 'real issues' (*Jahmali*, 'Real issues', 1998) and hiding the truth (Burning Spear, 'Subject in school', 1995, Anthony B, 'The mockingbird', 1997, or U Roy and Dennis Brown, 'Half me get', 2000) and to be domination tools implemented by 'the system'.

However, in the case of Jah Shaka, the sound system becomes more than just a medium of communication: it has to play a specific role within the community, transmitting a message but also bringing people together through the event, and creating a focus for networking. The notion of community here is vast and complex; it is not limited to, but includes, the local community. The community is one of multiple entangled levels, from the neighbourhood and the city to informal networks within the reggae and/or Rastafari movements in Great Britain but also, ultimately, between the different places of the diaspora as well as with Africa. Jah Shaka achieves this goal through different ways: primarily through the peregrinations of his sound system, which performs throughout Great Britain and beyond, but also through an international diffusion of recordings (both of live performances of the sound system, and of artists he produces on his own recording label), as well as, and maybe above all, through his social commitment with the 'Jah Shaka Foundation', which provides local schools and groups in Ghana, Ethiopia and Jamaica with books and diverse medical or work-related supplies and records. Therefore, the sound system is not only a crucial cultural event with multiple social and political functions (as shown by Stolzoff, 2000, about Jamaican sound systems), but it also becomes a grass roots space for concrete commitment within the community, taken here in the broad meaning of both the local and the global, linking together the different places of the diaspora as well as the diaspora with Africa.

In a way, Jah Shaka's sound system is a concrete example of the parallel evolution experienced by reggae and Rastafari since the 1970s, from the local to the global. Reggae music, through its growing success, expanded its audience beyond Jamaica, both within and outside the diaspora. Rastafari, following similar routes, had to deal with the interest and entry (or attempted entry) of non-Jamaican and then non-black individuals. For both movements, this evolution represented a challenge in terms of identity and openness: from a local to an international audience for reggae music, from a specific to a universal message for Rastafari (in biblical language, religious revelation had to shift from addressing one people to addressing all the people). This tension between a strictly African-Jamaican root and a universal exigency (the latter being accepted or rejected, depending on the individuals and groups) has been central to the evolution of both the musical style and the religious movement since the end of the 1970s, and it remains so today, especially in terms of boundaries and inclusion/exclusion.[32]

In the case of Jah Shaka, the response to this evolution is very clear, and is made by favouring inclusion over exclusion, while remaining intensely focused on the African-Jamaican roots of both reggae and Rastafari. For Jah Shaka, reggae music is a universal language that can be understood by everyone, and Rastafari is a faith that can touch everyone; and the disparity of the crowd that attends his dances is in tune with this position. The main goal of Jah Shaka, primarily through music and the sound system, is to create a network that connects the different places of the diaspora as well as the diaspora with Africa; moreover, this network, while remaining strongly grounded and focused on the black struggle, can be opened beyond the African diaspora as such through the participation of non-blacks. The notion of network is here simultaneously concrete and abstract, because the connections created are ideas as much as actions; the sound system is both a medium for the transmission of history, culture, and socio-political ideas and commitment, and a medium for building connections between people and places; it contributes to the creation of a spatial map that is at the same time physical and mental.

Concluding remarks

In a way, reggae music is a meaningful example of how the African diaspora built itself – and is still being built – through simultaneous roots and routes (Gilroy, 1993), as expressed by Keith Negus: 'The roots of the contemporary black experience can therefore be traced back to Africa and the sudden brutal disruption introduced by slavery. Yet, the subsequent routes that black people have taken and the cultural forms that have been created cannot be understood simply in terms of common origins in Africa'.[33] In reggae music, the relationship with Africa, with which I started this chapter, can be seen as the roots, while the modulation found in the displacements and movements followed by reggae music can be considered as the subsequent routes. Both participate, with equal importance, in the progressive construction of the notion of diaspora as well as of the sense of being in diaspora.

Reggae music in itself can be considered as a dynamic attempt, continuously renegotiated, to elaborate a simultaneous conceptualization and experience of 'what it means to be a or in diaspora', as well as, to use Hall's own terms (1995), to be 'twice diasporized'. Through its international success and spread, reggae has had to face multiple movements and shifts in relationship between the local and the global, while the notions of exile and diaspora were already central to its very emergence. There are three core aspects to the dynamic attempt thus described: (1) it transmits a collective memory considered essential to the very survival of the group; (2) it voices a discourse *of* and *on* the diaspoa; (3) it traces the space and movements of the diaspora.

Transmission of collective memory

The collective memory encompasses a very broad spectrum, from remembrance of the Middle Passage and of the past of slavery, through the evocation of the events and heroes of the black struggle (*Steel Pulse*, 'Tribute to the martyrs', 1979), to the identification with the biblical people of Israel, which is fundamental to Rastafari and features strongly in reggae lyrics (*Israel Vibration*, 'Streets of glory', 1978). This educational role of reggae music, claimed by the artists themselves, is coupled with an essential religious character of Rastafari as being 'the revelation of the truth' within a strong rhetoric of adversity. Music therefore becomes a medium of transmission, which reveals the truth concerning history, determines who are the enemies, and creates a continuity between past and present. And this transmission clearly considers the diaspora to be unified and, therefore, an expression of this continuity.

The debate on diasporic identities

This is mainly communicated through the lyrical content of reggae songs, in which can be traced the apparition and evolution of the notion of diaspora itself, as well as the emergence of a 'diasporic consciousness'. For example, the progressive shift from a 'mythical Africa' to a 'contemporary Africa' is found from the 1970s onward – or, rather than a shift, a non-conflictual accretion of different but co-existing levels of identification – and shows how the memory of a lost land was opened to the present multiple places of the diaspora and to a complex relationship that takes into account both the roots and the routes of the diaspora. One indicator is the apparition of African countries in the vocabulary used to talk about Africa, for example in Pablo Moses' 'We should be in Angola' (1978) or Buju Banton's 'Til I'm laid to rest' (1995) and 'Sudan' (2000). In a similar way, the socio-political references present in Jamaican reggae songs have progressively included black struggle heroes from Jamaica, the Caribbean, North America and Africa, as well as other figures, depending on the local context of the music for non-Jamaican reggae, for example in Mauritius, France or Great Britain.

This inclusion has contributed to the formation of a collective memory of resistance drawn from all the places of the diaspora, while music has simultaneously gained access to a diversified, multi-geographic audience – bringing Africa to the Caribbean, but also London to Kingston, for example – and acted as a medium for historical transmission in a multitude of back and forth movements within the diaspora.

Additionally, reggae music proposes a dynamic systematization of the diaspora that has been very concretely expressed over many years, from Bob Marley's evocation of a multi-dimensional unity (both vertical and horizontal, historic and diasporic) between the diaspora and Africa and within the diaspora itself (especially in 'Zimbabwe' and 'Africa Unite', 1979, but also in 'Buffalo soldier', 1983) to the questioning of the relationship between diasporic, ethnic and national identities that was made central in British, north-American or French reggae (for example, U Roy and Sister Audrey's 'True born African', 1991). The debate about relationships has been central to the defining of boundaries between the 'inside' and the 'outside', an issue which takes on crucial importance because of the internationalization of reggae audience; the notion of race, in relationship to both the question of the universality of the movement (or, on the other hand, its exclusivity) and the racism faced in Europe or the Americas, is indeed an important theme in reggae music,[34] and also remains a central, and maybe vital, issue for Rastafari.

The space and movements of the diaspora

The third category, illustrated in this chapter by the case of sound systems, concerns the spatial appropriation and the routes traced by reggae music through its concrete diffusion and displacements. Reggae traces the space of the diaspora by physically moving within it, through the distribution of recordings as well as the performances given by artists all around the world. To put it very simply, when an artist plays successively in Jamaica, the British Caribbean, New York City and throughout Europe, his music and the things he says on stage are travelling with him. Similarly, the distribution of records from Jamaica to Great Britain, to the United States, and back is a way of communicating within the diaspora. The international (or transnational) networks created in terms of musical diffusion and performance are travelled back and forth, thus connecting the different audiences and tracing the space in a multilateral way. As Louis Chude-Sokei says about reggae dance-hall: 'Here we can witness an attempt to connect the various points of black/Afro-Caribbean disembarkation into one transnational, commodity-based space. One postnationalist city of blackness – but with many, many suburbs'.[35] As a matter of fact, both Rastafari and reggae are characterized by their simultaneous presence in all the 'places of the African diaspora' (including Africa), and the permanent, continuous and multiple circulation of words, sounds and individuals within this space plays a part in tracing the diaspora, its very existence, and its identity.

A new dimension of this spatial mapping has emerged with the Internet; music is now present everywhere through this medium, and reggae fans organize networks for discussion, information and meetings through the medium of the Internet;[36] Irie FM, the Jamaican reggae station, can be listened to from any computer, whether it is in Wisconsin or on a Greek island. Music has never been so easy to diffuse and distribute, and whether it will lead either to a uniformity of what reggae fans listen to, or on the other hand to a multiplicity of sounds that will be found everywhere instead of remaining limited to their place of emergence only, is an open question, and one that deserves interest.

Notes

1. I am grateful to Terry Williams for the comments he provided at various stages of this work.
2. Auguste Comte suggests that 'our mental balance depends in a great part on the objects of our daily life, which do not change, or almost, offering us an image of permanence and stability' (Connerton, P., 2000, 'Lieux de mémoire, lieux d'oubli', in Huglo, M.P. *et al*, *Passions du passé: recyclages de la mémoire et usages de l'oubli*. Montreal: L'Harmattan, p. 57). Connerton adds that 'individuals remember the past together because together they occupy certain narrative spaces ... Our environment is not a simple external image, it cannot be separated from the history of our identities and is incorporated into it'.
3. According to Paul Connerton (2000), this is actually the main characteristic of our contemporary world.
4. Stokes, M. (ed) (1994), *Ethnicity, identity and music: the musical construction of place*, Oxford: Berg, p. 3.
5. Both the corpus and fieldwork were part of a Ph.D. in Sociology. For more details concerning methodological choices, see Daynes, S. (2001a), *Le mouvement Rastafara: Mémoire, musique et religion*, thèse de Doctorat en Sociologie: Ecole des Hautes Etudes en Sciences Sociales, Paris.
6. Daynes, 2001, pp. 365–94.
7. Chude-Sokei, L. (1994), 'Post-nationalist geographies: rasta, ragga, and reinventing Africa', *African Arts*, **27** (4), 80. Chude-Sokei distinguishes 'reggae of Bob Marley's generation' and 'ragga' of the 80s on this basis: according to him, 'instead of psychologically dwelling in an "elsewhere", the discourse of dance hall is an exploration and celebration of microrealities ... what artists call strict reality'. This analysis is very pertinent; however, it does not take into account post-1994 dance-hall, which shows great differences compared to 80s 'ragga' in terms of content.
8. This term has already been used, for example, by Capone concerning Brazil.
9. See for example Hall, S. (1995), 'Negotiating Caribbean Identities', *New Left Review*, 209, 5: 'questions of identity are always questions of representations. They are always questions about the invention, not only the discovery of tradition'; and Gordon, E.T. (1998), *Disparate diasporas. Identity and politics in an African-Nicaraguan Community*, Austin: University of Texas Press, p. 260: 'they had a strongly "African" *identified* culture'.
10. Slavery is one of the most prominent themes in reggae lyrics; see for example Burning Spear 'Slavery days', Culture 'Too long in slavery', Abyssinians 'African race', Bob Marley and the Wailers 'Crazy baldheads', Dennis Brown 'Jah can do it',

Gregory Isaacs 'Slave market'. It is worth noting that the way reggae artists speak about slavery is very intimate (in particular, the use of 'I' and 'we'), which creates both a generational closeness, which builds a vertical continuity, and a diasporic closeness, which builds a horizontal unity.

11. Jenkins, R. (1997), *Rethinking ethnicity: Arguments and explorations*, London: Sage, p. 169.
12. Music, as a combination of 'sounds and words', is indeed seen as having an inner power of action on the world, and can thus be used as a tool for education and struggle (hence the term 'warrior music', for example). See for instance Sizzla's 'No other like Jah', 1997: 'I must put you down / burning you with words / power and sound'.
13. Chude-Sokei, *op. cit.*, p. 80.
14. References to the return to a Promised Land are countless in reggae lyrics. See for example Hugh Mundell 'Jah say the time has come', Israel Vibration 'Streets of glory', Dennis Brown 'Milk and honey', Aswad 'Judgement day', Black Uhuru 'Leaving to Zion', Anthony B 'Seek Jah first', Luciano 'When will I be home' and 'Moving outta Babylon'.
15. I refer here to the work of Henri Desroche (1960, 'Les messianismes et la catégorie de l'échec', *Cahiers Internationaux de Sociologie*, **XXXV** (1), 61–84) about the 'sociology of Hope'. See also Desroche (1973), *Sociologie de l'espérance*, Paris: Calmann-Lévy, and (1974), *Les religions de contrebande*, Paris: Mame.
16. Taylor, P.D.M. (1990), 'Perspectives on history in Rastafari thought', *Studies in Religion*, **19** (2), 201.
17. As such, Rastafari cannot be considered strictly escapist. An essential rhetoric of hope and redemption does not annihilate dynamism, rather it reinforces and fuels resistance and revolution. Hurbon, L. (1986, 'New Religious Movements in the Caribbean', in Beckford, J. (ed), *New Religious Movements and Rapid Social Change*, London: Sage, p. 336) and Taylor (1990, p. 200) share this same view. Indeed rastamen do not consider return to nature as an escape, but as a necessary replenishment within the struggle against evil, as well as the only way to avoid contamination from it. Moreover, the articulation of the concept of Nature/Good with its antithesis Babylon/Evil, is part of a process of redemption: the degradation by man of the Creation of God leads to the end of the world; the quest for harmony with nature is hence in itself a proof of faith and a refusal of evil, which are essential in the active preparation for Armageddon.
18. Barkan, E. and Shelton, M.D. (1998), *Borders, Exiles, Diasporas*, Stanford: Stanford University Press, p. 5.
19. Cohen, R. (1997), *Global Diasporas: An Introduction*. London: UCL Press, p. ix.
20. Safran, W. (1991), 'Diasporas in modern societies: myths of homeland and return', *Diaspora*, **1** (1), 83–4.
21. Clifford, J. (1997), *Routes: Travel and translation in the late 20th century*, Cambridge: Harvard University Press, p. 249.
22. Ibid., p. 250.
23. Ibid., p. 247.
24. Ibid., p. 263.
25. Ibid., p. 269.
26. Said, E. (1984), 'Reflections on Exile', *Grana*, 13, Autumn, 159–72.
27. Including where English is not a first language, for example Japan, Continental Europe, French-speaking Africa, Latin America, or Mauritius. In terms of 'hybridization' Brazilian Samba-Reggae, Colombian Champeta, and Drum'n'Bass, are all good examples of the influence of reggae outside its own 'musical boundaries'.

28. Stolzoff, N. (2001), *Wake the town and tell the people: Dancehall culture in Jamaica*, Durham, NC: Duke University Press, p. 100.
29. Back, L. (1987), 'Coughing up fire: sound systems, music and cultural politics in S.E. London', *Journal of Caribbean Studies*, **6** (2), 214.
30. For example on a 2002 flyer: 'Jah Shaka is the spiritual doctor offering dub medicine for each and everyone'.
31. Of course, compared to recordings, attending a dance adds the dimension of performance, which in the case of sound systems also implies the notion of trance and the elaboration of a sense of belonging in terms of space and time.
32. These mechanisms are especially visible when looking at the construction(s) of the notion of race within Rastafari.
33. Negus, K. (1996), *Popular Music in Theory*, Hanover and London: Wesleyan University Press, pp. 106–7.
34. For instance, The Gladiators, 'Dreadlocks the time is now' (1978) and 'Eli, Eli' (1976), Hugh Mundell, 'Let's all unite' (1978), Morgan Heritage, 'Protect us Jah' (1998), Steel Pulse, 'Rock against racism' (1979), or French Djamatik Connections, 'Rouge' (1999).
35. Chude-Sokei, *op. cit.*, p. 84.
36. From Internet-based forums of discussion and 'clubs' to reggae websites or online record shops.

Chapter 2

Who is the 'other' in the Balkans? Local ethnic music as a *different source* of identities in Bulgaria[1]

Claire Levy

> A world with more cultural differences is more aesthetically
> pleasing and intellectually stimulating...[2]

A venomous snake and a dog met at a Balkan river-bank. 'You can swim, would you take me to the other side?' asked the snake. 'I will,' said the dog, 'but you're venomous, you can bite me.' 'Why would I do that?' said the snake, 'if you sink, I'll drown.' The dog thought for moment – it looked logical to him – and then agreed. The snake climbed on his back and when they reached the middle of the river, she bit him. 'Why did you do it?' asked the dog while sinking in the muddy turbulent waters, 'now you'll drown too.' 'Because we are in the Balkans,' said the snake.[3]

This story could be heard with the starting sounds of the 1998 CD album *Vavilon*, performed by the Bulgarian singer/showman Slavi Trifonov and the Kou-Kou Band. It was intended not so much as a metaphor of any dark and stereotyped sides of presupposed Balkan mentality but as a semi-dramatic, semi-satirical reflection on the strange metamorphoses in the problematic love–hate/friend–enemy binary, which is sometimes completely illogical, but nevertheless crucial in any identity process. The parable refers to a particular situation concerning musical belongings in Bulgaria. Those who have witnessed the heated public debates on the emergence of the most popular, locally-derived pop music genre in Bulgaria during the 1990s, labelled *chalga*,[4] are aware of the hidden smile in this story, intended to parody paradoxical understandings of the national musical identity, according to which this particular trend has been seen as an enemy, threatening the national culture because of its supposed primitivism and backwardness. The Kou-Kou Band is one of the most successful contributors to the emergence and definition of the genre, at least since their first visible crossover in the Bulgarian local mainstream with their 1994 album *Roma TV*. The band has written a number of subsequent hits of that kind (and because of this is a favourite target of *chalga*'s opponents), and its members have chosen this particular strategy for defending themselves. *Chalga* embraces the tools of music and verbal parody (or self-parody), instead of responding directly to the abusive allegations of 'destroying the national culture' which have been noisily aired in public.

Expressed, however, mostly by representatives of the so-called cultural élites, such abuses have revived an old national identity syndrome and a dilemma that has accompanied Bulgaria at least since the time of its liberation in 1878, after five centuries as a part of the Ottoman Empire – long enough to explain the visible 'oriental' cultural traces in the language and music of Bulgarian culture in the present. This dilemma is more political than musical, but it is also shared by other Balkan countries with a similar political history (and likewise located at the crossroads between East and West).[5] Underlying it are calls for a clear orientation of the national 'civilizational choice'. Which is the road to national prosperity? East or West? Orient or Europe? Or – translating the largely popular interpretations of this geographical binary – cultural backwardness or modern progressiveness? According to some of the most common ideological trends now penetrating the new Bulgarian history, such a dilemma is mainly rhetorical. Cultural élites in this country have repeatedly propagated and encouraged – in the name of the *right* cultural choice – acceptance and acculturation of the values associated with the European Enlightenment and the implicit idea of 'catching up' with the European West, which embodies the 'Promised Land' and is the rose-coloured icon of human progress. Such a choice, even today, presupposes, however, that the cultural heritage of Bulgaria in its broadest sense (its ethnically mixed culture, language, and music vocabulary, expressed in ways comparable with the lively local inter-ethnic exchanges taking place throughout the Balkans) is something different and dispensable. Instead of looking at the dilemma as a possible expression of complementary conditions, rather than as a choice between alternatives, that is East *and* West rather than East *or* West, cultural élites persist in trying – in the name of social, political, and cultural progress – to distance Bulgarians from some of the multi-ethnic traces of their past. To identify the national 'self' with the notion of a pure Bulgarian ethnicity is still the prevailing idea, while local ethnic groups who are excluded, especially the more numerous ones (Gypsies and Turks), are assigned the role of being the national 'others'.

What people enjoy in music and may embrace as a source of identity is certainly not necessarily rooted solely in their own country's local cultural traditions and environments. Yet the emergence of a new pop music in Bulgaria has served as a reminder of the past and retrieved above all the *beauty of the fading small remnants* of local traditions, which had been excluded and marginalized for years from public media and are now, along with the changes brought by social and political liberation since 1989, resurfacing in a very natural and powerful way, demonstrating that what is inherited through common memory cannot easily be deleted as if it had never existed. Called popfolk, ethnopop or just *chalga*, this new genre of pop music has revived a specific sensitivity to local cultural traditions and brought back the notion of exchange and transmission through ethnically mixed local practices, which have been bound together as part of a 'common stock' throughout the Balkans at least since the mid-nineteenth century, and are generally described at present as 'Balkan,' 'Oriental,' or 'non-western.' Infused with contemporary western-derived pop music techniques, but based predominantly on a variety of different local sources of ethnic music, including those derived from the vernacular musical practices of local Gypsies and Turks, which are more closely associated with the notion of the 'Orient', the genre could be identified as a local contemporary episode based on two continuums: Balkan urban folklore and contemporary 'world music' discourse. This new music development has become a sign of modern hybridity and a specific form of multiculturalism, similar to many recent popular musical developments that have appeared worldwide. Yet, while westerners are customarily attracted to the sounds of this particular genre, its growing local popularity within Bulgaria has been the subject of increasing ideological argument on the cultural identity of Bulgarians and their 'civilizational choice', a clichéd slogan which has again penetrated public space since the 1989 watershed and implied a clear national orientation towards western values and standards. Such an orientation, at least according to the ruling cultural élites, is supposed to ignore any oriental infusions in culture, especially in popular music, where they are more visible than in other forms of cultural expression. The fact is, however, that this point of view stimulates and reinforces, if not a racist, then at least a hostile attitude towards the bearers of any presumed 'non-Bulgarian' influences, which are understood to mean influences coming from the local cultures of Gypsies and Turks.

Needless to say, debates of this sort have revealed 'essentialist' views close to the rather anachronistic idea of the national as a single, frozen concept, while remaining somewhat vague with respect to the place of local minorities in the context of the national discourse. This point of view is evidently quite opposed to the idea of interpreting identities in a multiple, pluralistic, and flexible way, according to which the *inherited* and the *acquired* do not necessarily contradict each other and may construct the specific identities both of individuals and groups. Quite paradoxically, in this particular case, the inherited (the Balkan) was conceptualized as the culturally horrifying 'other', that is, as an enemy *inside* the nation, while the acquired (global, western-influenced and western-oriented pop music trends) was considered as a promising friendly sign *outside* the nation leading to modern civilization and future prosperity.

Against this background, *chalga* has become a problematic site, raising, along with issues of identity, issues of tolerance, pluralism, and cultural relativism. It is also problematic in terms of the moral panic it provokes and the revival of a very familiar highbrow syndrome directed (traditionally) against the nature of popular music and popular culture in general, especially as far as the cultural establishment is concerned. Hidden behind a concern for 'good taste,' threatened by 'that bad music,' the moral panic reinforced the notion of a (hopefully unrealized) racism, defined by Richard Schechner as 'a myth of desired cultural purity played out against "others" who are perceived as being not only different but inferior.'[6]

In the following commentary, I will argue that the process of identity is indeed problematic, but that the questions 'Who am I?' and 'Who are we?' are also a matter of state of mind, which is not always modelled independently, but, more often than not (at least as observed in the Bulgarian case) according to the will and the dictate of those in power who exert a hegemonic control of culture. In this context, it is important to consider the controversial role of cultural élites who are responsible for shaping and even falsifying canons for 'good' and 'bad,' 'pure' and 'phoney' in culture, endeavouring to direct and control natural developments in cultural property, that is, to point towards the *right* policies with respect to inclusion and exclusion in the process of identity. While agreeing that the concept of 'otherness' is more ideological than merely musical,[7] I shall, however, return to this issue after giving some consideration to the *chalga* continuum.[8]

Old new sounds: continuity and change

The word *chalga* is an abbreviated form of *chalgija*. Literally, it means 'playing', but it also refers to a small folk band, in which instruments new to the Balkans, like clarinet, fiddle, and accordion, were introduced. The word, incorporated into Bulgarian and into all Balkan languages, comes from Turkish (Arabic) and implies music played for pleasure that meets people's everyday needs. *Chalgija* also connotes a musical style developed in the context of Balkan urban folklore that emerged during the mid-nineteenth century and gave rise to a new level of professionalism in instrumental performance which marked a significant aspect of the transition from rural to urban cultures in the Balkan region. Performed predominantly by travelling Gypsies and Jewish musicians at fairs and other communal celebrations of the times, *chalgija* played a significant role in the emerging eclectic popular music of the time, freely exchanging and fusing diverse musical materials derived from various local ethnic traditions and from modern foreign urban popular music.[9] Based on the pleasurable notions of oriental tunes, *chalgija* features a specific melismatic manner of playing/improvising, the emotional potential of the oriental music modes ('sweet' *makams*), and rhythms often associated with the ancient dance named *kyucheck* (belly dancing).[10] It is interesting to note that during the first decades of the twentieth century, *chalgija* was brought to the United States by Jewish immigrants from Eastern Europe and shaped *klezmer* music to some extent.

Although marginalized for decades because of westernization (which, contrary to some current cultural and political interpretations, did not pass Bulgaria by), *chalgija* has never ceased to be performed in Bulgaria, especially in villages where the rural way of life was still very much alive and where urbanization and westernization were proceeding at a slower pace. The 1980s saw the first more visible revival of *chalgija* tradition, exemplified in the music of the so-called wedding bands. These bands involved traditional *chalgija* in a new synthesis, mostly by updating the sound without abandoning traditional instruments (especially the clarinet which remains basic) but adding new ones: electric guitars, electric piano, and acoustic drum kit, among others. Playing predominantly live, mostly at weddings, they developed a highly virtuoso style, sometimes qualified as Balkan instrumental jazz, as exemplified by the internationally successful clarinetist Ivo Papasov (Ibryama) and his Trakia orchestra.[11] The 1990s witnessed the second revival of *chalgija*, which eventually acquired the vernacular name *chalga* and inherited the sound and the virtuoso instrumental style of the wedding bands. Unlike these, however, in its new phase the genre developed the song as a more effective medium for dancing and mass participation.

Chalga brought back local sounds to the Bulgarian pop mainstream, which by the end of the 1980s was characterized mostly by western-oriented pop music styles. It was a product of the free market opportunities which opened up after 1989. For the first time, after 45 years of centralized policies, which ruled the national media (including radio, television and record production), private commercial enterprises became possible and this has resulted in the rapid growth of newly created independent recording labels, radio, and TV stations. Moreover, these enterprises began to promote ethnically based local music in response to the demand of large audiences in Bulgaria who, by that time, were strongly attracted to the pop music production of neighbouring Balkan countries, including Greece, Yugoslavia and Turkey. It must be pointed out that before 1989 there was a vacuum in Bulgaria in terms of an ethnically based local pop music as a result of a specifically conservative approach to Bulgarian folklore, which was most often interpreted as if it belonged in a museum, or in the spirit of the concert practices of classical music, which cut it off from everyday musical culture. In neighbouring countries, the ethnically based popular music tradition had been developing continuously, but the Bulgarian media which promoted pop music remained aloof from local sounds and, as a result, a gap was created between pop music practices and local folk and ethnic traditions.

The movement towards the 'local' and the 'indigenous' in the 1990s might be seen in part as an echo of the trend which has become internationally identifiable, at least since the late 1980s, under the label 'world music'. Yet the revival of indigenous sounds also renewed the dialogue with the Balkan past in Bulgarian culture, at the same time as it questioned a number of traditional social and psychological attitudes. Spreading throughout the country, the movement discredited the idea of the national as a frozen, static or non-dynamic category. It also contradicted the idea of cultural 'purity' and 'authenticity', and, along with the rising self-consciousness of the local ethnic minorities and their specific contribution to this particular genre, this musical practice initiated by itself a celebration of local multiculturalism, even if the concept has still to be acknowledged as viable.

As a fairly amorphous multi-ethnic and multi-dimensional genre, *chalga* continues to employ and update a variety of local ethnic forms of expression considered as belonging to the Balkans. It also continues to accumulate western pop music sounds and techniques, as well as their visual contexts. Yet, musically, it gravitates around two quite broadly identified streams, associated, generally speaking, with the concepts of traditional 'Macedonian' and 'Oriental' sounds.[12] Bulgarians rediscovered the vigour of these traditions as meaningful alternatives to the more sterile interpretations of the 'amusing' in music. *Chalga* became the most popular pop music genre, able to compete, for the first time in Bulgarian pop music history, with the irresistible global, western-oriented pop music of today. Roughly speaking, the 'Macedonian' sounds (pleasing tunes and supple dance rhythms in 7/8) could be qualified as 'Balkan country': not as a straight musical parallel with American country music, but in terms of the semantics of both musics, which feature a 'hidden conservatism' that corresponds to traditional patriarchal values. Such a semantics, observed similarly both in the songs of Dolly Parton or Johnny Cash and in the songs of the Bulgarian singers Yordanka Vardjijska or Ilia Lukov, dominates a significant part of the repertoire of popfolk singers. On the other hand, the 'oriental' sounds (identified with eastern melismatic tunes and the rhythms specific to the belly dance) have greater parallels with black American music, although (again) not in terms of straight musical similarities but in terms of their semantics, which imply specific suggestiveness and a body language that undermines the patriarchal idyll.[13]

Observed aesthetically, 'the new ethnically based pop music developed two main trends based on *quasi-realism* and *rabelaisian parody*.'[14] The one is associated with the language of glossy images, the 'soap opera,' and the forms of escapism particular to the naïveté of utopias, the illusion of story-telling, and the new myths of Bulgaria, and is customarily represented through reincarnations of the female temptress. By exploiting such concepts, female singers like Nelina, Gloria, and Zvetelina, among others, involved local folk traditions in a new artistic context, unusual for traditional folklore. The other trend, observed in the practice of groups like the Kou-Kou Band, mentioned above, or the male singing group Gypsy Aver, exploits musical and verbal irony and self-irony, situational parody, satire and hidden 'second meanings,' usually targeting contemporary social reality and the new pragmatic myths. Almost by rule, this trend involves male creative participation. Yet, regardless of gender, whether embracing forms of utopia or parody, the broad, flexible music and aesthetic territory of the genre of *chalga* (popfolk or ethnopop) has become a site where current 'western' myths and a sensitivity to the 'Balkan' past have met to create room for specific forms of contemporary self-expression. Based on the power of traditional sounds and on the healing power of humour, these forms brought – for many local people – the notion of celebration and a release from the hardship of everyday life.

Inclusion and exclusion

We may ask if there is anything like a *correct* policy of inclusion and exclusion in the process of cultural identity. Is it a matter of spontaneous choice under complex circumstances, or is it a matter of policy for larger communities, especially for national communities, in which people are connected in a more vague and imagined way? National identity is a category reasonably questioned nowadays by thinkers like Benedict Anderson,[15] yet the concept is not completely exhausted, especially in 'developing' countries like Bulgaria. Leaving aside social, economic and political arguments that keep the category still very much alive, it must be pointed out that its resilience is fuelled in part by the natural human need to feel 'physically at home'. The question, however, is one of how the concept of the national may be successfully updated, developed and reconstructed in the context, on the one hand, of an evident interior multi-ethnicity and multi-culturalism, and on the other hand, of a process of globalization which exposes cultures, communities, groups of people, and individuals to a variety of different sources of cultural identity. The 'other', the *different*, may be included or excluded on the basis of individual preferences, as is human, but is that choice always made independently? The following symptomatic cases provide material for reflection on this issue.

Those who watched the TV musical greetings to the world sent from different parts of the planet during the Millennium evening may remember the minutes given to the Australian greeting. Although I personally missed that greeting, which was part of a global media project titled '2000 Today' and transmitted simultaneously in 56 countries, I heard about it from my colleagues who were strongly impressed by the fact that Australia greeted the world with a performance of Bulgarian songs in a style popular in Bulgaria since the early 1950s, representing an arrangement of Bulgarian folklore in the standard way in which it is performed by the so-called folk ensembles. An investigation on the internet confirmed that my colleagues were right. The Australian performers were identified as a group named 'Mara' and the choir performing alongside them was called 'Martenitsa', a name which incorporates a term for Bulgarian holiday rituals. Certainly, there is nothing unusual in the fact that non-Bulgarians perform Bulgarian music. Such a practice may be observed, say, in Pittsburgh in the USA, or in Finland, and in many other places around the world. What impressed my colleagues as curious was the fact that Australians had chosen to greet the world on such a special occasion with non-Australian music. As it turned out, however, the same internet search showed that such a practice was not exceptional in the context of Australian music and culture, but part of a large multicultural movement over the last twenty years that had become an essential sign in the construction of national identity in that country. The role of Bulgarian music in this movement (evidently just one colour in the cultural rainbow) was due, according to the words of my virtual informant, not to the presence of Bulgarian immigrant communities in Australia but to the global attractiveness of this music. Evidently, this attractiveness, reformulated in the context of another, non-Bulgarian socio-historical situation, was received not as a sign of a 'far-away exoticism' but, thanks to the way of thinking by the local cultural élite, as a source of national cultural identity that had already been realized.

While this case is symptomatic in terms of the inclusion of the music of others in the construction of national identity, another case, drawn from recent Bulgarian experience, shows the exclusion of the music of others and gives an idea of which music the cultural élite in Bulgaria would admit as a source of national identity. A petition by citizens to the Bulgarian Parliament, initiated in December 1999 by prominent cultural figures, pleaded for a 'cleansing' of the national soundscape of what, for Bulgarians who signed it, were the 'bad,' 'vulgar' and – most importantly (!) – 'strange' sounds coming from the 'uncivilized' experiences of the local Gypsies and Turks. Neglecting the fact that these minorities are the biggest in Bulgaria, the petition expressed concern about an invasion by their music which might result in the 'gypsification' and 'turkification' of the Bulgarian nation. This event, which is not at all an exceptional episode, but a common kind of occurrence among many similar actions undertaken by Bulgarian cultural élites, is symptomatic not simply of an aesthetic concern, but of a prevailing idea concerning the concept of the nation. It also points to who is in control, at the national, public level, in modelling what are intended to be considered as 'high' and 'low' in culture and who, after all, is destined to be a 'stranger at home.'

The public war against *chalga* started in the mid-1990s, at about the time when the genre was booming across the nation, disseminated through the broadcasts of private radio and TV stations, although not through the national media. As Luben Dilov-Junior, one of the spiritual leaders of Kou-Kou Band, stated: 'Since its emergence, *chalga* has been a victim of stupid ideological speculation.'[16] Ethnic 'dirtiness' and musical 'commonplaceness' were among the qualifications most often used by guardians of a 'pure' national culture willing to dismiss *chalga* music. Strangely enough, even established pop and rock musicians, who until quite recently protested against censorship during totalitarian times, were now loudly crying against *chalga* and calling for new institutional controls to limit its access to media space.[17] In the pages of different newspapers and periodicals, it is not unusual to read slogans such as 'Down with *kyuchek*!' (the oriental belly dance), or 'Next elections I'll vote for the party which will ban *chalga*,' or warnings such as 'It wouldn't be surprising if soon the national anthem sounded oriental.' The antagonists of *chalga* also looked for arguments in the values of 'real' art, which they understand in light of their own preferences, whether in folk or other styles of popular music; these preferences however, often rarely go beyond slavish imitation of models from the global or western mainstream. It has been repeatedly and aggressively claimed that *chalga* is 'phoney' and brings 'bad taste', 'vulgar culture', 'kitsch', and other 'low', 'terrible', 'disgusting' characteristics to which 'our children are exposed.' Rock and pop performers of the 1960s were banned by classical music performers for offences of this nature; it was ironic to hear the formerly banned artists voicing these same criticism of *chalga* musicians in the 1990s. One wonders if the highbrow syndrome isn't after all a comfortable mask with which to hide interests that are somewhat less than sublime and rather more pragmatic or commercial.

All this public noise in Bulgaria seems to repeat situations that have already been seen in pop music history. What is happening today in Bulgaria is strangely reminiscent, for example, of the payola scandal in the USA during the 1950s when established pop-singers testified against the 'brutal', 'degenerate', 'phoney' and 'false' music derived from the 'non-civilized' music of black Americans.[18] As history tells us, rock'n'roll has been attacked many times, whether as an enemy of high cultural values, as a 'plot' of the godless communists (in the US during the 1950s), or as a 'plot' of western ideological propaganda (in Bulgaria during the 1960s).[19] There is no direct musical parallel, but *chalga* – with its specific cultural power – could be seen as the 'black music of the Balkans,' which apparently also threatens the *status quo* of some particular social sectors. The fact that this ethnically based music emerged in a post-totalitarian situation, which liberated the local culture from old ideological taboos and created a space for more visible identification of different local ethnic groups, has not changed the fact that the democratic process has not been effective enough in eliminating the negative attitude to the tradition of *chalgija*. Seen as a 'Gypsy thing',[20] as a phenomenon that is both non-civilized (non-westernized) and detrimental to the 'authenticity' and 'purity' of Bulgarian culture, *chalga* is attacked under the guise of the highbrow syndrome which has dramatically accompanied the history of Bulgarian culture since the time of its 'opening' to the 'high' Western European ideas in art and culture more than a century ago.

Some observers suggest that negative attitudes to traditional Balkan culture in general (of which the vernacular musical tradition of *chalgija* is a part) reflect the impact of one ideology taken for granted. Developed to serve the positive image of Western Europe in the age of modernity, this ideology constructed Europe's 'reverse others', that is, its others with negative connotations. In this sense, Maria Todorova states that 'by being geographically inextricable from Europe, yet culturally constructed as "the other" within, the Balkans have been able to absorb conveniently a number of externalized political, ideological, and cultural frustrations stemming from tensions and contradictions inherent to the regions and societies outside the Balkans.'[21] Thus, 'the Balkans have served as a repository of negative characteristics against which a positive and self-congratulatory image of the "European" and the "West" has been constructed.'[22] In his book *Europe*, Count Hermann Keyserling even stated that 'if the Balkans hadn't existed, they would have been invented'.[23] This paradoxical statement, expressed in 1928, implies again the motives for deliberate ideological construction of the 'other' – this 'other' who may serve as a negative mirror in the construction of the positive European self, even if this self is otherwise quite amorphous and controversial.

Whether or not such presuppositions have their well-grounded arguments and maintain their validity at present, it is not difficult to suggest that the national discourse in Bulgaria still very much excludes, or at least pushes to the margins, not the 'distant other' but that 'local other' who reminds us of the existence of particular Balkan stock in music. In Bulgaria today it is much more prestigious to follow musical canons from the 'distant different,' including what is heard, for instance, in the productions of Britney Spears or Marilyn Manson. In other words, the Western European and North American canons, and the idea of a 'pure' folklore, the folklore of ethnic Bulgarians, shape the idea of what should be called 'national values' in art and culture. The local multi-ethnic musical mixtures of the present provoke the highbrow syndrome and a capacity for sanction supposedly owned by the cultural élites. Without wishing to generalize too readily, it might be suggested, however, that such a paradoxical reception of the 'other' in which the 'local different' is considered as a horrifying enemy, is not only a Bulgarian national syndrome. People from other national cultures also embrace more easily the 'cultural other' or the 'different' that comes from afar and tend to be suspicious of the 'others' around them. An American I recall meeting on a visit to the USA was fascinated by specific asymmetric folk rhythms observed in Bulgarian folklore and tried to learn to play them, and yet he also wondered why I had so much interest in blues. It is also well known how North American cultural élites referred to rock'n'roll during the 1950s and to other musical genres derived from local 'horrifying others' which embodied the music of African-Americans. It would certainly be interesting to consider how Australians, while embracing the music of the distant Bulgarians, refer to their local 'different others,' that is, to the music of local aborigines.

Notwithstanding the preceding comments, because of trends in cultural globalization, which expose more and more people to a mosaic of different cultures, attitudes to the 'others' have progressively changed. The music itself re-affirms this condition, given that the process of music-making is often fuelled by intuition, not in response to ideological taboo and speculation. Moreover, modern creative attitudes are no longer dominated by single cultural canons. Since we live in an era of ex-centric attitudes, it is a function of late modernity to resist cultural essentialism, regardless of whether it derives from a Western European or North American canon. There is, in effect, another side to cultural globalization, one which stimulates not the McDonaldization[24] of the world, but cultural differences. Whether we like it or not, the process of globalization is progressing. Yet, the more intensive it is, the more evident is the need for the survival of ethnic memories. Although the category of 'world music' – a vague and quite amorphous label – was devised in the West, its emergence has none the less appeared to emphasize the need for cultural diversity emanating from stored or survived experiences from all over the planet. It has appeared to celebrate *the beauty of the small* and to stimulate cultural differences in a new flexible way through a variety of mosaics made of many ethnic fragments. World music has also appeared to avoid the hegemonies of the western world, which – in music, at least – were held until recently by dominant Anglo-American sounds. The roles of the 'different other' and the 'self' are often easily replaced or just mix with each other under the sign of an increasingly lively multi-ethnic traffic as geographical and cultural barriers are crossed. Modern people are learning to appreciate the 'different,' not solely as a source of the exotic, just for a change, but as a challenge to their own cultural identity. In a world in which behaviour in art is increasingly characterized by cultural, ethnic and aesthetic pluralism, the imposition of concepts that adopt a centric point of view already seem anachronistic. Considering things optimistically and not in a quasi-liberal populist way, I would venture to suggest that in the context of the new modernity the exotic is no longer thought of as a primitive or horrifying source of cultural difference. Nonetheless, the question remains as to whether or not cultural élites around the planet who, in their way, are responsible for setting the tone of public opinion and taste, can acknowledge the potential of such ideological developments.

Lest I be thought too idealistic, however, a postscript is necessary. While finishing these lines, my attention was caught by an announcement in a newspaper advertising a new radio station, under the name 'BG Radio,' scheduled to begin broadcasting shortly and – what a chance for local music! – its programmes would play Bulgarian pop music exclusively. Any pop music but *chalga*, that is! That was how the station owners defined their policy, and I would not argue with it. Any media – certainly! – must decide upon a specific profile. Yet their statement implies more than just a choice of this kind. It bites at the 'bad' music consumed today by at least half of the eight million Bulgarians in the country, and, just as in the fable told at the beginning of this essay, it brings back the bitter taste of hatred. Another bite, another venomous snake . . .

Notes

1. An earlier version of this text was published in Richard Young (ed.) (2002), *Music, Popular Culture, Identities*, New York and Amsterdam: Editions Rodopi.
2. William L McBride (2002), 'Cultural Differences and Cosmopolitan Ideals: A Philosophical Analysis', in *Globalization and Cultural Differences*, proceedings of the Fourth International Fulbright Conference, 19–21 May, Sofia: Fulbright, p. 29.
3. The story is recorded in Bulgarian as an introduction to the CD *Vavilon* performed by Slavi Trifonov & Kou-Kou Band (BMK, 1998). Translation into English by Claire Levy.
4. *Chalga* (also called 'popfolk' or 'ethnopop') is one of the names for a pop music genre that emerged during the 1990s. Similar genres are observed in Yugoslavia ('turbofolk') and Turkey ('arabesk').
5. Discussion on this issue concerning the Turkish popular musical genre known as *arabesk* is provided by Martin Stokes (2001), 'East, West, and Arabesk', in G. Boru and D. Hesmondhalgh (eds), *Western Music and Its Others: Difference, Representation, and Appropriation in Music*, Berkeley, Los Angeles and London: University of California Press, pp. 213–33.
6. Cited by Michael Atherton (2000), 'The Didjeridu in the Studio and the Dynamics of Collaboration', in Tony Michell *et al.* (eds), *Changing Sounds: New Directions and Configurations in Popular Music*, proceedings of the IASPM International Conference 1999, Sydney: UTS, p. 15.

7. For a critical definition of the terms 'otherness' and 'difference', see Philip Tagg's article 'Popular Music Studies versus the "Other".' www.theblackbook.net/acad/tagg/articles/cascais.html

8. See also Levy (2000), 'Interpreting *Chalga*: Old Indigenous Sounds in New Configurations', in Tony Mitchell *et al.* (eds), *Changing Sounds: New Directions and Configurations in Popular Music*, proceedings of the IASPM International Conference 1999, Sydney: UTS, pp. 84–89.

9. For a critical discussion on the *chalgija* continuum see also Dimitrina Kaufmann (1990), 'Ot vuzrojdemskata chalgija kum suvremennite svatbarskite orkestri' ['From Nineteenth-Century *Chalgija* to Contemporary "Wedding Bands"'], *Bulgarski Folklore*, 3, pp. 23–32.

10. 'Belly Dancing is among the oldest continuing classical folk dances in the world, evolving from the fertility cults of ancient society. A product of the traditions of Eastern music, over time it spread from its beginnings in Asia and Africa into Western Europe and the Mediterranean, catching on in America after its introduction in Chicago at the dawn of the 20th century, where the name "belly dancing" was adapted from the French "danse du ventre" (dance of the stomach). Associated with both religious and erotic traditions, it is traditionally danced barefoot, and with its emphasis on abdominal muscles and movement of the chest and hips, is designed to be performed primarily by women. The music accompanying the dance is most influenced by rhythms inherent in near- and middle-Eastern music, although contemporary belly dancers are increasingly open to influences of Western music as well.' www.allmusic.com

11. On 'wedding bands', see also Timothy Rice (1994), *May It Feel Your Soul: Experiencing Bulgarian Music*, Chicago and London: University of Chicago Press; and Gencho Gaytandjiev (1990), *Populjarnata muzika – pro? kontra?* [Popular Music – Pros and Cons], Sofia: Narodna Prosveta.

12. See Vesa Kurkela (1996) , 'Producing "Oriental": a perspective on the aesthetics of lower arts in the Eastern Balkans,' paper presented at the IASPM conference in Ljubljana.

13. See Claire Levy (2000b), 'Produtsirane na poslanija v suvremennata "etnicheska" muzika' [Producing Meanings in Contemporary 'Ethnic' Music], *Bulgarsko Muzikoznanie*, 3, pp. 69–89.

14. Ibid., p. 85.

15. See Benedict Anderson (1983), *Imagined Communities: Reflections on the Origin and Spread of Nationalism*, London and New York: Verso.

16. Luben Dilov-Junior (2001), '21 vek, chalgata I mediite' [21st Century, Chalga and Media], *Media & Reklama*, January, p. 14.

17. See Claire Levy (1999), 'Musik in post-diktatorischen Zeiten: Der Gestus des Anspruchsvollen oder einfach Zensur?', in Werner Pieper *et al.* (eds), *Verfemt, verbannt, verboten: Musik und Zensur-weltweit*, Lohrbach: Der Grune Zweig, pp. 98–100.

18. See Reebee Garofalo, 'Crossing Over: 1939–1989', in Jannette L. Dates and William Barlow (eds), *Split Image: African-Americans in the Mass Media*, Washington, D.C.: Howard University Press, pp. 57–121.

19. See Claire Levy (1993), 'Rok muzikata v Bulgaria: nachaloto' [Rock music in Bulgaria: the beginning], *Bulgarsko Muzikoznanie*, 3, pp. 9–16.

20. See Lozanka Peycheva (1998), '"Tsiganija" I bulgarska identichnost' [The "Gypsy Thing" and Bulgarian identity'], *Bulgarski Folkore*, 1–2 , pp. 132–36.

21. Todorova, Maria (1997), *Imagining the Balkans*, New York: Oxford University Press, p. 188.

22. Ibid.
23. Cited in ibid.
24. See George Ritzer (2000), *The McDonaldization of Society*, Thousand Oaks, CA:
     Pine Forge Press.

Chapter 3

'Power-geometry' in motion: space, place and gender in the *lyra* music of Crete

Kevin Dawe

> Moreover, and again as a result of the fact that it is conceptualised as created out of social relations, space is by its very nature full of power and symbolism, a complex web of relations of domination and subordination, of solidarity and co-operation. This aspect of space has been referred to elsewhere as a kind of 'power-geometry'.[1]

'Power-geometry' in motion

This article draws primarily on methods of analysis used by ethnomusicologists, anthropologists and ethnographers of musical performance; my research relies on extensive fieldwork experience both as observer and participant observer. I took lessons on local instruments and travelled with musicians to gigs all over the Greek island of Crete. I documented the activities of musicians and musical entrepreneurs in notes, interviews, recordings, photographs, and on film, in a variety of contexts from remote mountain villages to recording studios. Conducted over a ten-year period, my fieldwork was at its most intense during 1990, 1991, 1994, 1996, and 2000, and it is these years of research that I refer to in my discussion. Using both diachronic and synchronic methods of analysis to discuss musical processes at work in Crete, I look at the ways in which local notions of space, place and gender are mutually constitutive with the local music scene.

The notion that the three-stringed bowed 'fiddle', the *lyra*, has its origins in antiquity suits local constructions of Cretan identity well. Even today, on the Greek island of Crete there is an extensive folklore that grounds *lyra* music in a world of pastoralists and mountain villages, up where the air is pure and where Zeus was born. In this mountain 'refuge', the *lyra–laouto* ensemble[2] retains its power and influence as a manifestation of 'the heartland' and 'the body politic', as a man's or a shepherd's instrument, and as the 'national' instrument of Crete. *Lyra* music is nostalgic but progressive, rough and ready, yet refined, at once tough and sensitive. As all of these it provides for the polysemic construction of an island's musical identity and for the sensing and defining of a people and a place as Crete comes within the reach of global media, tourism and an ocean of social and economic opportunities. Music impacts on Cretan life largely through the apparatus of a local recording industry and a live music circuit. For many musicians these offer a rare opportunity to make money from music and there is never any shortage of young, willing and able musical entrepreneurs ready to participate. However, away from the club and tourist end of the market, it is the virtuosi who find a reasonably steady but never fully reliable niche locally through the recording and performance of *lyra* music (Dawe, 1998; 2000).

The stock sounds, metaphors, and images involved in the presentation, production and promotion of *lyra* music make powerful statements about Cretanness, roots, authenticity and difference within the Cretan world at large. I note the success of live recordings featuring the sounds and imagery of mountain village celebrations, for instance. The excitement and energy of a wedding or baptism celebration provides for an intoxicating and highly marketable package and is indicative of the *bravura* performances that inform Cretan music. After all, in 1990 a *lyra* music ensemble from Anoyia village reached the Greek Top Ten with an album of celebration music. It was not recorded 'live' in one of the village squares where weddings and baptism celebrations usually take place; it was recorded in the village's boarding school, and has an exceptionally 'clean' sound. However, since the late 1990s, commercial recordings of celebrations have aimed to capture all the excitement and energy generated by open air and energy-charged festivities, including phenomena such as gunfire, cries, whistles and yelps, which are left in the 'mix' and recorded on superior quality sound recording equipment.

At the heart of the matter is the crucial relationship between music and masculinity, most clearly played out and negotiated in, through and as *lyra* music.[3] Ultimately, this is a contested performance, where power and control are sought within the labyrinthine corridors of the music industry (in sound and image), in studios, at celebrations, in coffee houses, and in talk and gossip about music and musicians. *Lyra* music is thus performed in all kinds of places, but within well defined, acknowledged and accepted cultural spaces (from recording studios to mountain village squares). It is through music, then, that I consider the relationship between space, place and gender in Crete, and move to a mapping of its social and cultural co-ordinates. Sonic/verbal and visual aspects of musical practice are important contours on this map, as are gestures, postures and the kinaesthetics of musical performance and the iconic nature of instruments. Cretan musical phenomena are located not only within local and broader definitions of performance (music, poetry and drama are inextricably linked) but conflated with an omnipresent, all pervasive and largely village-based moral geography. The mapping of this moral geography onto everyday life (in rhetoric and hyperbole, sound and image) sets Cretan music, and most importantly Cretan men's music, apart from the rest of the world in thought, word, gesture, action and deed. Musical performance practice then is more than poetry in motion; *lyra* music is 'power-geometry' in motion and is the space 'full of power and symbolism, a complex web of relations of domination and subordination, of solidarity and co-operation'.[4] In order to demonstrate this point, and the applicability of Massey's model, I discuss a series of examples and vignettes (a wedding celebration, 'the mountains', 'the village') where space, place and gender can be seen to coalesce in, as, and through musical phenomena.

The wedding celebration

In this section, I recount the stages of a wedding celebration in Anoyia village which took place on 29 June 1991.

The procession

The musicians arrived from Crete's capital city, Iraklion, at four in the afternoon and proceeded to set up their equipment on a raised platform in the area reserved for such occasions. The area lay behind a small church set sideways onto the higher square and the Pasparakis neighbourhood. The bandleader was Dimitris Pasparakis (based in Iraklion) and the wedding was between a member of the Pasparakis family (the groom) and the Skoulas family (the bride). During the next hour, the musicians made four trips between this neighbourhood in the higher part of the village to the Skoulas neighbourhood in the lower part of the village, including a visit to what would become the house of the newlyweds. The purpose of the first procession through the village, involving all the men among the Pasparakis family and their friends, was to collect part of the dowry gifts for the groom from the bride's family.

The procession also signalled to villagers that the wedding had started and – apart from enemies gained in sheep rustling – all could join in. Rather, all men could join the procession, women could watch. The procession actively draws lines through the village, choosing neutral routes and those able to offer the best acoustic spaces (the *lyra* player leading the procession, accompanied by two *laouto* players, must at least try to be heard above the singing of the men). The steep and winding steps and alleyways of the village were traversed as the procession meandered down to the lower square where a crowd had gathered outside the Skoulas house. After ten minutes, the musicians emerged from the house with the bridal banners being carried before them and the baskets containing the dowry gifts being carried behind them. The bandleader began to play the 'melody for the groom' as the procession wound its way back up the steep hill.

The wedding service, in a large church located in the lower part of the village, began at six in the afternoon. The musicians sat outside and waited. When the newlyweds emerged, the musicians began playing the *Protos syrtos* dance for the bride and groom, joined by close relatives and more distant relatives (by now in 'traditional' village costume). This open circle dance demonstrated to the whole village that the two families were now joined. Therefore, throughout the processions and the dance of the newlyweds the use of space was crucial, in signalling, delineating, defining, reinforcing and demonstrating a masculine authority within the village and the lines of allegiance that joined the families. Space, place and gender were clearly linked.

The evening dance

The evening dance began at eight. Here, in the upper square of the village, the musicians and celebrants made full use of available space. There is no doubt that the incantations of the *lyra* and *laouta* create an intense, exciting and challenging performance dynamic at the evening dances which make up the longest part of Cretan wedding celebrations. 'Power-geometry' in motion. Although village and town celebrations are open to the whole community, the focus at them is upon the activities of men, musicians, dancing (highly complex, varied and physically demanding), the recitation of poetry, the firing of guns and other displays of *bravura*, and eating and drinking. In the public arena men are in control; even though women take up the dance, it is to the tune of a *lyra*-playing male. The *lyra* player comes to epitomize the control men have in these contexts; the sound and appearance of the instrument are worked by musicians. As they intervene in and oversee the proceedings, both man and instrument become symbols of authority, masculinity, village identity, Cretan-ness and 'tradition'. The incantations of the *lyra* bring the past into the present, expectations are met, and the revelry and excitement that is precipitated is on a Dionysian scale. Ultimately, the *lyra* itself becomes the focus of attention as man and instrument appear to become one. The unique and unmistakable sound of the *lyra* – aided and abetted by mini mixing desks and a PA system – cuts through the cacophony and revelry of the celebration, framing the event, pulling in the community, reinforcing a sense of the liminal but keeping everything under control.

Inextricably linked to the instrumental improvisations that drive the performance dynamic described above are the verbal improvisations of the *lyra* player and male guests, as well as whistles, cries and gunfire. The essential interplay between all these elements creates a community of *machismo* at the celebration – a sense of solidarity, as well as a flirtation with the liminal, where a crossing of accepted social boundaries is enacted, played with even, but always contained. The *lyra* is at the epicentre of this complex performance dynamic, and its sound is the prime mover. The instrument and its repertoire have evolved with, and are inextricably linked to, the intricate rituals, spectacle and display of the celebration. The music stopped with the first hints of sunrise in the leaden black sky. The mauve hue that gradually appeared and spread over the countryside eventually became strong enough to reveal the debris covering the area of the celebration. An exhausted crew of musicians made their way unsteadily off stage at six that morning. But their duties were not over. They walked to the house of the newlyweds, who had by now consummated their marriage, and began singing rhyming couplets called *mantinades* for the next two hours.

In the next sections, I elaborate upon Cretan notions of 'roots' epitomized by the wedding celebration. Here, I focus on local folklore made up of talk about music, rhetoric, hyperbole, and a vision of 'the heartland'. In this heartland, the *lyra* and its music, the mountains, mountain villages, the inhabitants of these mountain villages, along with their celebrations, are woven into the fabric of a complex and timeless world that evokes a powerful and all pervasive sense of place. I begin to detail the ways in which talk about music is indicative of local notions of the ways in which space, places and gender relate to one another.

The mountains

Cretans on the western half of the island often relate styles of music to the island's topography. They describe the music of the eastern, less mountainous part of Crete as 'softer' and 'slower'. Only *skopoi tou gambrou* (melodies of the groom) exist in western Crete, in contrast to *skopoi tis nefes* (melodies of the bride) in the east, so I was told. A local moral geography was therefore conflated with a gendering of this geography, a male, 'tough', dominating part of the island contrasted with a female, 'weaker' and dominated part. This indigenous theory of place was developed much further and I have listed the main features below:

- in the west, the men are difficult, just like the mountains;
- life is fast for the shepherd; sheep run fast, they hide often invisible in the uneven terrain. They must be chased and found;
- shepherds wear traditional trousers that are less baggy in the west, along with tough knee boots which help them move fast through the low undergrowth of prickly, unyielding vegetation;
- the shepherds do not eat much, having thin, lean, tall and athletic bodies;
- the shepherd's *bastouna* or 'crook' is jagged in the west where it is said to be a trademark of the owner's life, reflecting life's ups and downs, and the mountainous terrain; shepherds are the same as their crook; in the east, life is easier and the crook is smooth.

Music continues to feature in this construction of a local moral geography. It is said that the *lyra* forms part of the shepherd's baggage when he goes into the mountains to stay for long periods of time to pasture the sheep. He also carries the *floyera* (small flute), eating utensils and a repair kit for clothing and boots. The *lyra* is carried in a special shoulder bag along with changes of clothing. When he dies the *lyra* is put away into this bag for ever, for its owner has gone to the mountains, for ever. The shepherds live in small villages high up in the mountains, in hamlets of drystone round huts, known as *mitatos*. They live off the meat of their flocks and relax by drinking *tsikoudia* or *raki* while one of them plays the *lyra* or *floyera*. This is the usual romantic vision of the life of shepherds in the mountains, fuelled by a number of books (for example, see Ivanovas, n.d., redeemed by its wonderful pictures).

The shepherds are said to be alert to the power of sound in the mountains. They use the acoustic space of the mountain landscape practically and symbolically, where the power of sound is said to be a means of overcoming physical, mental and supernatural challenges. The belling of flocks (goats and sheep) is said to protect them from evil spirits whilst acting as a locating device. Magical power is attributed to the sound of the bells. On our way to one of the coffee houses in the mountain village of Anoyia, one dark and cold January evening, Manolis Kalergis (owner of the Pension *Mitato*) stopped me dead in my tracks in response to my question about the meaning of *lyra* music. He stood in front of me and pointed a finger at me, saying, 'Listen! Listen! Do you hear the animals?' He raised his eyebrows, smiled, and walked off. The cries of the livestock and the sound of their bells filled the air, echoing through the valleys like whale song through thermal layers in the ocean (in the same manner, the sound of the *lyra* cuts its way through the social and acoustic environment of the wedding celebration). How could I have been so stupid? I had failed Manolis. I had overlooked the ways in which the *lyra* is tied to the land and to the mountains in the Cretan imagination, and practically to the acoustic ecology of the mountains and the social spaces that Cretans have created within them. My auditory and perceptual skills were clearly below par and not 'tuned-in'.[5] After all, the instrument is often described as a product of the mountains. It is ideally made from mountain wood. It has a body, a neck, eyes, a heart, a soul and a voice that cries out like the spirits and animals of the mountains.

In the same way that instrument makers are said to craft the *lyra* 'to work in the mountains', the shepherds 'craft' their animals. The dogs and the cats that the shepherds keep up in the mountains are physically modified to meet the demands of the working life imposed upon them. Shepherds say that they cut a dog's ears short to keep the flaps out of its ear hole so that it can hear better and also cut its tail short so that it does not become caught in the thickets. A kitten will be given *tsikoudia* (the local firewater) only a few days after birth. If it lives, it tends to grow very large legs and a small body. This will enable it to move quickly, and to catch the hundreds of mice that live off the carob trees grown by the shepherds.

I was also told that the *lyra* is the first instrument of Crete because it 'fits' the bodies of, or is suitable for, the small-framed Cretan people. The relationship between instrument and body is the subject of intense cultural elaboration, an approach mirrored and often foregrounded in much visual culture, dress, kinaesthetics and even promotional imagery. The original Minoan population is said to have been, on average, five feet tall. On Crete most vegetables and fruits are small due, so I was told, to the poor soil. Weapons were also small. The small Cretan knives were put forward as an example. Like the *lyra*, they must be portable and light if they are to be of use in Crete's difficult mountainous terrain. One older man complained about the size of 'the long *bouzouki*', which he said was designed for the long-limbed peoples of Turkey and central South Asia, and not fit to play Greek (and especially Cretan) music. Most of the above information was gained from interviews with the people of Anoyia village.

The village

Typical in the Milopotamo region of Crete is the settlement pattern whereby populations are concentrated in large communities located on mountainsides and hilltops, with vast tracts of land between them. There is an absence of cultivatable land, near what looks more like a town than a village, so one has a feeling of urbanization. In Anoyia,[6] coffee houses, restaurants and shops line the streets in close proximity to each other. One could be standing in a neighbourhood of Iraklion that has detached itself from the urban sprawl. The concrete facades and steel shutter blinds of the cityscape are absent, but the presence of many buildings in a state of near-completion mirrors urban development and reveals a speed-building ethic. One can see the mountains through a foreground of old shepherds' houses, small concrete apartment blocks and an occasional Swiss-style chalet. The breathtaking panoramic views of the mountains and the island below, with the coast visible on a clear day, are obscured and privatized for the consumption of upwardly mobile locals, those working away in Athens, and one or two foreign residents. By no means was Anoyia the hermetically sealed world that I had expected, even though local rhetoric suggests that villages are timeless places where nothing has changed for hundreds of years and shepherds pride themselves on their adherence to a pastoral way of life up in the mountains. Here, 'just like the air, men are pure and uncontaminated by practices not recognisable to them as Cretan'.[7]

The purity of Anoyia was championed in relation to and at the expense of the reputation of other places. This is the art of the put-down or *campanilissimos* described by Bernard (1976) and observed by Herzfeld (1985). Inter-village rivalry in Crete often appears in the form of references to the inhabitants of the other village as *kolotourke* ('bloody Turks') or *skatobarbare* ('shit barbarians'). This binary categorization of 'them' and 'us' is one that is constantly able to expand and incorporate other groups, so that nearby villages are thought of as being full of 'Turks'. Outside threats to the village of Anoyia have always been met with fierce resistance, whether from Arab, Turkish or German forces. However, the inhabitants of the island have always sought refuge in the mountains. And, whether in the mountains or on the plains, there is also a 'threat' from other villages in the form of sheep rustling.

Other 'places' in the area around Anoyia (which means, according to villagers I talked to, 'I go up'), villages such as Livadia ('field') and Krana ('the name of a tree'), were talked about by Anoyians and other townsfolk as 'wild places full of wild people'. I was warned several times not to and visit them: 'Don't go *there*, they will kill you!' However, having survived several trips to these 'wild places' (my motorbike crunching spent shotgun and pistol cartridges into the dust as I rode through the main streets after a wedding celebration had taken place), I discovered that they featured on the same musical circuit as Anoyia. It was Nikiforos Aerakis who played for these two other villages (amongst others in the area of the mountains) at wedding and baptism celebrations. I was advised to go back to Anoyia to study 'the tradition', as the villagers I spoke to in Livadia, Krana and the nearby village of Zoniana considered Anoyia to be superior in terms of its music, dance and poetry. They also described Anoyia as 'a place full of sheep rustlers'.

In Anoyia, I had several conversations with the semi-professional *lyra* and *bouzouki* music group, 'The Black Sheep'. They knew of the musicians I had met from the village of Axos and dismissed it outright as 'a tourist village'. They were keen to tell me that of one thousand people in Anoyia, they estimated that at least eight hundred and fifty would have learnt to dance, though only some would have learnt to play instruments. This predilection for the dance and a willingness to join in celebrations was said to be typical of most villages around Mount Psiloritis. And 'of course' Anoyia and Sfakia district (in south-west Crete, incorporating the White Mountains, where 'they have many guns') were the last bastions of *paradosiakos* (traditional) and *to rizes* (roots) music.

These examples of the construction of social space are typical of those informing discussion of what are regarded as the 'remoter' areas of Crete, particularly the Milapotamo region around Anoyia. In trying to decipher this rhetoric, and in doing so noting Cretans highly developed and particular sense of place, I find the comments of Edwin Ardener useful: 'The actual geography is not the overriding feature – it is obviously necessary that remoteness has a position in topographical space, but it is defined within a *topological* space whose features are expressed in a cultural vocabulary.'[8]

The Anoyian topological vocabulary is all-enveloping, often glossing over the intricacies of village relations to 'actual geography' and the outside world. The outside world might as well be a village across the valley, villages on the plain, coastal towns, the east of Crete, the rest of Greece or 'the East'. Anoyia is not just a village; it is seen as a *kósmos* or 'world' where one may live out one's entire life, and local moral and musical discourses are interwoven into the rhetoric that maintains this ideology. After all, other places are not so good (Greger, 1985; Feld and Basso, 1996). This complicated rhetoric links 'tradition', 'roots', 'remoteness' and 'danger' in conversation; and one must also note Herzfeld's remark that in Crete this is likely to be an 'androcentric localism, in which the collective identity is imbued with specifically male pride'.[9] And it is crucial to recognize that Anoyian topologies make up one of the most powerful contributions to the cultural geography and 'power-geometry' that informs the boundaries of the Cretan musical universe.

Conclusions

The ideas put forward in the preceding sections can be supported by further analysis of a range of phenomena informing Cretan musical life, as they bear upon local notions of space, place and gender. For instance, one need only look at the ways in which the physical features of musical instruments inform the cultural make-up of the Cretan landscape. The workshop of the instrument maker is yet another point on the Cretan musical map where the co-ordinates of space, place and gender meet. This is the place where the wood of the mountains meets the technology of the town.

The workshop is organized systematically into a place where craftwork, retailing and social space are combined to create a particular type of world associated with instrument making in Crete.[10] This is a place where business is done, but done in a determined Cretan way, and mostly by men. The workshop is a cultural space and a social world as much as a place of work and business. It is also engendered space. Dimitris Agrimakis, now semi-retired, has worked in Iraklion as an instrument maker for 45 years, moving between three shops. One of the most striking features of the Agrimakis workshop is the big display boards hung on the walls. Attached to these pin boards are memorabilia that the Agrimakis family has collected and been given over the years that it has been making musical instruments. These displays are storyboards, telling the life history of not only the Agrimakis family firm but of Cretan music. The signed portraits (all male musicians) and business cards feature many of the well-known faces, figures and names making up Cretan music history. Many are now dead, so the boards take on the role of a memorial to Cretan music and its musicians. This is history enshrined. The memorabilia also act as credentials for the Agrimakis workshop, a seal of authenticity, rooting it into Cretan music history whilst drawing attention to the firm's continued engagement with 'the tradition', and how it supplies its performers with first-rate instruments. The workshop, like Cretan record shops and musical instrument shops, offers musicians and enthusiasts a place of refuge in a rapidly changing world.

The landscape of a music shop is to some extent crafted from the shapes and contours of its instruments. In Crete, as elsewhere, the musical instruments in some shops represent a diverse range of musical traditions, cultures, places and times. The layout of the shop can tell us much about how musical instruments fit in with local values in relation to the world at large. The music shop can become a kind of geo-political landscape. Certain instruments prove to be not only icons of ethnicity but engendered. The guitars at the back of the shop can be seen as symbolic of the 'wall of sound' of guitar culture that is reverberating within, and getting ever louder within, local contexts around the world. At the moment the culture of the guitar is being played out behind or beside Greek instrumentation. Beneath the relatively inexpensive collection of 'copy' guitars a fairly expensive *lyra* was hanging. However, those Cretans interested in buying a good quality *lyra* would visit a workshop like that of Agrimakis. Besides the one good quality *lyra*, a few inexpensive ones are here for those with more of a casual interest in *lyra* music, such as tourists or guitar players. One needs to acquire 'local knowledge' to decode the meanings saturating such establishments as they become manifestations of the ways in which space, place and gender are thought about and interact in relation to musical practices in Crete.

I hope to have demonstrated the applicability of a social geographic model (Massey, 1994) to research that connects ethnomusicology and popular music studies. Musical poetics or poetry in motion is 'power' in motion too. So much so, that the force of the Cretan musical experience needs channelling. These channels are capable of carrying large currents and charges to all peoples and places on the island of Crete. Media and transport are but two devices that aid the flow. I have discussed other media, such as live performance in processions and celebrations, retailing, instrument making, folklore, talk, gossip and rhetoric, where the co-ordinates of space, place and gender are musically plotted, where boundaries are put in place, and notions of what constitutes the inside and the outside are defined. Local music connects, has co-ordinates, and maps the contours of a 'local gender culture' (Massey, 1994, 188) whose ideas lie at the very heart of a complex social and cultural system.

Notes

1. Massey, D. (1993) 'Power-Geometry and a Progressive Sense of Place', in J. Bird *et al*. (eds), *Mapping the Futures*, London: Routledge, p. 265.
2. The *lyra* [lira] (plural: *lyres* [lires]) is a three-stringed, upright, bowed lute; the *laouto* [lauto] (plural: *laouta* [lauta]) is a four-course (8 strings grouped in pairs), plucked, long-necked lute.
3. Robert Walser writes of the rock arena/record as places where heavy metal guitar players play with and define virtuosity in both technical and social terms. Ultimately, the exercise is empowering for men as the boundaries of their world-without-women is explored, negotiated and contested (Walser, 1993). Here and elsewhere I use Michael Herzfeld's ethnography of the performance of masculinity in a Cretan village as a touchstone (Herzfeld, 1985).
4. Massey, *op. cit.*, p. 265.
5. Steven Feld's work amongst the Kaluli tribe of Papua New Guinea has raised some very interesting questions about the interrelationship between a people and a place, and music and the environment. The Kaluli have no concept of music, recognizing sounds, arranged in categories, that are to varying degrees shared by the natural elements, animals and humans. They assume that every member of the community will become a competent producer and maker of the natural and cultural sound patterns in a rainforest environment that demands acute auditory and perceptual skills (Feld, 1982; 1990).
6. Agriculture is by far the main source of income for Anoyians, with more than 120,000 sheep being husbanded in the mountains in any year and around 250,000 kilos of olives and grapes being produced every year in the lower valleys and plains. These details were relayed to me by the Assistant Mayor who presided over the extensive

and apparently well-kept statistical records in the Mayor's office. In fact, there is an agricultural co-operative with its own vet and a women's weaving association. With all this administration and ministry, it is hardly surprising that Anoyia is, in fact, a small agro-town rather than a 'village'. It had an all-year-round population of 2322 in 1991, as well as a registered population of 5000.

7. Herzfeld, M. (1985), *The Poetics of Manhood: Contest and Identity in a Cretan Mountain Village*, Princeton: Princeton University Press, p. 38.
8. Ardener, E. (1989) *The Voice of Prophecy*, ed. Malcolm Chapman, Oxford: Basil Blackwell, p. 214.
9. Herzfeld, *op. cit.*, p. 38.
10. I have attempted to engage in both ethnomusicological and ethnographic processes in a study of guitar making in Spain and in an investigation of the role of the *lyra* in Cretan society. Elsewhere, I have described the social, cultural and physical make-up of the workshop of instrument makers (Dawe and Dawe, 2001). To varying degrees, the guitar workshops I visited in Granada were arenas of spectacle and display. The shop part of the establishment is often decorated with memorabilia, from personal photographs to signed portraits of famous guitar players, where the animated discussions, negotiations and banter between the maker, his friends and his customers bring the scene to life. The rapid-fire verbal exchanges between Manolo the guitar maker and his friends and customers in his shop was part of his 'fine tuning' (we relaxed and got to know him better) and a means of bringing the material culture of the shop to life. Stories and exchanges tended to bounce off the equally colourful walls of the workshop, which were decked out in eye-catching displays of guitar memorabilia. With the photographs that lined the walls of his shop, Manolo tried to create a faithful representation of his past, his achievements, and the people he had met and shared stories with (some of whom are now dead, so consequently particular photographs take on the role of a shrine). These pictures provided a visual counter-point to the verbal exchanges going on in the shop (Dawe, 2001). Furthermore, these and other social relations that have come to be intimately involved in the material practices and rituals of guitar construction show the workshop to be part of the local musical network of the city and a point in national and international musical networks. It is a social centre as much as a retail outlet. This is quite unlike the world of Attilio, the Sardinian instrument maker interviewed by Lortat-Jacob. Attilio's workshop 'without being a completely secret place, had a more private character . . . Literally embracing nature, turning its back on social places and spaces for display, it confined Attilio in an industrious solitude' (Lortat-Jacob, B., 1993 *Sardinian Chronicles*, The University of Chicago Press, p. 43). See also Dawe (2003).

Chapter 4

Interrogating the production of sound and place: the Bristol phenomenon, from Lunatic Fringe to worldwide Massive

Peter Webb

I was really keen to get in some of the New Wave stuff, I feel we'd really missed out on using that influence. Everybody working in Bristol now has some connection to that period. I remember fucking about with Lunatic Fringe, a punk band in Bristol, performing *Anarchy In The UK* in Sefton Park Youth Club where Roni Size was working. There's a core of that whole punk-reggae connection in Bristol. So for the first few weeks in the studio I was sampling Gang of Four's *Entertainment*, Wire's *Chairs Missing*, The Ruts, 999.[1]

Fresh Four was like our group, we developed our sound in the 1980s, with thanks to Smith and Mighty. They helped us out with Studio equipment etc., and we kind of taught ourselves how to make music. We were making beats and mixing breaks together back then, it was later on we met up with Die, then after that Roni and then formed Full Cycle, and later Reprazent. We've always been into the 'Bristol sound'. But it's progressed, there's a Bristol D&B sound as well now, which is definitely different to the London sound. London is a lot more industrial, techno-influenced and dark-sounding. Which is great, I mean, I love it, but I couldn't listen to it all night. Our thing gives us our identity. I'm glad we do come from Bristol because otherwise we might be forced to conform to what everyone else is making, it's good that we're from the country because I think it influences our sound.[2]

It probably went back to the punk thing, why we told Branson to fuck off. I was into that, the idea behind the whole thing and it's still there; a lot of people carry their morals from that time.[3]

Contained within these statements are clues to the conundrum of the importance of place, location and identification with different elements of popular music genres and their influence on the sound of a locality's popular music. D, Suv and Rob Smith are all important informational nodes in the cultural landscape of Bristol's popular music scene. D illuminates the importance of punk and reggae and the connectivity that many who are still working in the popular music scene in Bristol have to that period. Suv hints at the importance of location in influencing the type of sound, comparing the dark, industrial D&B of London to the more melodic, jazz- and reggae-influenced D&B of Bristol. He also points out the element of conformity that exists in scenes which I want to argue comes from the development of the musical milieu in those locations and the musical 'fields' that they operate within. Rob Smith shows the importance of certain ethical and moral attitudes that come from the punk era and ethos. He still feels strongly about and respects the do-it-yourself philosophy, the anti-corporate stance, having a weariness of 'selling out' and a hatred of the flash insubstantiality of the mainstream pop world (Marcus, 1993; Savage, 1992).

There have been a number of academic studies that have interrogated elements of localized music scenes, most notably Sara Cohen (1991) in *Rock Culture in Liverpool* and Ruth Finnegan (1989) in *The Hidden Musicians: Music Making in an English Town* (a study of music making in Milton Keynes). Sara Cohen gives us a sense of the problems of being a musician and the problem of bridging the gap between commerce and creativity. She addresses many issues that are common to all musicians entering the music industry. She discusses notions of creativity, success and interaction, but confines the importance of location to the social settings within which bands operate through the studios and rehearsal rooms they use. Throughout the book you glimpse the importance of location but nothing tangible as to the interaction between place, individual subjectivity, creativity and production. Ruth Finnegan (1989) describes different musical worlds in Milton Keynes and how they overlap. She identifies how important music is in the individual's own expressions of their identity and how central music is in the structuring of everyday contemporary life. However, there is little interrogation of how place or locality impacts on the music that develops there.

I have set out this chapter in the following way. First, I want to give a flavour of the theoretical material that I feel is most useful to our understanding of the development of popular music in particular locations. I will outline the importance of the term 'milieu' and the situating of a phenomenological perspective *within* a cultural field of production approach as defined by Bourdieu (1993). I will then discuss the development of the city of Bristol, giving some demographics and some history – these elements are important for understanding the fabric and cultural geographic make-up of the city. Next, I will outline the developments of different musical spheres within the city: the 'Dug Out' club, reggae, jazz, punk, alternative rock, new wave and pop. Elements of these spheres then moved into a new orbit with the constant mixing of styles and musical signatures. I will then discuss this process in the section entitled '"Mash up": mixing it up in a Bristol fashion'. This section introduces the term Producer Led Outfit (PLO), which describes a model of creation and production that would soon be used in many popular music spaces and locations in the world, and is characterized by guest appearances, collaborations, multiple projects for individual musicians and a changing music industry (for a fuller discussion see Webb, 2003). Finally, I will return to the theoretical themes that are touched on at the beginning of the chapter and try to give them life through their interaction with the material discussed in the preceding sections.

Music and the milieu

Within popular music studies there have been few attempts at providing a framework for theorizing the production and development of musical milieux in particular locations and the impact of those milieux on the narrative of place and the aural productions that come to be associated with them. There has been a lot of work on location and particular elements of music production, creation and narrative (Cohen, 1991; Finnegan, 1989) but writing and theorizing on the intersection of music and place is still developing outside the popular narratives of locational scenes (for example, Johnson, 1996). Cultural geographers and some popular music theorists have begun this task (see Leyshon *et al.*, 1998; Mcleay, 1998; Stokes, 1994; Straw, 1991; Bennett, 2000) and to these debates I add this chapter. To do this I feel we need to think in ways that combine different traditions of theory in order to give us a multi-perspectival understanding of the ways in which different combinations of forces are *played with by*, and *play with* individuals and milieux in the formation and development of particular social phenomena. If we look at the work of Bourdieu on the 'cultural field' and situate that around a phenomenology that illuminates fine-grained individual experience, we can progress some way towards understanding the social phenomena of popular musical milieux. This approach can lead us to understand the importance of location, association, narrative and production.

A useful starting point for this type of analysis is Jorg Durrschmidt's (2000) book *Everyday Lives in the Global City*. In it he presents the theoretical tools to understand the development of globalization and the culture of global cities. Taking his cues from phenomenology, he guides us through the development of subjectivities and life worlds (Goffman, Schutz, and so on) and how globalization has impacted on these forces. He defines milieu thus:

> Milieu shall be defined as a relatively stable configuration of action and meaning in which the individual actively maintains a distinctive degree of familiarity, competence and normalcy, based on the continuity and consistency of personal disposition, habitualities and routines, and experienced as a feeling of situatedness.[4]

Developing this further through a discussion of Scheler, Schutz, Goffman and Cassirer, he suggests that in order to understand the time-space distanciation, the disembedding and re-embedding of people's life worlds (Giddens and Beck, 1991, 1992) and the deterritorialization (Appadurai, 1990; Lash and Urry, 1993) of the late modern period, we need to examine people's phenomenological space. The narrative and biography of individuals is 'the logical starting point for an empirically grounded phenomenology of Globalisation'.[5] I want to argue that the theoretical make-up of this approach has elements within it that can give us cues to develop an understanding of the importance of place and locality in the creative production of particular types of popular music that then come to be associated with a specific locality or (more usefully) a particular milieu situated within a cultural field of production (Bourdieu, 1993). In particular, Schutz's concepts of 'relevancies' and 'typifications' are of central importance for a temporal ordering of the theory of place. I will discuss the five functions of relevance and typification, as presented by Schutz, and show their importance for illuminating the development of particular musical milieux. These five functions are:

1. that they determine selectivity in facts and events;
2. that they transform unique individual actions into typical functions that lead to typical ends;
3. that they act as a scheme of interpretation and orientation which constitutes a universe of discourse amongst the actors;
4. that the scheme of orientation and interpretation has a chance of wider recognition if it is standardized or institutionalized;
5. that a socially approved system of relevancies and typifications provides a common field through which individual members live and order their lives.

I will show how this particular notion of relevance and typification can describe the development of individuals and the milieux they associate with, how the orientations of these individuals and milieux become standardized and establish a sense of congruency, and how a developed milieu can then become part of a standardized canonical narrative about a place that becomes nationally, and in this case internationally, recognized. To interrogate this further I first want to present a picture of Bristol and the development of its music culture in order to illuminate the importance of place, whilst at the same time illustrating the influence of national and global musical trends in relationship with the creative musical milieu within the city. I will then discuss the usefulness of Durrschmidt's approach and particularly the importance of Schutz's work, and then try to situate the phenomenological experience within the wider notion of a 'cultural field' (Bourdieu, 1993) to explain why certain genres, productions and influences come to be associated with particular locations. This theoretical approach could be seen as the unfolding of a series of overlapping and interlinking spheres that have different relevancies and levels of influence at different historical and biographical times.

Bristol: the city and its population

Bristol is the largest city in the South West of England, with a population of approximately 407,000. The metropolitan area (including Bath) has a population of 1,000,800. Historically a county in its own right, it lies between Somerset and

Gloucestershire. Its full title is the City and County of Bristol. A few miles from Bristol's centre two motorways intersect. The M4 from London to South Wales bridges the river Severn. The north–south M5 skirts the city at the industrial centre called Avonmouth (on the river Severn) and provides a direct link to Birmingham, Manchester and Liverpool (northwards) and Exeter, Plymouth and Cornwall (southwards).

Five per cent of the population of the city of Bristol are from ethnic minorities, compared to 5.5 per cent nationally. The 25–44 age group is the biggest group in the city, repesenting 30.9 per cent of the population. Bristol's industry centres on the service sector. Its main areas of employment are the financial services, real estate, renting, retail, distribution, hotels and catering, and repair work. These areas account for 62.8 per cent of all business sites in Bristol. In line with the national average, 81.1 per cent of businesses employ 1–9 persons. The larger industrial sector is now confined to Rolls Royce, which makes aircraft engines, and British Aerospace, both based in Filton, Bristol. Other big employers are the city's two universities: the University of the West of England and the University of Bristol. These two academic institutions bring tens of thousands of students to the city each year. Students have quite a large impact on the economy of the city and also on its music life. Promoters are known to scale down promotions out of term time, especially in the summer. Based on the population of working age in private households, student halls of residence and NHS accommodation, Bristol has 82.1 per cent in employment, 9.6 per cent in self-employment and 7.9 per cent unemployed. However, leaving out individuals on government training schemes and unpaid family workers, the employment rate is 71.9 per cent. Eleven per cent of the population are in receipt of income support (government-paid benefit for those out of work). For full-time employees the average weekly gross wage is £447.80 for males and £321.50 for females (bearing in mind that average wage figures are usually distorted upwards by high wage earners). Bristol has the lowest proportion of detached houses in the South West (5.3 per cent of all housing); 41.4 per cent of houses are terraced, and 26.3 per cent of houses are semi-detached. House prices in Bristol are on average the most expensive in the South West; they are higher than in other major UK cities, excluding London. The types of crime most frequent in Bristol are burglary, theft and handling stolen goods, and criminal damage. Bristol has two football clubs, Bristol City and Bristol Rovers, and a rugby club, and is 'home' to Gloucestershire county cricket club. These facts are highly relevant. The two football clubs, for example, create deep divisions and have a major impact and influence on the city's residents, including its musicians.

Bristol's history and culture

Bristol's skyline and landscape are dominated by the engineering and architectural work of Isambard Kingdom Brunel. His suspension bridge looks over the city; his ship, the SS *Great Britain*, is a major tourist attraction and his architecture, for example the Gothic façade to the old Temple Meads railway station, is a central feature of a number of well-known Bristol buildings. Another important figure in Bristol's economic and cultural development was Edward Colston. He was born into a merchant family in Bristol in 1636 and was a member of the Royal African Company. They were a shipping company involved in the triangular slave trade: ships from Bristol would sail to the west coast of Africa and trade goods for slaves. They would then take the slaves to the Caribbean or North America to work on plantations (some owned by Bristol merchants) and then sail back to England with goods and money from this trade. Colston was also a member of the Society of Merchant Venturers, the leading mercantile organization in Bristol that leased the wharves and quays from the city corporation, as it was then known (now the City Council). He made many philanthropic gestures within the city. He set up almshouses for the poor, a number of schools and put money into regenerating public buildings. His religious (High Anglican) and political (Conservative, Tory) leanings heavily affected his work. He demanded, for example, that the poor who were accepted into his almshouses adhered to a very strong religious and moral code. His schools still exist – the Colston Boys school in Stapleton and the Colston Girls school in Cheltenham Road – as do many of the almshouses and buildings that he invested in. There is a central street named after him as well as the city's largest music venue – the Colston Hall. The hall started life as a 'sugar house', refining sugar from plantations owned by Bristolians in the Caribbean. In 1708 it became Colston's first school for poor boys – the Colston Hospital. Now it is the biggest venue in Bristol, with a capacity of 2121; it is Bristol's main concert hall for classical music but also has jazz, rock and pop concerts through private promotions. The Colston Hall still causes a lot of controversy in Bristol; Massive Attack refused to play there because of its links with Colston and the slave trade. A recent debate and survey in the local paper, the *Bristol Evening Post*, has shown that the controversy still haunts this venue (*Bristol Evening Post*, 1 May 2002). Massive Attack have been part of a vocal campaign calling for a name change for the venue. The *Evening Post* suggested that a majority wanted the name to stay the same, giving some acknowledgement of Colston's role in Bristol's history. It has consistently been debated by the City Council whether the hall is capable of fulfilling the city's live arts objectives. Various initiatives to improve the city's concert hall provision have so far failed to provide another venue capable of offering better service. The City Council has yet to develop a coherent strategy to support or fund popular music in the city. The city's musical successes all begun as group and private ventures or creative projects that were self-funded until some commercial success was gained (for example, Portishead's beginnings on the Enterprise allowance scheme).

The city centre is divided between two main areas, the shopping centre at Broadmead and the old centre which lies around the floating harbour. The harbour is an area where small craft and barges are moored around a road and pedestrian system dominated by a statue of Neptune, fountains and a mast sculpture representing Bristol's sailing history. This area has a large number of cafés and bars, an arts centre and cinema called the Arnolfini, and a multi-media centre called the Watershed. Moored around the corner from the Arnolfini on 'The Grove' is the 'Thekla' or 'Old Profanity Showboat' as it was originally known, a boat that has been turned into a venue and for many years now has been a centre for DJs and bands. Moving away from the centre to the west of the city you find Park Street, the trendy shopping area. It boasts many clothing stores, cafés, bookstores and a number of record stores. Imperial Records, Replay, Break Beat Culture and the newly opened FOPP store cater for a wide variety of musical tastes. The top of Park Street is dominated by the Gothic architecture of the University of Bristol's main buildings and the city's museum. This area used to be the location of Bristol's main early independent record shop, Revolver. The shop spawned the Vital Distribution company in its back room and Daddy G of Massive Attack used to work there, giving him access to a very wide musical palette. The Smiths, Cocteau Twins, Mantronix, Miles Davis, Dennis Brown and Crass could all be heard in the space of a few hours in Revolver. Beyond the relative calm of Park Street and around the outskirts of Bristol there is a wide variety of working-class areas such as St Pauls, Bedminster, Knowle West, Hartcliffe, Southmead, Fishponds, Kingswood and Barton Hill, to name a few.

Bristol's musical spheres

The legendary Dug Out

In terms of the music scene, one club in particular has a legendary place in Bristol's folklore and was used by many of the different sections of Bristol's population. The Dug Out was a club situated on Park Row, just north of the the the city centre, mid-way between St Paul's and Clifton, Southville and Cotham. It was an ethnically mixed club, with Rastas, African-Caribbeans, Clifton Trendies (named after the area in Bristol which is culturally and economically very middle-class, these 'trendies' dressed well and were into soul, funk, jazz and later hip hop), Punks, Soul Boys and Girls – a real mix of people from some very different demographic areas of the city. The music varied from The Clash to hip hop, soul, funk and reggae, and there was an upstairs video lounge where one could watch a whole variety of trendy films and music videos. The place brought together many of the people who would become the architects of some of Bristol's greatest popular music. Grant Marshall, later of Massive Attack, was the club's DJ for a while, and then in the early 1980s the Wild Bunch (which included Grant) began DJ-ing there. The Dug Out brought together a variety of people who were influenced by reggae, roots, soul and punk, especially some of the combinations of sounds that The Clash had mixed together (from *London Calling* to *Sandianista*). It was closed in 1986 when the police and traders in the area complained vociferously after some violent incidents, which, it was argued, had gestated in the club. The decision was seen by a number of commentators (local press, etc.; see Phil Johnson, 1996) as evidence that the authorities were not impressed by the mix of people that the club attracted. This further reinforced some of the anti-establishment, anti-racist, punk ethos that still informs the attitudes of many in the Bristol music scene. The Dug Out had been a melting pot of identities, ideas, musics and tastes. Venues in different areas of Bristol continued for many years to provide the sort of mix that had characterized the Dug Out. St Paul's had its 'Blues'; illegal drinking clubs (such as Ajax) with DJs, that stayed open until early in the morning; pubs such as the Star and Garter and The Inkerman, which seemed to ignore licensing laws completely, and had a great set of DJs who played roots, reggae and ska. Clifton had good pubs and a great party scene; many parties would attract the crowds that had been to the Dug Out and further enhanced the cultural mixing that went on in the city. Montpelier had pubs full of punks and bohemians, teachers and social workers, and again great house parties. Southville and Bedminster had the harder working-class neighbourhoods and pubs, and a number of well-known squat and house parties. This particular firmament is still evident in Bristol today although there is no longer the same focus in terms of a single nightclub that can be seen to express it. Time spent in the city and hours spent going to different types of nightclub, different concerts and different venues will reveal a multiplicity of influences: the fruit of a multiplicity of individuals. It is only through this sort of in-depth research that one can piece these elements together.

There are many different strands to the music scene in Bristol. Russ Conway, a pianist, had massive success in the 1950s and 1960s working with Dorothy Squires and Gracie Fields and won a silver disc in 1959, becoming Britain's biggest selling artist at that time. He was Bristol's only known popular music performer until the 1970s. From this time on the many different strands of the Bristol music scene began to develop. I will now briefly discuss a few of these that have helped develop the form that has become known as the 'Bristol sound'. (For a fuller discussion of the different musical scenes within Bristol see Webb (2003), the entry on Bristol in *Encyclopedia of Popular Music of the World – Locations Volume*, Continuum.)

Reggae

Bristol has a vibrant reggae scene which developed in the 1970s when various DJs, sound systems and bands would play in venues such as the Bamboo Club, Blue Lagoon, The Dockland Settlement, a variety of 'blues' venues such as Ajax and then more recently the Malcolm X Centre and The Black Swan in Stapleton Road, Easton. In the early days there were two main bands to come out of Bristol: Black Roots and Talisman. Black Roots came from the St Paul's area of Bristol and had a long-lasting impact on the British reggae scene. They were championed by John Peel and Kid Jensen on Radio One and recorded many sessions for both DJs. They released ten albums in their career and were seen all over the UK at festivals, venues and on the college circuit. Talisman were a multi-ethnic band who were also played on John Peel's Radio One show and became favourites on the festival circuit. Other local reggae acts contained characters who would become local legends. Restriction had a young guitarist called Rob Smith who would later team up with Ray Mighty to form Smith and Mighty. They also had a young engineer called Dave McDonald who would later become the 'fourth' member of Portishead (referred to as such because he was an engineer rather than a musician). There are still many reggae bands in Bristol, Devan (a former member of Talisman) and his band One Drop being one, but today much more in evidence are the sound system crews and producer-led acts. Armagideon are a St Paul's based sound system who have produced many of their own albums (they have toured often with Massive Attack as their support act). One man, Gaffa, writes the music and does the systems, aided occasionally by others, including legendary horn players Vin Gordon, Deadly Headly and Bobby Ellis (Vin Gordon also played with Black Roots). Other systems and DJs important to Bristol's scene are the Roots Spot Crew who include DJ Stryda, Kama Dread, Addis and Henri and Louis (who have played with Smith and Mighty). Legendary reggae singer Horace Andy also is connected with Bristol through his continuing work with Massive Attack. Sound system music has always had a big effect on Bristol's musical consciousness. Systems like Jah Shaka's, the Mad Professor and, more recently, Irration Steppas have always been part of the musical architecture of Bristol's nightlife.

Jazz

Bristol has a long history of jazz musicians and clubs. Each year there is a jazz festival in King Street between the Old Duke and Llandogger Trow pubs. The Old Duke, a firm favourite with 'trad' jazz lovers, regularly hosts 'trad' gigs, featuring among others Acker Bilk. Two of Britain's most famous jazz musicians also come from Bristol. Andy Sheppard lived in Bristol and first started playing there with a quartet called Sphere. He then played with many other groups including Klaunstance, who played regularly at Bedminster's Albert Inn. He moved to Paris for three years, returning to the UK in the mid-1980s, and became one of the rising saxophone stars. He has released records on Blue Note, Island's Antilles label, and recently the independent label Provocateur Records. Keith Tippett is one of Britain's best jazz pianist/composers. His long history includes work with Robert Fripp and King Crimson and a huge variety of jazz musicians. He started the Rare Music Club in Bristol where he brought together musicians from the jazz, classical, global and folk contexts to play, perform and improvise together. It ran successfully until 1995 when it closed down. It is now open again and running a series of events at a variety of Bristol venues. One of those is the beautiful St

George's church just off Park Street in central Bristol. The church hosts a variety of concerts from Radio 3 classical sessions to more contemporary music from the likes of the Brodsky Quartet, Björk, Dead Can Dance and of course Keith Tippett himself. The Bear pub in Hotwells is another location on the jazz map of Bristol: it has hosted many be-bop, modern, avant-garde and improvised sessions and provided slots for all of Bristol's jazz community. It hosts the be-bop club which receives grants from South West Arts and the Musicians Union. Another figure on Bristol's jazz scene who is particularly illustrative of the many links and cross-fertilization that occur in Bristol between various elements of the music community is Andy Hague. He is known as a jazz trumpeter, drummer and composer, and has backed many of the UK's leading jazz figures including Andy Sheppard, Don Weller and Peter King. He is now gaining recognition as a composer and has released two CDs of his own material. He has also played on both Portishead LPs and performed live with them. Portishead's Adrian Utley also started his musical life playing in many of the local jazz bands and jams, and is seen by some as one of the great jazz guitarists. Some of the first Roni Size singles, and his early DJ sets, are heavily influenced by jazz. The jazz stage at Glastonbury, where Roni Size did some of his early DJ sets in the back stage bar, is always heavily populated by individuals from Bristol's music scene and the jazz influence always in evidence. It is run and programmed by Bristol promoters and crewed by Bristol crews. From the Pop Group through to Reprazent there is a tangible jazz presence in the music.

Punk, alternative rock, new wave and pop

The first attempts to crystallize a specific Bristol music scene were made in 1978 with the formation of a label called 'Heartbeat Records'. It was initially run as a partnership between Tony Dodd (who ran Tony's Records on Park Street and was a gifted guitarist) and Simon Edwards (a local musician and manager). Tony soon decided to concentrate on the shop leaving Edwards as the sole owner. They brought together a good selection of local talent and put out the *Avon Calling* LP (released in 1979). The music on this LP was a combination of new wave, punk, alternative rock and pop. John Peel (presenter of the late night prestige Radio One show) played many of the tracks from the album and the label subsequently released fourteen singles and five albums. Many of the musicians featured on this label went on to become influential artists and major players within the UK's popular music scene and become part of influential Bristol bands. The Numbers were a punk/new wave band from Yate (a large conurbation on the outskirts of Bristol, one of the biggest housing estates in Europe), whose guitarist Angelo Bruschini went on to play with the Blue Aeroplanes and is now with Massive Attack. The Blue Aeroplanes, formerly the Art Objects, were an alternative guitar band (much loved and praised by REM) fronted by a poet, Gerard Langley, who still releases solo material and Aeroplanes material today.

The Bristol punk rock scene was a very important part of the musical architecture of the city. One band, called Vice Squad, contributed a song titled 'Nothing' to the *Avon Calling* compilation. They were one of the more visually and musically striking bands within Bristol's growing punk scene at the end of the 1970s through to the early 1980s. The main punk bands to emerge then were The Cortinas, Disorder, Lunatic Fringe, Chaos UK, Court Martial, The Undead and a band who were not from Bristol but whose main members lived in the city, The Amebix.

Bristol became very influential in the British and European anarcho-punk scene between 1980 and 1985. Many bands from Europe came over and played at places like the Docklands Settlement, The Stonehouse and later the Demolition Diner and the Tropic Club, whilst Bristol acts such as Disorder and Chaos UK became popular attractions all over Europe, America and especially Japan. Bands such as Crass, Flux of Pink Indians, The Subhumans, and Conflict all came to Bristol, forging links with the city and individuals within it, and were part of a growing underground scene. The scene had its own lifestyle politics which included squatting and the formation of many squatters' rights groups, vegan and vegetarian groups (witness the growth of cafés and organic food suppliers such as Harvest Natural Foods in Bath, the Better Food Co, Essential Foods and Nova Wholefoods in Bristol), anarchist politics (Class War, and at some points Direct Action, had a strong base in Bristol) and even housing co-operatives (one, called 'The Diggers', set up in Montpelier and St Paul's, and obtained grants to buy and rent out property). These trends were characteristic especially of the Montpelier, St Paul's, St Werburgh's and Easton areas, where one would be guaranteed to see plenty of 'crusties' (dreadlock hairstyles, Doc Marten boots, coloured hair, and so on) with dogs on strings shepherding their flocks of fellow 'crusties', dogs and occasionally children down the city's more colourful streets. Animal rights also began to flourish, and groups such as the Animal Liberation Front and the Hunt Saboteurs found many a recruit in Bristol. D and Angelo Brushini from Massive Attack, Dave McDonald from Portishead, Rob Smith and Ray Mighty, from Smith and Mighty, and Tricky were all fairly active participants in the punk scene and absorbed much of its ethos and musical sensibilities.

'Mash up': mixing it up in a Bristol fashion

During this period a band emerged who were to be incredibly influential and who would spawn numerous critically acclaimed acts. The Pop Group were formed in 1977 by five young men who seemed at the time to be a part of the Clifton scene (a more upmarket area of Bristol). Mark Stewart, Gareth Sagar, Bruce Smith, Simon Underwood and John Waddington welded together influences from funk, dub reggae, jazz, the avant garde and punk to provide an overtly political and radical sound. They caught the attention of the national music press and played with a huge variety of acts, supporting the likes of Johnny Thunders, Linton Kwesi Johnson and This Heat. They released three albums between 1980 and 1981 and then broke up, but their influence was huge. Nick Cave cited the tracks 'She's beyond good and evil' and 'We are all prostitutes' as some of his favourite and most influential music. The cross-pollinating music that these bands were developing continued with Mark Stewart, who went on to work with Adrian Sherwood's On-U Sound label, collaborating with various Jamaican reggae artists and New York's legendary Sugar Hill Gang as 'Mark Stewart and the Mafia'. Stewart is often referred to as the godfather of the Bristol Sound, and his powerhouse, distorted hip-hop rhythms, dub and funk bass, atmospheric sampling, and haunting, screaming vocals have now been aired on five albums for Mute (a London-based label, the home of Nick Cave and Depeche Mode, amongst others). Other ex-members of The Pop Group also went on to have influential careers further developing the unusual blends of music that Bristol has become known for. Bands such as Rip, Rig and Panic, Float Up CP, PigBag and Head came and went, and various former Pop Group member played with The Slits, Public Image Ltd and James Blood Ulmer.

As Mark Stewart became influenced by the sounds of hip hop and turntablism from New York, combined with the reggae sound systems that were quite familiar to Bristol, so were other individuals in the city's music scene. The Wild Bunch were a sound system who combined the talents of Grant Marshall, Nellee Hooper, Miles Johnson, Robert Del Naja and later a young Andrew Vowles. The Wild Bunch's sound system essentially started off playing in St Paul's where there were plenty of underground venues for them to play. They maintained a residency at the Dug Out club, and then a series of parties established the Wild Bunch as the best sound system in town, although others such as 2Bad Crew, City Rockers, Plus One, FBI, UD4 and the Wise Guise were all active and influential in the scene. This whole development marked the beginning of a radical change in the way music was made in the city. The traditional guitar, bass and drums group was being replaced by the 'posse' or 'crew' who worked around a sound system: one or more DJs, some MCs (Masters of Ceremonies), singers and sometimes even graffiti artists. This later evolved into a small production unit as the availability of computer-based studios, samplers and studio outboard equipment became cheaper and more widely accessible. This became a template that was then adopted by many artists. I would call it a production unit or Producer Led Outfit (PLO). Most of the nationally recognized acts in Bristol adopted this approach. It marked an essential change in the nature of music industry production, especially in most forms of dance music. The development of PLOs meant that the creative core of a group was much more explicitly identified. One, two or three individuals would be at the centre of a group's writing and production. They would use the available technology (computers, samplers, sound modules, decks, and so on) to craft and orchestrate their set of songs or pieces. Some PLOs would have a singer as a core member, while others worked with a variety of guest vocalists. They would then think about bringing in other musicians if they wanted to develop a live show, so that their songs could be given a live airing. Massive Attack are a classic example of this approach. Their live shows started off as DJ and vocalist sets (that is, a sound system) and then, as their career progressed, became a full live band show (drummer, bassist, keyboards, guitarist, percussion, vocalists and DJ). This approach gave individual musicians greater control over writing and greater freedom to experiment with different projects that they could guest with. This method of music production is now commonplace in popular music, especially in the dance music sphere. It was also a development that meant record companies could sign one, two or three individuals as a project and then pay session fees or small royalties to guests, though this presented its own particular problems for musicians and the industry. (For more on the development of PLOs see Webb, 2002.)

The Wild Bunch signed to 4th and Broadway and released one single. It contained the tracks 'Friends and countrymen' and 'The look of love', a Burt Bacharach and Hal David classic which was stripped down to bass, drums and vocal. This track in particular provided the basis of what became a central feature of something that would be described by journalists as the Bristol Sound and then later as Trip-hop. The Wild Bunch then split. Nellee Hooper went off to work with Soul to Soul, Miles Johnson went to work in Japan, and Grant Marshall (Daddy G), Robert Del Naja (3D) and Andrew Vowles (Mushroom) became Massive Attack. They released a single produced by another local crew, Smith and Mighty, called 'Any Love'. Smith and Mighty were the next element to push Bristol further into the national and international pop consciousness. Between 1988 and 1989 they released 'Walk on By' and 'Anyone Who Had a Heart'. These were two more Bacharach and David classics, but Smith and Mighty's trademark reggae bass, discordant piano, eerie vocals and tense, electric production stamped these songs with a particularly Bristol feel. They produced a classic but relatively unsuccessful album for local singer Carlton, gave a young Bristol crew, Fresh 4 (whose members later formed Reprazent and the Full Cycle label with Roni Size), a top-ten hit with a cover of 'Wishing on a Star' and released various tracks on their own Three Stripe label. Smith and Mighty were then signed by London Records, a partnership which ended after a four-year battle when the record company refused to release the band's album. Smith and Mighty, who many felt had been cheated of the fame they deserved, returned to the underground to release material on their own label, as Smith and Mighty, and also as More Rockers (a more 'drum and bass' approach). In early 2003, they were with Studio K7 of Germany.

The early to mid-1990s belonged to what might be described as the holy trinity of the current Bristol music scene – Massive Attack, Portishead and Reprazent – and the various groupings and offshoots from these acts. Massive Attack's *Blue Lines*, *Protection* and more recent *Mezzanine* albums have placed them among the most influential English artists. They used the template of a production unit and took it into new territory. The three core members craft ideas out of samples, collaging and mixing sounds together. They enlist musicians to add parts in, invite guest vocalists to contribute and then they cut and mix the final product.

Portishead, who emerged from the fringes of this scene also used the PLO template and produced an album, *Dummy*, that was a huge international success. Their core members were Geoff Barrow, who was a tape operator in Massive Attack's studio and an aspiring DJ; Adrian Utley, who had been working for years on the Bristol jazz scene as a guitarist; Beth Gibbons, a local pub band singer who had met Geoff at an Enterprise Allowance Introduction Day; and Dave Mcdonald, who had earlier played with Rob Smith of Smith and Mighty in the local reggae band Restriction and worked at PIJ Studios (situated in Jamaica Street, Bristol) and around the city as an engineer. The music they produced combined influences from film composers like John Barry, Ennio Morricone and Bacharach, with hip hop rhythms and vocals influenced by Janis Joplin and Billie Holiday. They went on to release a second album, entitled *Portishead*, which continued their success. Roni Size, a young DJ who had been getting into the rave scene, met another DJ called Krust who had been in Fresh 4. They formed a label called 'V Records' with London producer Jumpin Jack Frost who had played in Bristol many times at Massive Attack parties. Soon they started their own label called Full Cycle and produced some of the most cutting-edge 'jungle' or 'drum and bass' music to come from the UK. A crew has developed around them, including singer Onallee, DJ Suv, DJ Die, DJ Krust and MC Dynamite. These individuals all produce their own music and also came together to form Reprazent with a full band playing behind them. They enlisted local musicians such as Rob Merrill on drums (who has played with Sheep on Drugs, Arthur Baker, Monk and Canatella, Smith and Mighty), Si John on bass (who has played with The Federation, Monk and Canatella, Finger) and occasionally Portishead drummer Clive Deamer (another stalwart of Bristol's jazz scene). Reprazent's first album won the Mercury Prize in 1996. Their second, *In the Mode* (released in 2000), gained them an even bigger audience. Throughout their releases one can hear the jazz, heavy reggae bass and occasional punk and new wave influences seeping through. Massive Attack's initial crew has also spawned a number of acts, the best known of which was Tricky, whose debut single had been co-written by Mark Stewart (formerly of The Pop Group). His *Maxinquaye* album became a huge seller and pushed Tricky into a limelight that led to four further albums and a part in Luc Besson's film *The Fifth Element*. Shara Nelson, the voice of Blue Lines, also left to pursue a solo career.

During this time many other artists were springing up. Nick Warren and Jody Wisternoff emerged as Way out West, The Blue Aeroplanes continued to make music, bands such as Strangelove emerged as a promising indie rock band. Labels such as Cup Of Tea, Hope, Sarah Records, Earth Recordings, Breakbeat Culture, Tech Itch Records, Independent Dealers and NRK introduced such acts as Statik Sound System, Monk and Canatella, Crustation, Receiver, Flynn and Flora, The Field Mice, Staircase, Decoder, Technical Itch, Jamie Anderson, Kosheen, and The Experimental Pop Band. Bristol had gone from a relative backwater where most people felt that the Wurzels and Fred Wedlock were the height of West Country musical production to a city which was talked about all over the world.

Theorizing the development of *the* Bristol sound

This exploration of the cultural background of the city of Bristol and the various music scenes which have developed there is crucial to an understanding of the nature and importance of the influence of locality on popular music. We can see the threads that have woven together to create some of the musical palettes which, as we have seen, contribue to the 'Bristol sound'. We have to understand the influence of the national and the global and their intermingling with the local. If we take the music of some of the most important groups associated by the media with the Bristol Sound then we can see these musical cross-pollinations quite clearly. The Pop Group, Mark Stewart and the Mafia, Massive Attack, Portishead, Tricky, Reprazent, and Smith and Mighty provide plenty of examples of music that audibly and visually represent this. I am not just referring to the sound itself, but also to the artwork, promotional photos, comments and actions by the artists themselves. As an example, The Pop Group's single 'We Are All Prostitutes' (1979, Rough Trade, RT023) is musically a cross-pollination of funk, jazz and punk/new wave. The label of the record has a star on it with the words *organize*, *participate* and *demonstrate* emblazoned boldly around it, directly echoing and maybe imitating the artwork of Crass, the anarchist punk band who had been releasing records since 1978. Most of the artwork that accompanies Pop Group material has that punk, agit-prop critical feel to it.[6] D from Massive Attack talks about the direct influence of punk/new wave records on the creating of their *Mezzanine* album. The promotional campaign for the most recent Massive Attack album, *100th Window* (released 2003), contains anti-war, anti-poverty, anti-economic exploitation and sloganeering material which would not have been out of place on a Crass or Clash poster or record sleeve.

If we look at the influences and environments to which the individuals involved in these bands were exposed we begin to see the relevant catalogue of audio, visual and temporal elements that have seeped into their work. Tracing their individual histories and movements across and through different spaces of musical, artistic and aesthetic development, and how the narrative of each particular milieu became entwined and utilized in their music can provide us with a theoretical understanding of the gestation of specific musical milieux. If we turn again to phenomenology, Durrschmidt describes Schutz's notion of 'relevancies' as:

> ... the ordering of the individual's environment into spatio-temporal segments that are relevant practically to the individual's varying tasks at hand. The system of relevances that frames the individual's every day life carries the index of his or her 'biographical situation' – life plans, projects, skills and abilities and corresponding stocks of knowledge.[7]

This quote emphasizes one central element of this chapter. Throughout it I have discussed the development of particular music scenes and important narratives evident within Bristol's cultural life. The intermingling and fermenting of these various elements are evident within the biographical narratives and the aural/visual narratives of the city's music producers. The 'biographical situation' of the individual and the 'corresponding stocks of knowledge' can be traced, mapped and illuminated by reference to the complex development of local and global elements that I have described in this chapter. It can also explain the peculiar nature of some of the musical production that has become associated with the city, such as the dominance of heavy, dub-reggae-type bass, jazz melody and vocal techniques, the melodic influence of punk/new wave and the dissonant chords and dance beat dominance of hip hop. We are again reminded here of the wide antennae of the cultural producer.

Durrschmidt goes on to describe how Schutz suggests that these relevancies are by no means confined to the immediate surroundings, in this example to the artist's immediate surroundings. By use of technical devices the individual's manipulatory sphere is constantly expanding and being linked to spatially distant individuals and events. We can read 'technical devices' as radio, television, telephone, video and now of course the Internet. Here we have a useful conceptual tool for understanding the interactions between the local and the national or the global. Throughout the discussion of Bristol's cultural and musical history I have referred to the development of genres, all of which have links to national and global musical trends. Their particular constellation and trajectory within Bristol itself and how this affected the sound of this city is what is important to us in this chapter. Schutz's phenomenology can help us analyse how these developing strands became individually identified, were typified into a group, became schemes of interpretation and orientation for musical creativity, became standardized for a period of time as the dominant way to produce music within a specific cultural grouping in the city, and then were challenged and sometimes relegated to a 'last year's thing' status. In *On Phenomenology and Social Relations* (1970), Schutz discusses the concept of relevancies and typifications. He suggests that systems of relevance and typification exist at any given historical moment. They are part of the social heritage and are passed down through education (informal and formal) to the members of the 'in-group'. The 'in-group' can be conceived as the particular milieu, which in this case, is the musical milieu around the individuals who produced the music that became the dominant form for a period of time. We are, of course, part of many milieux: musician, lecturer, father/mother, sportsman/woman, politician, handyman/woman and so on, each overlapping and affecting the other. For Schutz the main milieu we are involved in shapes the understanding and outlook that we have. At the beginning of this chapter I described the five important functions of these relevancies and typifications. I have used these as a basis for looking at how individuals working and living in a particular musical milieu come to orientate themselves:

1. Relevance and typification determine selectivity, that is to say the way we make choices when faced by facts or events. When we make music, or perpetuate a particular style of music, we are likely to be more tuned-in to some tracks and styles than to others, depending on our own taste in terms of style, mood and genre. These tastes are shaped by the ideological, ethical and musical influences we have acquired.
2. Relevance and typification transform unique individual actions of unique human beings into typical functions of typical social roles, resulting in typical motives aimed at bringing about typical ends.[8] This can be seen as the way that the individual once attracted to a grouping begins to act in the required way and finds similar relevancies with that grouping.
3. Relevance and typification function as both a scheme of interpretation and as a scheme of orientation for each member of the in-group, and they constitute a universe of discourse among them. We could interpret this as the way in which the musical style, language, dress sense, attitude, body language, aesthetic and general ambience of a genre becomes a marker of identity within the group who are developing it.
4. The chances of the establishment of congruency between the typified scheme used on the one hand by the actor as a scheme of orientation, and on the other hand by his fellow men as a scheme of interpretation, is enhanced if the scheme of typification is standardized, and the system of relevancies institutionalized.[9] We can see this as the establishment of the particular genre or style firstly within a specific locality and secondly within the wider culture of the music industry. Examples of this are the institutionalizing of scenes such as the Manchester Sound, the Mersey Beat, the Bristol Sound, the House Sound of Chicago and so on.
5. The socially approved system of typifications and relevancies is the common field within which the private typifications and relevance structures of the individual members of the group originate. This is so, because the private situation of the individual as defined by him is always a situation within the group, his private interests are interests with reference to those of the group (whether by way of particularization or antagonism), his private problems are necessarily in a context with the group problems:[10] the individuals within the group have interests which are sometimes conflicting and sometimes consensual, and these are resolved within the system of typifications and relevancies of the group.

We could look at Cohen's discussion of the role of women and relationships that existed and developed within and around the bands she studied in Liverpool through this particular element of theory.[11] She discussed the ways in which relationships between men and women were worked out in the context of, or in direct opposition to, the bands' milieu. We could also analyse the conflicts that often exist within bands and scenes depending on their particular reading of their biographical situation. For example, when Massive Attack were discussing the making of their *Mezzanine* album, 3D and Daddy G were using some openly punk/new wave influences. Mushroom, the third member, had this to say about punk:

> 'I was never down with punk,' says Mushroom ... Growing up in St George (area of Bristol), midway between St Pauls and Barton Hill, punk has a whole other resonance for Mushroom: more Oi! and Ain't no black in the Union Jack than Agitprop and Rock Against Racism. 'Punks and Psychobillies and skinheads were pretty much the same thing to me,' he says. And in such statements you get a sense that the roots of the rift that developed in the band during the making of *Mezzanine* were as much ideological as aesthetic.[12]

Finally I want to suggest that, in order to understand how a particular genre becomes institutionalized and associated with a particular locality, we need to have some understanding of the struggle that takes place within musical milieux and within the wider music industry. Theoretically we can turn to Bourdieu's notion of the cultural field to conceptualize the struggle that occurs on a cultural capital and economic level:

> The Class relations of the cultural field are structured around two divisions: on the one hand, between the dominant classes and the subordinate classes, and on the other, within the dominant classes between those with high economic capital as opposed to high cultural capital, and those with high cultural capital as opposed to high economic capital.[13]

I am suggesting two things here: firstly, that we see the popular music scene as a cultural field, which contains struggles occurring within it for authorship, dominance and success; secondly, that within and at the heart of the field are the phenomenological selves of the individuals, their narratives and histories, which are constructed from interaction at the peculiarly local level and at the more universal national or even global level. The players in the scene battle it out, not only with each other but also with the wider music industry, in order to get recognition and finance. The Wild Bunch became one of the main party sound systems in Bristol, often in competition with other systems. They began to get national attention as they took the sound system to London and did parties with systems like Soul to Soul. Then they managed to negotiate a record deal and elevated their status further. This is clearly the case with the development of most movements, scenes and location-specific genres (see Haslam, 1999; Reynolds, 1998). The national attention was focused on Bristol with the Wild Bunch then Massive Attack, Smith and Mighty, Portishead, and later Tricky and Reprazent. These artists and their particular milieu, affected by punk, reggae, jazz and hip hop and the ways that those scenes had developed in Bristol, but also in conversation with national and global scenes, created their own particular brand of musical cross-pollination. There were many other musical forms and influences in Bristol but these artists became the dominant ones partly because of their profile in the local scene and then because of their acceptance and elevation by the national and then the global music industry.

Artists whose careers develop like this have the opportunity to become the representation of the locality. The idea of becoming the 'representation of the locality' can be usefully analysed through a look at the narratives of the individuals involved. Ruth Finnegan, in *Tales of the City* (1998), discusses the way in which narrative evolves: it moves through a temporal or sequential framework (the Bristol time-line of reggae, jazz, punk/new wave, the Dug Out and hip hop), this provides an explanation and a coherence (recognizable markers of development and location-specific points with reference to communities, historical events and cultural practices); this in turn gives us a text that is generalizable (analysing different locations from specific narratives of the actors and finding similarities) and which is told within recognizable generic conventions (music journalism, popular journalism, local story-telling and academic accounts). The narratives provided by individuals like D, Rob Smith and Suv are not just individual tales, they also reflect the development and sequential recording of Bristol's musical milieu. They provide us with clues to the genesis of various strands of the sounds of Bristol.

Conclusion

Bristol has become a thriving centre for music production. Its artists have often had to struggle due to the lack of an industry infrastructure within the city, but the music they have produced has been some of the most influential of the last decade. The particular mix of influences that seep into a lot of the music to come out of the city says a lot about the city itself. The combinations of reggae, hip hop, funk, jazz, punk, film soundtracks and alternative rock can be said to be present in a number of cities within the UK but artists in Bristol have combined them in very particular ways. The genre, which was named by music journalists 'trip-hop' (Reynolds, Energy Flash) was a combination of slow hip hop beats, heavy dub-reggae-influenced bass lines, big string arrangements that were either sampled from film soundtracks or composed, indie/alternate rock guitar lines, jazz trumpet or sax flourishes and soulful jazz-influenced vocals. This genre has been incredibly influential worldwide, particularly in Northern Europe, America and Japan. Many of Bristol's artists can now be heard on film soundtracks, advertisements and promotional videos for a wide range of companies. Through artists such as Massive Attack, Portishead, Reprazent, Mark Stewart, The Pop Group, Smith and Mighty, the Blue Aeroplanes and many more, Bristol has a very particular brand of musical production that is partly inspired by the peculiar development of the city itself. Its population, demography, economy and culture, in conversation with musics and scenes that have developed nationally and globally, have given these artists a particular inspiration and orientation to produce the music for which the city is now famous. Through the perspectival prism of some aspects of the phenomenological tradition, combined with the developed post-Marxism of Bourdieu, we can begin to conceptualize the production of these musical practices and the importance of location in understanding their development and trajectory.

Notes

1. 3D on Recording their album *Mezzanine, Mojo Magazine*, July 1998, p. 62.
2. DJ Suv of Full Cycle and Reprazent, *International DJ*, January 2002, p. 49.
3. Rob Smith, from Smith and Mighty, on why they refused to sign to Virgin Records 'Straight Outa Bristol', in Johnson, P. (1996), *Massive Attack, Portishead, Tricky and the roots of 'Trip Hop': Straight Outa Bristol*, London: Hodder and Stoughton, p. 183.
4. Durrschmidt, J. (2000), *Everyday Lives in the Global City*, London: Routledge, p. 18.
5. Ibid., p.17.
6. The Pop Group website. See websites lists on p. 85.
7. Durrschmidt (2000), *Everyday lives*, p. 19.
8. Schutz, A. (1970), *On Phenomenology and Social Relations*, Chicago: University of Chicago Press, p. 120.
9. Ibid., p.121.
10. Ibid.
11. See Cohen, S. (1991), *Rock Culture in Liverpool: Popular Music in the Making*, Oxford: Clarendon Press (chapter 8: 'The Threat of Women').
12. *Mojo Magazine*, July 1998, p. 61.
13. Storey, J. (2001), *Cultural Theory and Popular Culture*, London: Prentice Hall, p. 177.

Websites

Alpha: www.alphaheaven.com/bandwidth.html
Bristol History and links: http://bristol.netgates.co.uk
Bristol Sound: www.bristolsound.co.uk
Full Cycle: www.fullcycle.co.uk
Heartbeat Productions: www.heartbeat-productions.co.uk
Hombre Records: www.hombre.co.uk
Hope Recordings: www.hoperecordings.co.uk
Massive Attack: www.massiveattack.co.uk
The Pop Group: http://ccwf.cc.utexas.edu/~edge/pop_group/index.html
Portishead: www.portishead.co.uk
Roni Size and Reprazent: www.ronisize.com
Shugar Shack Records: http://www.sugarshackrecords.co.uk
Smith and Mighty: www.smithandmighty.co.uk
Statik Sound System: www.statiksoundsystem.tv
Wurzels: www.users.globalnet.co.uk/~gunning/ajculter.html

PART 2

Rap and Hip Hop:
Community and Cultural Identity

Chapter 5

The emergence of *rap Cubano*: an historical perspective

Deborah Pacini Hernandez and Reebee Garofalo

Introduction

Given the international dispersion of rap, we should not be totally surprised that it has found its way into Cuba. Notwithstanding US efforts to isolate its neighbouring island nation, the rap scene, centred in Havana, has become a significant, if still marginalized, feature of Cuba's popular music landscape – especially among black youth – both in the form of recorded rap from the USA and, more recently, in the form of an indigenized *rap Cubano*.

Rap in Cuba offers particularly interesting possibilities for analyzing the international circulation of rap and its embedded meanings. One critical question is how rap's clear and unambiguous origins in the USA – the country most responsible for Cuba's economic hardships – are reconciled with Cuban rappers' strong sense of national identity. Young Cubans know rap originated in the USA, and that US rappers continue to be its most important innovators. They acknowledge US rappers as their models and express their desire to achieve comparable sounds – even as they insist that their *rap Cubano* is quite distinct. How are the conflicts between their nationalism and their desire to emulate their US counterparts resolved?

Race also affects how Cuban rappers – most of whom are dark-skinned and would be identified as black in the United States – imagine rap and its association with the USA, since they perceive it as the particular creation of the oppressed US African-American minority, rather than a more generic – and multicultural – US phenomenon, such as rock. (Interestingly, like most North Americans, Cubans seem unaware of the crucial contributions to rap's early development by Nuyoricans and West Coast Chicanos,[1] although they are familiar with island-based Puerto Rican rappers such as Vico C.[2]) Accordingly, in the context of a country where the official discourse is that racism has been dismantled by the Revolution, and where focusing on racial differences can be seen as a threat to the integrity and unity of Cuban national identity, young Cuban rappers' conceptions of their own racial identity and its relationship to their musical practices can be expected to be quite different from that of their African-American counterparts.

It has been widely accepted in the United States that the aggressive and defiant sound and style of US rap account, at least in part, for its appeal to young people growing up in an increasingly oppressive, alienated and conflict-ridden US society.[3] The rap phenomenon in Cuba, however, demands a more nuanced analysis of facile homologies such as rap, oppression and social protest. How is 'dissent' imagined and articulated within a tightly controlled revolutionary society which is socially and ideologically progressive, yet economically and politically besieged? And why have young Cubans chosen rap as their preferred vehicle for social analysis rather than Cuba's own, homegrown music of social commentary, *nueva trova*?

Finally, rap's presence in Cuba raises questions concerning the new international system referred to as globalization. How does rap in Cuba, a socialist country (moving reluctantly towards state capitalism), whose position within the global system is marginal at best, illustrate the global culture flows described by Appadurai and Clifford?[4] Urban Cubans are very well educated and perceive themselves as cosmopolitan,[5] yet they have little access to the trappings of cosmopolitanism. Far from being bombarded with images and products from multiple metropolitan sources, Cuban youth are able to catch only fragmentary, highly decontextualized glimpses of non-Cuban cultural forms such as rap. To what extent, then, does embracing rap reflect young Cubans' desire to go beyond (while not necessarily relinquishing) a narrowly-defined national identity, and to locate themselves within a broader international cultural community? In short, how has scarcity as opposed to ubiquity affected the circulation and meaning of an internationalized musical form such as rap within Cuba?

History

The arrival of rap in Havana must first be understood within the broader historical context of other styles of US popular music, particularly rock, that have circulated within Cuba for decades. Prior to the Revolution, economic, political and cultural ties between Cuba and the USA were very close.[6] Habaneros in the 1950s were quite familiar with US popular musics of all sorts, including rock and roll. After the Revolution and the ensuing US blockade all music from the USA, but especially rock, became tainted as music of the enemy and began to disappear from public view. A small, underground rock scene remained, comprising mainly young fans with access to records (which were highly valued), and a handful of musicians who had managed to obtain the necessary instruments and equipment to play at private parties.[7]

Despite such limiting conditions, young Cubans have managed to stay abreast of musical styles in the US, from doo wop to the Beatles, to soul, funk, art rock, disco, alternative, metal, and, more recently, rap. Since the primary mechanisms for the diffusion of these musics have been informal networks rather than Cuba's official cultural apparatus or the organized efforts of the international music industry, rap, like rock before it, became an underground (that is, marginal, not forbidden) phenomenon, rather than a mass and/or state-supported one. Rap thus took its place in the uneasy cultural history of Cuba's long, and largely unsung, relationship with US popular music.

Following the dissolution of the Soviet Union and Cuba's reluctant conversion to a 'mixed' economy, pragmatists in the government began acknowledging that the younger generation's keen interest in non-Cuban forms of popular music was not necessarily in conflict with the goals of the Revolution. Accordingly, rap was viewed with relatively less widespread public and official disapproval than rock had encountered in previous decades. Cubans also recognized rap's aesthetic divergences from rock; as music videos from the USA made clear, rap was explicitly associated with an oppressed African-American minority. Thus, when rap took root in Cuba, its undeniable racial associations stimulated (if not forced) Cubans to deal with issues of racial coding and identity in a way that rock never had.

In the USA it is impossible to talk about rap without making reference to race, and to rap's importance as a vehicle for oppressed African-Americans to express their grievances and desires. In Cuba, where the subject of race was, at least until recently, seldom discussed publicly,[8] Cubans typically account for variations in musical preferences and practices among different social groups in cultural rather than racial terms. In Cuba, rap was seldom described to us as 'a black thing' by rap fans and musicians, although it is quite obvious, extrapolating from interview data and our own observations, that most Cuban rappers and fans are black. The fact that rap in Havana, as in the USA, has also become popular among Habaneros of all colours, and that a number of white rock musicians have incorporated elements of rap into their music, has made it possible to avoid emphasizing racial differences by seeing rap as a youthful rather than a racial phenomenon. Nevertheless, while we are aware of the pitfalls of viewing Cuban culture through a US lens, it seems clear that the development of Havana's rap scene has had clear and significant racial dimensions, which will be explored at length below.

The Cuban rap scene

In the USA, early hip hop was a DJ-based music; it was the creative transformation of the turntable from a mere playback device to a full-fledged percussion instrument that established 'break beat' music as a new cultural form.[9] Cuba, however, had neither turntables nor black vinyl, making it impossible for these exotic new sounds to be duplicated within Cuba. Thus, while Sugarhill Gang's breakthrough 1979 hit 'Rappers Delight' arrived in Cuba not long after its US release, and breakdancing subsequently also enjoyed a surge of popularity, young Habaneros found themselves ill-equipped to become active producers in a hip hop movement based on unavailable technology.

Young Havana rap fans were exposed to some rap in (government-sponsored) youth-oriented discotheques, such as Pabesco or La Piragua, or neighbourhood cultural centres, which might play a few commercial rap songs and/or videos during an evening. The most devoted fans, who preferred less accessible rap, congregated as well in private gatherings called *bonches*. These *bonches* can be considered the seeds of today's Cuban rap community.

In spite of their relative cultural isolation, dedicated fans were able to acquire a solid understanding of developments in contemporary rap outside Cuba, as well as a good sense of its historical development. Most of the young fans we talked to recognized the names of early hip hop DJs like Afrika Bambaataa and Grandmaster Flash, and they also recalled second-, third-, and fourth-generation US rappers like RUN-DMC, Public Enemy, and Queen Latifah, respectively. An all-female rap group was also able to rattle off a whole list of female influences from TLC and En Vogue to Salt N Pepa, Monie Love, and Da Brat. Puerto Rican rapper Vico C was also cited as a favourite, because he rapped in Spanish.

As the *bonches* grew into events too large to be contained in private homes, around 1994 an enterprising rap entrepreneur and would-be DJ named Adalberto Jiménez, then 32 years old, was able to obtain a public space for hip hop gatherings, which was referred to informally as *el local de la Moña*. In Cuba, *moña* has become a generic term for rap, and rappers and rap enthusiasts alike are known as *moñeros*.[10] From the beginning, La Moña, as organized and DJ-ed by Adalberto, was a travelling party. All of the venues for La Moña, however, have been in Old Havana, a traditionally black (and infrastructurally poor) neighbourhood, whose central location has made getting there easier for *moñeros*, who come from all over the city.

La Moña initially charged a small (5 peso) admission and sold drinks, but otherwise it functioned more like a social club than a commercial venture. When we visited La Moña in January 1999, it had recently been relocated to a tiny club called La Pampa, which held but a fraction of the audiences drawn by the previous open air sites. Admission at La Pampa had jumped from 5 pesos to 20 pesos (almost a dollar), which many young Cubans could not afford. Still, La Moña remained the only place in Havana where *moñeros* could hear every weekend the latest 'underground' rap, and where they could mingle with the city's most dedicated rap fans.

The emergence of *rap Cubano*

Havana's rap scene may have developed around imported recordings, but it was inevitable that young *moñeros* would themselves begin rapping; after all, they had been raised in a culture rich in Afro-Cuban musical resources that highly values orality, the ability to use language creatively and spontaneously. For years, the lack of equipment discouraged *moñeros* from trying to organize into professional rap groups, although many had begun rhyming verses among friends and on street corners. This changed in 1995, when the first Festival de Rap Cubano was

Figure 5.1   DJ Adlaberto Jiménez behind his mixing console (*Credit:* Deborah Pacini Hernandez)

Figure 5.2　　La Pampa, the location of La Moña in January 1999 (*Credit:* Reebee
　　　　　　　　Garofalo)

announced. This event, which was organized as a contest, offered young would-be rappers a socially-sanctioned public venue for displaying their talents, thereby stimulating the creation of 'professional' groups.

The festival took place in Alamar, a huge housing project in East Havana. Unlike West Havana (where La Moña is located), which includes the more racially-mixed, infrastructurally better-off neighbourhoods originally built and inhabited by the city's bourgeoisie, East Havana is a relatively new, densely populated, and predominantly black district. Alamar and its neighbour, Guanabacoa, are both massive housing projects constructed by workers' brigades after the Revolution to house Havana's poorest families, most of whom were black. These neighbourhoods are less well endowed with middle-class amenities (such as theatres, night clubs, and parks) than West Havana, but they are rich in youthful energy and creativity. A collective of organizers called Grupo Uno, from an East Havana district cultural centre, came up with the radical idea of organizing a Cuban rap festival.

To the Cuban establishment, rap, like rock, was perceived as a foreign import, and while it was never forbidden, neither was it promoted or encouraged. One of the festival's principal organizers, Rodolfo Rensoli, a highly articulate, university-trained cultural worker, had acquired experience organizing rock concerts in East Havana in the late 1980s. He realized that, in order to obtain official support, Grupo Uno would have to organize the rap festival in such a way as to distance it from the political pitfalls that had beset rock:

Figure 5.3   Site of Festival de Rap Cubano in Alamar (*Credit:* Reebee Garofalo)

Rock was much misunderstood here, for being a genre that wasn't considered national ... that it was associated with the so-called *diversionismo ideologico*, ['ideological diversionism']; that it brought with it capitalist influences, deviances of all sorts, physical and moral. And since we had suffered that ourselves before, we approached the Asociación Hermanos Sais, which is an institution for young artistic talent from throughout the country – like a union, an association of young artists – that is very connected to the UJC [the Communist Youth Organization]. With this connection, it was easier to get the project going. We didn't just do the rap festival, we organized other kinds of activities as well, in which rappers were linked to other kinds of artists and media people.[11]

While Grupo Uno was able to obtain official support for the festival, they were not given much to work with in terms of equipment, logistical support, or publicity. The amplification equipment made available to them was inadequate for the venue (a large concrete open-air theatre) and the festival was given little media attention. Fortunately, the effective circulation of information by word of mouth, from *bonche* to *bonche*, was already an established practice, so in spite of these difficulties, the rap festival was a tremendous popular success. Hundreds of young *moñeros* converged in Alamar from all over the city, and for the first time were able to see and hear on a public stage rap in their language, with texts reflecting their local realities. That first year, top honours went to Primera Base, a group whose name, 'First Base', invokes a reference both to baseball, Cuba's national sport, and their view of themselves as pioneers in establishing a base for rap in Cuba.

The 1995 Alamar festival, by all accounts, was a crystallizing moment in Cuban rap, spawning Havana's first performing rap groups. Alamar has continued to host the festival, which became an annual event, but in the wake of its success, scores of rap groups have proliferated in neighbourhoods throughout Havana, many of them composed of youngsters of all colours, barely into their teens. The Alamar festival has also stimulated rap festivals and concerts in other parts of Havana, typically in local cultural centres. East Havana, however, has remained rap's stronghold, and the Alamar rap festival is still considered the most important. All of Havana's best-known rap groups of the 1990s – Primera Base, Amenaza, Instinto, Grandes Ligas, Obsesión, and so on – have appeared at one or more of the Alamar festivals.

Moreover, the Alamar festival has been the only one to attract attention from the international rap community, including US rappers and journalists. In 1997 Paris attended the festival, although he did not perform. The following year, Dead Prez and Black Star performed at the festival. Their appearance bestowed an unrivalled legitimacy on the festival. As rap scholar Murray Forman has observed, these artists, the first US rappers to visit Cuba, represented a contingent of highly politicized, pro-black rappers who have been very vocal on issues such as prison reform and the slaying of Amadou Diallo (personal communication). The 1998 festival was also attended by a group of hip hop journalists from the USA, who reported on the event in journals such as *Stress*, *Vibe*, and *The Source*. Indeed, they

Figure 5.4   Members of Primera Base and Grandes Ligas (*Credit:* Deborah Pacini Hernandez)

were so impressed by the vibrancy of the Cuban rap scene that they formed a group called Black August, which organized a series of benefit concerts in New York City to raise money for purchasing equipment – microphones, turntables, tape decks, and so on – that would enable Cuban rappers to develop themselves professionally.[12]

The lack of technical resources noted by Black August was constantly cited by rappers themselves as the principal obstacle to the development of Cuban rap. The emergence of *rap Cubano* coincided with a time when US rap had moved to a new technological plateau of samplers, sequencers, and digital drum machines. Cuban rappers, in contrast, began to develop their craft by fashioning Spanish rhymes over primitive backing tracks recorded on cassette, which were produced at great personal and financial sacrifice. For their first song, for example, one group paid a producer $30, the better part of a month's wages, for a single three-and-a-half minute backing track. It should also be noted that these 'backgrounds' seriously limited improvisation; when the tape was over, they would have to stop singing until the tape was rewound. Good quality demos or videos that would have permitted Cuban rappers to demonstrate their talents to the fullest were far beyond their means.

Because rap still occupies a marginal position within the Cuban popular music landscape, most Havana rap groups are limited to free performances at neighbourhood cultural centres rather than clubs patronized by dollar-laden tourists. Rappers seldom appear on television, and when they have, it has been often been thanks to personal connections. The first television show to invite rappers to perform was *La Mitad de Hoy*, produced by Abigail García, whose husband Julian Fernández, a veteran of the highly acclaimed *nueva trova* ensemble Grupo Moncada, was producing background tapes for Havana rap groups such as Primera Base and Grandes Ligas. While rappers are not paid for appearing, television has provided a fortunate few groups with the legitimacy of national exposure.

Until recently, the Cuban label EGREM were still uninterested in Cuban rap, and fewer than a handful of Cuban rap groups had managed to obtain a contract either with one of Cuba's jointly owned labels (primarily with Spanish companies), or with other foreign labels willing to invest in production costs. Approaching the new millennium, only Primera Base, winners of the first festival, and SBS, a rap/salsa fusion group, actually had recordings for sale in Cuba, both with Spanish/Cuban joint ventures: No Problem Records and Magic Music respectively. 'This may give rise to the same old story of Cuban talent being discovered by foreign enterprises,' chided visiting journalist Kofi Taha. 'Cuban record labels should look into rap so these talents stay with local labels.'[13]

Race, gender, and dissent in *rap Cubano*

Given such trying conditions, what could have accounted for rap's appeal to young *moñeros*? They cited rap's energetic, compelling beats, the rhythmic cadence of its lyrics, and hip hop style as the most attractive features of the music. They also mentioned their admiration for US rappers' posture of assertiveness. In this connection, it is important to note that rap began to surface in Cuba precisely during the ascendancy of gangsta rap in the United States; artists like Ice-T, Ice Cube, Snoop Doggy Dog (now known as Snoopy Dogg), Dr Dre, 2Pac, and Notorious B.I.G. were regularly mentioned as models and favourites, even by women, and DJ Adalberto reported that these artists were among the most popular at La Moña.[14] When we observed that these artists were among the most criticized for their aggressiveness, violence, and misogyny, our Cuban respondents expressed surprise and informed us that they didn't understand the lyrics. Cuban rappers simply borrowed the stylistic elements that they found most appealing and adapted them to their own purposes.

As for the themes explored in Havana rap, the rappers we spoke to were unanimous in expressing their belief that rap lyrics should be socially relevant and constructive; these were generically referred to as *temas sociales*, or social themes. Cuban rappers' *temas sociales* commented on a variety of issues from the particularities of daily life in Cuba, to broader social issues such as AIDS and globally-relevant themes such as the destructiveness of war. But if young

Habaneros felt the need to express their views on social issues, why didn't they turn to *nueva trova*, Cuba's own, well-established genre specifically associated with social and political commentary? *Trova* had developed in the context of the socially conscious pan-Latin American 'new song movement' of the 1960s, which tended to employ lyrics that were self-consciously literary, formal and schooled, often reflecting affinities with poets such as Neruda and Vallejo.[15] So, while *nueva trova*'s lyrics touched on the themes important to rappers, *moñeros* considered rap to be better-suited to this purpose, because, as one member of Grandes Ligas observed, rap was 'more pure, more of the street'.[16]

Cuban *temas sociales* are often sophisticated rhymes which incorporate an analysis and critique of complex issues, but they are not oppositional in the sense that the term is understood in the USA. Gangsta rap emerged from the most disaffected sectors of US society, where the police and the government are viewed as the enemy. Young Havana rappers, on the other hand, have grown up with a very different relationship to the state. While there is no guarantee of free expression and the state does not take kindly to direct criticism, Cuban rappers are aware that their government has provided free education and healthcare, and a more equitable distribution of resources. Under these circumstances, dissent has a different experiential meaning for Cuban rappers than their counterparts in other parts of the world.[17] While there is certainly frustration with bureaucracy and dissatisfaction with scarcity in Cuba, *moñeros* did not seem to feel that they were more subject to these problems than other ordinary Cubans, and certainly not because of their race. Indeed, most of the rappers we talked to were intensely proud of their country and its accomplishments.

In this regard, Havana rappers were like a loyal opposition; they were aware that they have been part of a social experiment that has provided them with both opportunities and hardships, and they seemed confident that what they had to say about it mattered. Therefore, while rappers might expound on the problems the dollar economy has created for Cubans, or address the issue of prostitution, Cuban rappers were quick to point out that it was always done 'in a positive way'. For example, in describing their song 'Jinetera' (about women who consort with dollar-carrying foreigners and exchange sex for money, consumer goods, or simply a night on the town) a member of Primera Base noted that 'what she's doing is negative, but it is a product of circumstances', arguing that the rap was written from 'the perspective of a criticism made with love.'[18] Amenaza's Pando was emphatic about his responsibilities as a rapper: 'We want to let people know how to behave, in a positive way, always a positive message. We never talk about violence, about killing. We try to give a new message in a positive way and with the principles of the Revolution which made us develop.'[19] All this may sound a bit rhetorical, but one of the things that virtually all US observers have noted about rap in Cuba has been its incredibly positive energy, and a certain 'old school' optimism; US rap displayed similar features before it became commercial, when it was still an undiscovered street culture in the South Bronx.

In spite of such genuine optimism, the difficulties, for young people supportive of the Revolution's goals, of articulating alternative viewpoints and even critiques of their own society should not be underestimated. As one young musician noted, 'Protest is a difficult topic. We avoid the political parts, because that would be to put ourselves in a difficult situation for no good reason. Because in the final analysis, we were born here and whatever problems this system has, we have our food, our support.' In fact, as producer Pablo Herrera insightfully observed, young Cubans who have grown up under the Revolution are unaccustomed to expressing dissent:

> The discourse of the Revolution has been that this is the very best that we can have, and there's no way we can criticize it because it's the best in the world – which is true. In that sense the Revolution did not develop in people a sense of critical thinking, so people do not have a way of criticizing, analyzing something ... The reason is that Cuba has always been at war with the US, which means that there's no space for other discourses, because it might rock the foundations of the Revolution.[20]

Other themes common in US rap were also conspicuous by their absence in Cuban rap. MTV rap videos display the material wealth of US rappers, but Havana rappers have not followed suit. There is not much point in boasting about trendy liquors, fancy cars or brand name clothing in their lyrics, since most of these items are unavailable to most Cubans. More importantly, there is little celebration of violence and no rampant misogyny in Cuban rap. We were told, for example, about a handful of Havana rappers who made some aggressive raps about street fighting, but these songs were dismissed as simple posturing. Such lyrics were seen as either irrelevant – since US levels of street violence are unknown in Havana – or unnecessary and counterproductive. As one rapper from Obsesión observed, 'you can live in a violent context, but you don't have to sing about it.'[21]

US rap has also received much attention for its harsh treatment of women. In Havana, however, in spite of lyrics critical of some female behaviours (such as the *jineteras'* surrender to materialism), and in spite of the persistence of machismo and male chauvinism in Cuban society, most *moñeros* agreed that Cuban rap lyrics did not attack women as a group. There were even a few raps such as Primera Base's 'Malo' which criticized destructive behaviours in men including the mistreatment of women. Furthermore, we encountered a number of progressive female rappers who were highly respected by their peers and fans.

The first all-woman group to make a public impact in Havana was the Guanabacoa-based group Instinto, who won second prize at the second Alamar festival. Subsequently, other all-women groups emerged, such as Ambar and Atracción. There are also mixed groups that included a female rapper; for example, the female MC Magia was one of three rappers in the group Obsesión, which won first prize at Alamar in 1998. While Instinto's sense of rhyme and assertiveness were the products of their own experience, their incredible professionalism and riveting stage presence resulted from untold hours of honing their craft under the tutelage of Silvia Acea, a conservatory-trained pianist and artistic director with a highly developed political consciousness, who had performed and travelled with a number of Cuba's best musicians, including the well-known Afro-Cuban rock group, Síntesis. Under such mentorship, it was not surprising to find *temas sociales* playing a central role in the group's raps. Doris, from Instinto, described the sort of themes the group incorporated into their lyrics as follows:

> We do *temas sociales*, but also about love, the relationship between men and women in domestic space, but in a disarming way – not being disrespectful ... We try to always elevate woman [*llevar en alto el nombre de la mujer*], to defend her in everything she does and says, to make people see that we women have value in society, that we have substance, that we can do anything, that we can even rap. We will not permit men to speak badly of women.[22]

As for the issue of race, Cuban rappers, unlike their US counterparts, do not think of themselves as victims of institutional racism; like most Cubans, they perceive racial prejudices as the vestiges of past structures carried over from pre-Revolutionary times. Therefore, while there were some raps about race consciousness and pride, raps about racism were more likely to be denunciations of the evil effects of racism in general, than a pointed critique of its presence in contemporary Cuban society. The topic of race was so sensitive that, as Raquel Rivera noted when she attended the 1997 Alamar festival, 'when producer Pablo

Figure 5.5   Instinto performing at Café Teatro, January 1999 (*Credit:* Deborah Pacini Hernandez and Reebee Garofalo)

Herrera described rap as "an Afro-Cuban phenomenon" at one of the festival's afternoon colloquiums – all hell broke loose'.[23] The first publicly performed song directly to address the issue of racial difference in Cuba was Amenaza's 'Achavon Cruza'o', which they performed at the 1997 festival. Pando stressed that Amenaza's analysis of race prejudice was 'not against the government, it's against our mistakes. We talk about them, but always in a positive way.' The song, which as it happens, is about the experience of being mixed-race in Cuba, still generated considerable controversy because it openly challenged the official orthodoxy that racial differences were irrelevant in Cuba.

As Cuba becomes less isolated and Cuban rap finds a voice on the international stage, it is inevitable that Cuban conceptions of identity and racial unity will be put to the test. To help young Havana rappers gain perspective on such difficult issues, rap enthusiasts like DJ Adalberto Jiménez, Rodolfo Rensoli, producers Pablo Herrera and Julian Fernández, and Silvia Acea serve as guides and mentors. These individuals, ranging in age from the mid-30s to the 50s – all of whom have some degree of African ancestry – have well-developed political and social analyses, which include an understanding of the importance of race. As Pablo Herrera observed: 'Rap, if it's well used, could be the one thing that would make black people in Cuba have more of a consciousness around who they are, and where they are coming from ... not to rebel against the system, but to become a better part of the system. And when I say system, I mean the revolution for social change.'[24]

What part, then, has race played in the construction of *moñero* identity? While it is manifestly evident that most Cuban rappers are dark skinned, music in general is not racially coded in Cuba, nor is rap explicitly referred to as 'a black thing' in the same way it is in the USA. The lack of public discourse on race in Cuba has meant that most *moñeros* do not readily articulate a sense of themselves as culturally or socially distinct from other Cubans on account of their race. As rap producer Julian Fernández asserted bluntly, 'we don't have a concept of blackness in Cuba.'[25] Nevertheless, there is an understanding, which some attributed to the influence of music videos, that rap, at least in the US, has been primarily a music made by and for blacks. DJ Adalberto, for example, observed, 'In Cuba people watch ... music videos. If a rock group is shown, in general the musicians are all white. But if a rap group comes on, the musicians are all black, so that's what people perceive. That attracts the race. [*Eso llama a la raza.*]'[26]

Cuban rappers expressed a keen interest in participating in the international rap arena, but while such an impulse could easily be read as an awareness of their place in diasporan culture, there were few such references on the part of the rappers themselves. As Pablo Herrera noted, 'I don't think they see themselves in those terms ... One of the main reasons they don't identify themselves as Africans is because of racism and slavery, and they don't want to attach themselves with poverty and poor people, people with no resources.'[27] Thus, even as young Cuban rappers have become more conscious of their racial identity in local – Cuban –

terms, their perceived relationships to people of African descent still seem to be located in the historical past rather than the present. Their identification with contemporary diasporan communities and cultures – the sort of trans-Atlantic diasporan consciousness posited by Gilroy[28] – seemed to be less important to the young rappers and fans we spoke to than their sense of cosmopolitanism, of being part of a larger international community. This is not to say, however, that Cuban rappers and their fans have no racial consciousness; rather that it exists as part of, not in opposition to, their national identity.

Nationalism and the politics of music

If Cuban rappers' themes are primarily local, their overall sound and style continue to be closely modelled on their US counterparts; indeed, in 1999 they were quite forthright to us in their admiration for US rappers as the originators of the genre, and in their desire to achieve a similar quality of sound and image. How, then, did Cuban rappers reconcile their unabashed esteem for US rappers with their strong sense of nationalism? There appeared to be several strategies for negotiating such tensions. First, they knew rap was made outside the USA as well, so rap was not perceived solely as a US product. As one of the rappers from Instinto observed, 'We learn a lot from them [non-Cuban rappers] – but not just from North America, also from Latin America, and Europe. There's an expansion of rap in the whole world.'[29] More importantly, they perceived their rap to be distinctly Cuban because it was in (Cuban) Spanish and because its lyrics spoke of Cuban realities. Instinto, for example, incorporated texts about the Afro-Cuban deity Obatala. Finally, Cuban rappers have sought to indigenize rap by adding Cuban rhythms and instruments. Amenaza won the Grand Prize at the third Alamar festival when they added bata drums to a backing track lifted from Ice Cube's 'We Know You Do It.' Amenaza also made a background tape using Compay Segundo's song 'Chan Chan'.[30] Producer Julian Fernández used a Macintosh computer to create an original background tape for the group Grandes Ligas, laying down a foundation of unmistakably Cuban rhythm tracks, one with *maracas*, another with a *shekere*, and another with a *tumbadora* playing a *guaguanco*.

Another group called SBS (from the English 'Sensational Boys of the Street,') attempted to integrate rap with salsa. As the first rap ensemble to own their own instruments – that is, keyboards and synthesizers, not drums or turntables – SBS had the advantage of being able to play live backing tracks for their rhymes, and opening up possibilities for improvisation on stage that were not shared by groups limited to pre-recorded cassettes. Owning instruments also allowed them to experiment with non-Cuban musical styles, including *merengue* and dancehall. They were invited to open the show for the popular salsa group Charanga Habanera at the 1997 International Youth Festival, which was attended by thousands of young people from all over the world, as well as broadcast on Cuban television. Since then, they have recorded a CD, *Mami Dame Carne* (Magic Music FMD 75181), and have received extensive attention from local media. As a result, SBS has 'crossed over' to a national Cuban audience – the first Cuban rappers to achieve popularity outside of Havana. SBS's fusions, however, have not been well received by hard core *moñeros*, who have roundly criticized the band for distorting rap in order to achieve commercial success – in effect, for selling out.

Rap groups have also experimented with other strategies to further develop their craft and advance their careers. The availability of rock musicians who can play live backing tracks is particularly attractive to rappers with little access to the normal tools of the rap trade. Rockers, for their part, have recognized rap's appeal to young audiences, and have invited rap groups to appear with them on the same stage, sometimes providing them with live accompaniment. A few rappers, in turn, have incorporated elements of rock into their music. For example, Primera Base's song 'Igual que tú', which they performed at the 1997 festival and which appears on their first CD, *Igual que tú* (No Problem Records, CD 9492), has white rocker/rapper and producer Athanai singing along. Athanai, it should be noted, also produced Primera Base's first CD.

Rap, both US and Cuban, has also influenced Cuban rockers. Garage H, a Cuban garage band inspired by the likes of Rage Against the Machine, has made rap an integral part of its music. Signed in 1997 to a Basque record label specializing in protest music, they invited Grandes Ligas to record a number with them, making their CD *Sin Azucar* (Esan Ozenki-Gora Herriak, EO.098 CD) technically the first Cuban recording to include rap. Athanai, with his own rock band, has also incorporated rap, including one song on his first CD *Septimo Cielo* (No Problem Records, NP 19734) in which he raps about being a 'blanco rapero' (white rapper) without the taint of inauthenticity that accompanied Vanilla Ice. Because of the technical scarcity that accompanies rap in Cuba, the divide that separates rock from rap in the USA is less rigid in Cuba; if anything, these musics are further joined in their degree of marginality.

As the youthful audience for rock and rap gains a more prominent voice in Cuba, however, recent evidence suggests that their influence could lead to a change in the official status of these musics. At a meeting of artists in Havana in May 1999, the new Minister of Culture, Abel Prieto Jiménez, who is himself distinguished by his youthfulness and long hair, conceded that 'the approach of rockers as well as rappers in their music has been very Cuban.' Prieto concluded: 'It's time we nationalize rock and rap,'[31] by which he meant that rockers and rappers should come under the aegis of state representation, as do other musicians. Since all professional musicians in Cuba are employees of the state – and Cuban law now permits certain freedoms in terms of negotiating performances and record contracts – this could be a major development in the professionalization of *rap Cubano*. In 2000, EGREM agreed to a joint venture that included Pablo

Hererra and an unnamed New York rap producer.[32] Their first project, a twelve-act compilation of *rap Cubano* called *The Cuban Hip Hop All Stars, Vol.1*, was released on Papaya Records in 2001.

Where, then, do we position rap in the hierarchy of contemporary Cuban cultural practices? Officially, Cuba continues to recognize its African heritage through the active promotion of traditional Afro-Cuban genres such as *rumba*. When the voice of social commentary is called for in official circles, *nueva trova* remains the political voice of Cuba. On the popular front, if La Moña and the annual Alamar rap festivals represented important milestones for rap in Cuba, the majority of young Habaneros in 1999 continued to prefer Cuban popular dance music, particularly a close relative of salsa known within Cuba as *timba*, played by internationally popular bands such as NG La Banda. *Moñeros'* preference for rap did not mean they rejected salsa, which was perceived as practically synonymous with Cuban national identity. Asked if he still liked salsa, one *moñero* responded: 'We're Cuban, aren't we?' But the salsa made in Cuba is considered local, unique to Cuba, and quintessentially Cuban; it expresses a more locally-defined identity rather than a broader cosmopolitan identity, defined by Turino as: 'the imaging of oneself as part of the globe and transnational markets'.[33] By embracing rap, young *moñeros* – like rockers, but in contrast to *salseros* – participate in an underground, socially-distinct community linked to a cosmopolitan urban culture that transcends Cuba's borders.

In short, if salsa expresses Cuban nationalism, rap expresses *moñeros'* desire to participate in a broader, cosmopolitan international community. Clearly, there is the sense that people consider themselves to be a part of something larger than narrowly conceived identities would permit. Cuban young people have few options for expressing the difficulties of growing up in a society caught in the tug of war between socialism and capitalism, rap's hip hop beats, style and attitude continue to allow them to articulate their dual experiences of negotiating the complicated realities of daily life in Cuba on the one hand, and participating in global modernity on the other.

Notes

1. Cross, Brian (1993), *It's Not About a Salary: Rap, Race and Resistance in Los Angeles*, New York and London: Verso; Flores, Juan (1992–93), 'Puerto Rican and Proud, Boyee', *Centro: Bulletin of the Centro de Estudios Puertorriqueños*, Winter, 337–46; Rivera, Raquel (1996), 'Boricuas from the hip hop zone: notes on race and ethnic relations in New York City', *Centro: Bulletin of the Centro de Estudios Puertorriqueños*, Spring, 202–15.
2. Rivera, Raquel (1997a), '*Festival de Rap Cubano: Son de la Moña*', *The House in Your Face*, **2** (6) 36–37.
3. Lipsitz, George (1992–93), 'We know what time it is: youth culture in the 1990s,' *Centro: Bulletin of the Centro de Estudios Puertorriqueños*, Winter, 297–307.

4. Appadurai, Arjun (1990), 'Disjuncture and Difference in the Global Cultural Economy,' *Public Culture*, **2** (2), 1–24; Clifford, James (1992), 'Traveling Cultures,' in Lawrence Grossberg, Cary Nelson and Paula Treichler (eds), *Cultural Studies*, New York, pp. 96–116.
5. Perez, Louis (1992), 'US–Cuban Relations', paper delivered at the Thomas Center, Gainesville, Florida.
6. Guille Vilar, interview with authors, 1997.
7. Humberto Manduley, interview with authors, 1997.
8. Cf. de la Fuente, Alejandro (1998), 'Race, National Discourse and Politics in Cuba: An Overview,' *Latin American Perspectives*, **25** (3), 43–69.
9. Garofalo, Reebee (1997), *Rockin' Out: Popular Music in the US*, Boston: Allyn and Bacon; Toop, David ([1984] 1991), *Rap Attack 2: African Rap to Global Hip Hop*, London: Serpent's Tail.
10. *Moña* is also the generic Cuban street term for black musics, particularly those from the US, including older African-American styles such as soul or funk, which have long been popular in Havana. In thinking about black musics generically, without reference to specific point of origin, *moña* can be considered, as Waxer considers salsa, a cosmopolitan concept. To Waxer, 'cosmopolitanism' means 'of the world', something that is simultaneously local and global. Although the term is conventionally used to denote sophisticated élites, it is useful for its pliability in referring to ideas, practices and things which are shared in many places, without having a single point of origin or reference' (Waxer, Lise (1998), 'Cali Pachanguero: A Social History of Salsa in a Colombian City', Ph.D. dissertation, University of Illinois at Urbana-Champaign, p. 32). In this regard, Cubans' use of a generic term for black musics resembles the practice in Brazil, where black musics from the USA are all referred to as *funk*, regardless of whether they fit within that category from a US point of view (Charles Perrone, personal communication), and in Cartagena, Colombia, where musics from any part of the diaspora are referred to as *música Africana*, or as *música terapia* (Pacini Hernandez, Deborah (1996), 'Sound systems, world beat and diasporan identity in Cartagena, Colombia,' *Diaspora: A Journal of Transnational Studies*, **5** (3), 429–66).
11. Rodolfo Rensoli, interview with authors, 1999.
12. Taha, Kofi, 'Black August hip-hop benefit concert to create US–Cuba cultural exchange,' Black August press release (1998).
13. Taha, Kofi (1999), 'Cuba's union rap,' *The Source*, August, 52.
14. Bierma, Paige (1996), 'Hip Hop Havana,' *Vibe*, March, 94–98.
15. Manuel, Peter (1998), *Popular Musics of the Non-Western World*, New York: Oxford University Press.
16. Grandes Ligas, interview with authors, 1999.
17. Elflien, Dietmar (1998), 'From Krauts with attitudes to Turks with attitudes: some aspects of hip hop history in Germany,' *Popular Music*, **17** (3), 255–65.
18. Primera Base, interview with authors, 1999.
19. Amenaza, interview with authors, 1997.
20. Pablo Herrera, interview with authors, 1999.
21. Obsesión, interview with authors, 1999.
22. Instinto, interview with authors, 1997.
23. Rivera, Raquel (1997b), 'Rap Cubano,' *Stress*, December, 11–12.
24. Pablo Herrera, interview with authors, 1999.
25. Julian Fernández, interview with authors, 1997.
26. Adalberto Jiménez, interview with authors, 1999.
27. Pablo Herrera, interview with authors, 1999.

28. Gilroy, Paul (1993), *The Black Atlantic: Modernity and Double Consciousness*, Cambridge, MA: Harvard University Press.
29. Instinto, interview with authors, 1997.
30. Members of Amenaza journeyed to Paris where they formed a new group, Orishas, and released a CD, *A Lo Cubano* (EMI/Chrysalis-Spain, 7243 5 21410 2 8, 1999)
31. Cantor, Judy (1999), 'Portrait of the Artist as a Communist Bureaucrat,' *Miami New Times*, 24 June.
32. Sokol, Bret (2000), 'Hip-Hop and Socialism: In Cuba the Revolution will be Rhymed,' *Miami New Times*, 20 July. www.miaminewtimes.com/issues/2000-07-20/kulchur.html/printable_page
33. Turino, Thomas (1995), 'Musical nationalism and professionalism in Zimbabwe,' paper presented at the 40th annual meeting of the Society for Ethnomusicology, UCLA.

Chapter 6

Doin' damage in my native language: the use of 'resistance vernaculars' in hip hop in Europe and Aotearoa / New Zealand

Tony Mitchell

In his book *Spectacular Vernaculars*, Russell A. Potter applies Deleuze's notion of a 'minor language' (in the context of Kafka's use of 'Prague German') to the heteroglossaic, marginal vernacular forms of African-American rap, which he sees as a de-territorialization of 'standard' forms of English. Potter regards rap as a form of 'resistance vernacular' which 'deform(s) and reposition(s) the rules of "intelligibility" set up by the dominant language.'[1] In this chapter I examine the use of languages other than English in rap music outside the USA as examples of 'resistance vernaculars' which re-territorialize not only major Anglophone rules of intelligibility but also those of other 'standard' languages such as French and Italian. In the process, I also argue that rhizomatic, diasporic flows of rap music outside the USA correspond to the formation of syncretic 'glocal' subcultures, in Roland Robertson's sense of the term, involving local indigenizations of the global musical idiom of rap.[2] This assertion of the local in hip hop cultures outside the USA also represents a form of contestation about the importance of the local in opposition to perceived US cultural imperialism which corresponds to what Lily Kong (1999) has described, in reference to popular music in Singapore, as 'inscribed moral geographies.'[3]

I start with an example from Zimbabwe which challenges the standard rhetoric about the Afro-diasporic and Afrocentric aspects of African-American rap and hip hop.[4] In the title track of their US-produced 1992 EP *Doin' Damage in My Native Language*, Zimbabwe Legit, brothers Dumisani and Akim Ndlouvu, provide English translations of key expressions they employ in their Zimbabwe regional tribal dialect Ndbele.[5] These English expressions – 'Power to the people,' 'the ghettos of Soweto,' 'You know where to find me, in Zimbabwe' – serve two purposes for the Anglophone listener: they locate Zimbabwe Legit firmly in their county of origin as well as close to South Africa; they also prioritize the group's native dialect as the main source of their art of rhyming, which finds local equivalents for certain rhetorical attributes of African-American 'nation conscious' rap. The back sleeve cover and the CD itself highlight and celebrate words in Ndbele as a form of 'concrete poetry,' but Zimbabwe Legit's raps also incorporate Shona, the more 'standard' language of Zimbabwe. So the linguistic 'damage' done by Zimbabwe Legit is directed not only against the language of their colonizers, English, which they need to use to remain accessible in the USA, but also against standard linguistic practices in Zimbabwe. And their concern with linguistic authenticity is also linked to broader notions of authenticity and Afrocentricity. In another track called 'To Bead or Not to Bead' they criticize US rappers who assimilate African fashions such as beading their hair:

> To me, Afrocentricity is kinda spiritual
> Many MCs I see are hypocritical
> 'Cause in the past, rappers were into braggin'
> But at this time, Africa's the center of attention.
> Everyone is cashin' in on the fashion:
> To bead or not to bead, that is what I'm askin'.
> Some MCs would rather be Italian
> Now sportin' beads and a black medallion
> Medallion on your chest, but do you feel it in your heart?
> Jump off the bandwagon and pull the cart.[6]

The fact that this particular track is entirely in English, and includes an apparent reference to the rhetorical embrace of the Mafia by US 'gangsta' rappers, indicates there is little confusion about who its targets are. But despite their inventiveness and their 'authentic' African origins, Zimbabwe Legit were a distinctively minority voice in the chorus of African-American hip hop in 1992, and subsequently disappeared without a trace from the US music industry. An entry about them on the Rumba-kali African hip hop website describes them as the first African hip hop crew to break into the US and European market. Its two members were college students who settled in the USA and secured a record deal and an unreleased album produced by Mr Lawng (Black Sheep). Dumi is now part of a new crew called the Last 8th, and calls himself Doom E. Right.[7]

Another marginalized African rap group who share Zimbabwe Legit's multilingual dexterity are Positive Black Soul, a duo from Senegal who first appeared on a track on Baaba Maal's 1994 album *Firin' in Fouta*, and who rap in a combination of English, French and Wolof, thus managing to address two major global linguistic groups in the African diaspora as well as their own locality. The group regards prominent Senagelese singers such as Baaba Maal and Youssou N'Dour, who have come to global attention in the 'world music' boom, as traditional and national source material, in the same way that African-American hip hop artists look to James Brown and George Clinton. In their track 'Respect the Nubians,' Positive Black Soul identify themselves in English in relation to African-American rap as 'a brother man from another land known as the motherland.' In 'Djoko' ('Unity'), rapped in a mixture of Wolof and French, they address more local concerns, describing themselves as a 'a brand new [political] party ... we are underprivileged, but we want the good life.' Their multi-lingual rhymes enable them to address their immediate constituency as well as the USA and the world at large: the album sleeve contains the lyrics to all their tracks in English. Unfortunately the USA, with its widespread aversion to foreign-language films and music, did not seem to be listening, and the first album by this most innovative of African rap groups did very poor business in the English-speaking world, as they were running against the flow of dominant US rap paradigms. Positive Black Soul nonetheless made inroads into France and they have inspired a subsequent generation of vibrant young Senegalese hip hop artists, most of who likewise rap in a mixture of Wolof and French, and are featured on the 2000 French release assisted by Youssou N'Dour and entitled *Da Hop: Le son de Dakar*. The cohort of groups and individuals on this compilation combine mellow, syncopated, polyrhythmic elements of traditional Senagelese music with rapid-fire ragga-style raps, and includes Bideew Bou Bess (in a collaboration with former Fugee Wyclef Jean which gained airplay in France), Jant Bi, WA BMG 44, Peace and Peace, Daara J, Boul n' Baï, Lakalé Posse, Bugz Bunny and others. The French hip hop market has also provided a conduit for a number of Algerian hip hop groups, and even for expatriate Cuban hip hop, as represented by the Paris-based posse Orishas.

Deleuze's notion of the 'rhizome' is aptly applicable to hip hop culture and rap music, which has rapidly become globalized and transplanted into different cultures throughout the world. The rhizomatic, diasporic flows of rap music outside the USA correspond to the formation of hybrid 'glocal' subcultures, in which supposedly global musical forms are indigenized. This rhizomic process is expressed directly in the distinctively macaronic hip hop of another rap group, the ironically-named Silent Majority, who are based in Geneva in Switzerland and rap in a mixture of English, Jamaican patois, French, Spanish, and Swahili. Referring to themselves as 'funky multilinguals' – an apparent riposte to Cypress Hill's rather inaccurate self-characterization as 'funky bilinguals' – Silent Majority foreground their collective linguistic dexterity in a track entitled 'Dans une autre langue' ('in another language'). In it, guest Spanish rapper MC Carlos from the bilingual Lausanne-based group Sens Unik states his position in relation to the global flow of hip hop and its assumed US origins:

> OK!OK! Rap is American
> But if American was yellow my music would be Chinese music
> Sayonara! What's goin' on?
> I do it in Spanish and if you translate 'ola' [hello]
> 'Ola' to all the people who respect
> the echo that my kind of rap makes
> And I can't say what it is
> Señor C is proud of his Latin blood
> Boum! Bam! on the road
> Music is contagious and rhythm is a plant
> That grows from New York to Martignan.[8]

This use of the trope of rap music as a 'plant' neatly corresponds to Deleuze's notion of the rhizome and serves to emphasize the 'glocalization' of rap, which, although a worldwide phenomenon and a universal language, is, like African-American rap, still very much concerned with roots, family, locality and neighbourhood. As Sens Unik's MC Rade puts it in the same track, code-switching from French to English: 'Our music is not a pale copy of the USA, Lausanne on the map, rhymin' is the art, part of a global thing.' Perhaps one of the most peripherally exotic and marginal examples of the global linguistic indigenization of rap as a 'resistance vernacular' is the Nuuk Posse from Greenland, a country with a population of 50,000. The Nuuk Posse, who have been recording since 1992, use their distinctly minority language Kalaalit (Greenlandish), along with Inuit, Danish and English, and incorporate local cultural elements such as whale singing and throat song to rap about, among other things, the domination of their country by the Danish language.[9]

The variety of ethnic origins among French rappers, from Senegal and French West Africa to the French Caribbean to the Arab populations of North Africa and other parts of Europe, is notable. The origins of French hip hop in the immigrant and working-class housing projects of the *banlieues* (outer suburbs) of French cities, as displayed in Matthieu Kassovitz's 1995 film *La Haine* (Hate), are also a distinctive and defining feature. A broad variety of musical inflections, ranging from hard-core rap to reggae and raggamuffin, distinguish French rap from US rap and give it features more in common with British and Italian hip hop. The 'adaptation' period of French hip hop in the 1990s involved the growth of hard-core rap and Zuluism (based on Afrika Bambaataa's Zulu Nation), where US models were adapted directly to French realities, but other concepts, such as Afrocentrism, could not be translated wholesale into the French context. Prévos shows importantly how French rappers like IAM attempted to circumvent the 'return to Africa' ideology prevalent among some US rappers, in order to avoid playing into the hands of French right-wing anti-Arab movements like Le Pen's National Front. Consequently IAM constructed an elaborate 'Pharaonic' ideology and mythology which boasts about Africa, but not black or Arabic Africa, rather adapting the Africa of Ancient Egypt into a religious symbology. They also mythologize their native Marseilles, a marginalized city with a high non-European immigrant population, as 'le côté obscur' (the obscure side) of France, and rap in Marseilles dialect.[10] But generally, as Steve Cannon has noted, there is in Afro-French rap 'a closer physical and therefore less mythical relationship of (black) rappers in France to the "*pays d'origine*" [African homeland] than in the USA'. Cannon also notes that, despite only 6 per cent of the population of France consisting of non-European immigrants, rap and hip hop have become a vital form of anti-racist expression for ethnic minorities:

> studies of hip hop in France in the 1980s and 1990s suggest that not only is the most numerical participation in both production and consumption of hip hop 'products' among people of minority ethnic origin, but also that hip hop in France is

characterized to a great extent by its role as a cultural expression of resistance by young people of minority ethnic origin to the racism, oppression, and social marginalization they experience within France's *banlieues* and in its major towns and cities.[11]

Rap's rich impact on the French language was also illustrated by the publication in 1998 of a controversial dictionary of French urban slang partly derived from French rap, *Comment tu tchatches?* (How do you talk?) by a Sorbonne professor, Jean-Pierre Goudaillier. This charts the language of the French *banlieues*, known as *cefron*, 'a melting pot of expressions that reflect the ethnic make-up of the communities where it is used, borrowing words from regional dialects as well as Arab, Creole, Gypsy and Berber languages'.[12] It also reveals French rappers and North African immigrant youth to be talented linguists who often speak French and *cefron*, as well as their native language at home, rather than being the illiterate and uneducated subclass portrayed in the French mass media. Elsewhere, Prévos has pointed out, the use by French rappers of the 'reverse' slang languages 'verlan' and 'veul', in which words are syllabically reversed, represents a hip hop vernacular which contests the rules of standard French.[13] Combined with the use of borrowings from English, Arabic, gypsy expressions and words from African dialects, the vernacular of some North African immigrant French rappers displays a rich linguistic dexterity which constitutes another highly polyphonic form of 'resistance vernacular'.

As in a number of other non-Anglophonic countries, the first compilation of rap music in Italy was almost entirely in English. Called *Italian Rap Attack* and released in 1992 by the Bologna-based dance label Irma, it included a brief sleeve note by radio DJ Luca De Gennaro declaring that 'rap is a universal language, in whatever language and whatever part of the world it is performed.' But in fact the only Italian-language track on the compilation was Frankie Hi NRG's 'Fight da faida,' with its half-English, half-Italian refrain urging resistance against Mafia blood feuds. This track deservedly became the most re-released and most famous Italian rap track of the 1990s. It was a courageous declaration of resistance against the Mafia, which became one of the dominant polemics of 'nation conscious' Italian rap, in marked contrast to the celebration of Martin Scorsese's Italian-American mafioso stereotypes in US gangsta rap. Frankie Hi NRG's barrage of internal rhymes also illustrated the greater facility for rhyming that the Italian language had over English, while his use of a brief burst of a woman rapping in Sicilian dialect was also a first:

> Father against father, brother against brother, / born in a grave like butcher's meat; / men with minds / as sharp as blades, / cutting like crime / angry beyond limits, / heroes without land/fighting a war / between the mafia and the camorra, Sodom and Gomorrah / Naples and Palermo / Regions of hell / devoured by hell flames for eternity, / and by a tumour of crime / while the world watches / dumbly, without intervening. / Enough of this war between families / fomented by desire / for a wife with a dowry / who gives life to sons today / and takes it away tomorrow, / branches

stripped of their leaves / cut down like straw / and no one picks them up: / on the verge of a revolution/to the voice of the Godfather, / but Don Corleone is much closer to home today: / he sits in Parliament. It's time to unleash / a terminal, decisive, radical, destructive offensive / united we stand, all together, now more than ever before, / against the clans, the smokescreens, the shady practices maintained by taxes, / lubricated by pockets: / all it takes is a bribe in the right pocket / in this obscene Italy . . . / . . . you gotta FIGHT THE FEUD!!![14]

Although there are Italian posses based in the major cities such as Rome and Milan, a notable feature of Italian rap is a tendency to manifest itself in smaller and more marginal regional centres. If Turin and Naples became major localities for rap music, Sicily, Sardinia, Calabria and Puglia were just as important. A nationwide network of *centri sociali* (social centres), which were often set up in occupied buildings, became the focal point for Italian hip hop culture. As Italian rappers began experimenting in their native language, they also Italianized US hip hop expressions like 'rappare' and 'scratchare', even 'slenghare' (to use slang) and began to rap in their local regional dialects. Some rappers also revived the oppositional political rhetoric of the militant student groups of the 1970s, and in some cases began to excavate Mediterranean regional folk music roots which had been neglected since the Italian folk music revival of the late 1960s. A distinctive musical syncretism also emerged among the Italian posses, pushing out the parameters of hip hop, which more often than not became fused with raggamuffin reggae, dance-hall and ska influences. This led to the coinage of the term 'rappamuffin' in a 1992 Flying Records compilation of Italian rap and ragga entitled *Italian Posse: Rappamuffin d'Azione*. The Sud Sound System, based in Salento on the southern Adriatic coast, took this even further, referring to their hybridized music as 'tarantamuffin', referring back to the traditions of the tarantella and the traditional women's dances based on responses to the bite of the tarantula spider. As a result, they were subjected to prolonged analysis and interpretation by the French ethnomusicologist George Lapassade and his Italian collaborator Piero Fumarola, who among other things drew comparison with the Marseilles-based Marsilia Sound System. But as Felice Liperi has indicated, the use of dialect in Italian rap was partly a consequence of the choice of polemical subject matter:

> Clearly the motivation was not only cultural, it was also technical. Italian DJs and musicians who chose the musical idiom of rap, which is based on the relation between words and rhymes, found dialect a more malleable language in which to combine rhythm and rhyme. But it is also true that once they found themselves talking about the domination of the mafia in the south and urban disintegration, a more coherent use of the language of these localities came spontaneously. Dialect is also the language of oral tradition, and this brings it closer to the oral culture of rap.[15]

This is particularly evident in the work of the Bari-based group Suoni Mudù, who superimpose a street map of Bari on their name and enact a mock Mafia murder on the cover of their polemical 1996 mini-album, *Mica casuale sarà* (Hardly by Chance). The CD cover includes the lyrics in both Barese dialect and 'standard' Italian to their track 'Citt e camina (L'ambiente)' ('City and Hearth, Where I Live'). This begins with an address to local Christian Democrat and neo-fascist politicians and then proceeds to mark out a criminal cartography of Bari:

I'm telling you Matarrese of the Christian Democrats
I'm telling you Lattanzio of the Christian Democrats
I'm telling you Formica of I don't know which party any more
I'm telling you Tatarella of the MSI [a right-wing neo-fascist party]
Those who live on crime in the underworld
Have identified with the mafia since they were children
Poor us, poor us
The die is cast, the die is cast
A conspiracy of silence rules in Libertà
Organized crime rules in San Pasquale
There was a co-op in Japigia which sold drugs
In Carrassi a bag gets snatched every two metres
In the Madonella they skin you alive
You'd better keep your eyes open in the old town of Bari
Watch out in the Cep too, they'll knock your teeth out
What we call 'paranza' [corruption, literally 'fishing trawler'] in Bari
Has another name in other places, but it doesn't make any difference
The same brutal system afflicts our whole society
I know the perpetrators of this hell
The real 'paranza' is firmly established in the government
They wheel and deal with no sense of shame
They speculate on your grief
Dealing, speculating, prohibition
The die is cast, the die is cast
Cops, mafia, even the 'ndrangheta and the camorra
They'll destroy everything because they always
Get you below the belt
What else can we say
You already know all this
The criminal underworld are tyrants
They live in squalor, they're an ignorant bunch
Ask me for two hits, there, give him two hits
People are ignored, it's a lousy mistake
Poor us, poor us
This one's got a knife in his pocket
That one's got a gun in his pocket
They're the Libertà mob from Libertà
The die is cast, the die is cast,
The die is cast, and its made of drugs[16]

These are similar sentiments to those expressed in 'Fight da faida,' but they are articulated very differently. The loping ragga beat gives the track a sense of grim resignation as well as denunciation, and the sung refrains ('poor us' and 'the die is cast'), which use a female voice, draw on local musical idioms to express a sense of grief. Barese dialect is also used for its musical attributes, as in the line 'Ask me for two hits, there, give him two hits,' which is the onomatopoeic 'Dì dù, da dà, de dù.' As Plastino has noted, 'dialect is also used for its different musicality with regard to Italian, for the greater possibilities of rhythmic and musical organization of phrases which it allows'.[17] The use of local expressions, the perorations through the main precincts of Bari and the roll call of politicians also give the track a specificity and sense of locality which 'Fight da faida' lacks. Suoni Mudù provide a detailed and intimate cartography of the Bari criminal underworld which is fleshed out by their idiomatic use of the 'minor language' of Barese dialect. 'Fight da faida', on the other hand, like the Rome-based rappers Menti Criminali (Criminal Minds), addresses the whole of Italy by using standard Italian. As Menti Criminali put it, 'my rhymes are written in Italian so that what I experience and feel is clear from Sicily to Milan.' But this kind of clarity often involves sacrificing a sense of local identity which is vital to the regional diversity of Italian rap. In the case of the Sardinian group Sa Razza, rapping in Sardinian dialect becomes a question of defending their local (and national) pride. As they put it in their track 'The Road': 'We prefer Sardinian slang rap. You have to defend your pride in being Sardinian, brother. That's why we're rapping, here the only hope is for my people to survive. Survive on the road.'[18] For the Sicilian group Nuovi Briganti, rapping in the dialect of Messina is a way of maintaining contact with the poor and dispossessed people of their locality, who have difficulty expressing themselves in 'standard' Italian:

> we are based in one of the most devastated areas of the city, and the people in the neighbourhood have difficulty expressing themselves in Italian. They've been used to speaking dialect since they were children. And they were our first reference point, the people who have followed us since we began. And rap is about communication.[19]

A more paradoxically polemical use of Italian dialect as 'resistance vernacular' occurs in a track by the Calabrian group South Posse, who were based in Cosenza until they disbanded in 1995. In 'Semplicemente immigrato' ('Simply immigrated'), Luigi Pecora, an Italian of Ethiopian origin, also known as Louis, uses the dialect of Cosenza as a way of expressing his adopted Calabrian 'roots'. As Plastino has stated, here 'dialect serves the function of identifying the privileged interlocutors of a discussion, the people of Cosenza, and challenging them to a dialogue. At the same time ... it is a way of elaborating a personal style.'[20] Influenced by the dialect ragga-rap of Sud Sound System, Pecora wrote 'Simply Immigrated' in dialect as a way of expressing his ability to belong to Cosenza, and to get closer to the inhabitants, whom he addresses as 'brothers':

> Many people say all the world's your home town
> Too many people say go back to where you came from
> I'm telling you what the fuck do you want me to do
> I came here to work and mind my own business

I'm telling you it's all about egotism
It's the law, the law of I don't give a shit
I know very well
The problem's not that simple
It's very complicated to begin with
But maybe that's the reason
There's a problem
It represents a reason to help your brother
I'm telling you, imagine if you were in my position
You'd feel it in your ass
You'd feel it
I'm telling you, do you really think
He'd come all this way if he didn't have to
Think about it, you've got history on your side
He hasn't been helped by history
I'm telling you it's grief, so much grief
Grief, grief, grief, you see how much grief
If you had to emigrate you'd know what it's like
But now we're better off, now it's a different story
We have to care about others now [21]

The simplicity of the language used here is abetted by musical repetitions of particular words, and the shifts from the direct address of 'I' and 'you' to 'he' and then 'we' indicate a dual identity with both the immigrant and the native Italian. The use of dialect here is strategic, an act of defiance, and to emphasize this Pecora reverts to the standard Italian of the first two lines in the second verse. As Plastino notes, this mixture of dialect and Italian corresponds to 'the way a young person from Cosenza talks today, which is what Luigi Pecora wanted to identify himself with to communicate more clearly ... The reference to "roots" is made to indicate the need to establish an exclusively linguistic relationship to one's region.'[22]

But South Posse also use dialect to rap about racism, in the context of both the discrimination against southern Italians by northern Italians, and the exclusion of those immigrants of African origin expressed in standard Italian words like 'extra-comunitario', which is the euphemism used to describe all people who come from outside the European union. What is notable in most of these examples from Europe is that it is often MCs from regional or immigrant backgrounds who make particularly idiosyncratic contributions to dialect, slang or patois forms of standard languages such as French and Italian, as well as mixing and switching different 'resistance vernaculars' in the form of immigrant languages 'macaronically' to express transnational and translocal linguistic hybrids.

Maori rappers in Aotearoa/New Zealand, which is on the antipodes of Italy, illustrate another peripheral use of indigenous language as 'resistance vernacular'. The native inhabitants of Aotearoa, the Maori, constitute about 13 per cent of the four million inhabitants of Aotearoa, but 40 per cent of Maori are in the lowest income group, and 21 per cent are unemployed, compared with 5.4 per cent *pakeha* (Europeans). Seventy-five per cent of the Maori population is under 30 years of age, but 40 per cent of Maori youth are out of work and four out of ten leave school without qualifications. Since the 1980s, increasing steps have been taken by Maori towards a renewal of their cultural and social traditions, and to regenerate *te reo Maori* (the Maori language), which is only spoken by about 8 per cent of the inhabitants of Aotearoa. This establishes it as a 'minor language', although it is the language of the indigenous inhabitants of Aotearoa, the *tangata whenua* (people of the land). The syncretization of aspects of traditional Maori *waiata* (song) and imported African-American musical forms is one which many Maori popular groups and performers have pursued in different ways and to varying degrees throughout the history of Maori popular music. Given the implausibility of entertaining strict notions of authenticity and purity in relation to Maori cultural traditions (or to any contemporary indigenous musical forms), the combination of traditional *waiata* and US popular musical forms is part of a cultural project of self-assertion and self-preservation which links itself with a global diaspora of expressions of indigenous ethnic minorities' social struggles through music.

Maori rappers were quick to adopt the trappings of hip hop culture and to explore its affinities with indigenous Maori musical and rhetorical forms, illustrated by the way concepts such as *patere* (rap), *whakarongo mai* (listen up) and *wainua* (attitude) are easily assimilated into hip hop discourse. The first Maori rapper to release a recording was Dean Hapeta (also known as D Word, or *Te Kupu* in Maori), with his group Upper Hutt Posse. Hapeta was part of a 'lost generation' of Maori youth who had not had the benefits of learning the Maori language at school, as is now customary, and had to learn it himself. This informed the militancy with which he uses the Maori language in his raps as a form of protest. As he has stated, 'Although I love and respect Hip-Hop, being Maori I only take from it what doesn't compromise my own culture. But in spite of this I have found them both very compatible.'[23]

Hapeta and other Maori and Pacific Islander rappers and musicians have substituted Maori and Polynesian cultural expressions for the African-American rhetoric of hip hop, while borrowing freely from the musical styles of the genre. (And it is an indication of the strong position traditionally held by women in Maori and Pacific Islander societies that the misogynist aspects of US hardcore rap are totally absent from its Maori and Pacific Islander appropriations.) The result is a further syncretization of an already syncretic form, but one which is capable of having strong musical, political and cultural resonances in Aotearoa. In their 1996 album *Movement in Demand* (a title derived from Louis Farrakhan), Upper Hutt Posse weld together Maori traditional instruments and militant *patere* and *karanga* (raps and calls to ancestors) and invocations of the spirits of the forest (Tane Mohuta) and the guardian of the sea (Tangaroa) with Nation of Islam rhetoric. The album also draws on the group's reggae and ragga inclinations, funk bass rhythms, blues guitar riffs and hardcore gangsta-style rapping which switches from English to *te reo Maori*. One of the album's tracks, *'Tangata Whenua'* ('The People of the Land') is entirely in Maori. This meant risking virtually no radio or TV airplay, as the national media in New Zealand in 1996 still tended to regard the Maori language as a threat to its Anglophone hegemony. Nonetheless Hapeta completed a powerful video for *'Tangata Whenua'*, which told the story of a polluted river, a consultation with a *kaumatua* (elder), traditional Maori gods destroying a factory, and an expression of Maori sovereignty. It was previewed on a Maori-language television programme which is broadcast on Sunday mornings. The track begins as follows:

> Papatuuaanuku is my mother, the land
> Ranganui is my father, he is the sky above
> Listen now to this very important thing – a root of the world
> A foundation level of my genealogy
> It is Io-mayua-kore, the first parent
> Live! You all! My people
> Pursue the spirit of the fire
> Make correct the words, the work
> Cause the wrongs of Tauiwi [the foreigner] to pass away
> So the desires, dreams, can flow
> Of the hinengaro [conscience]
> So wise thoughts can rise up also
> People of the land, the durable lineage
> People of the land, the root and the authority
> People of the land, the glow of the breath
> People of the land – the everburning fire[24]

The track starts with a woman doing a *karanga* (call to ancestors), and includes the sound of the *purerehua* (bull roarer), a traditional Maori instrument associated with funerals. It draws on key concepts in Maori philosophy, which are familiar to some *pakeha*, such as *whakapapa* (lineage), *mana* (integrity), *tangata* (man) and *kaupapa* (strategy or theme of a speech). It also draws extensively on Maori oral traditions and rhetorical figures. The track is not translated into English on the lyric sheet of the album, which suggests that it is addressed to Maori only, although most New Zealanders know the meaning of the term *tangata whenua*. Hapeta has since released an entire solo album, *Ko Te Matakahi Kupu* ('The Word that Penetrates', 2000), in separate *te reo Maori* and English versions, and followed this with an entirely Maori language album by Upper Hutt Posse, *Ma te Wa*. In 2002 he released Maori-language versions of ten earlier Upper Hutt Posse tracks, suggesting that *te reo Maori* had gained a much stronger foothold in the intervening decade. (Indeed, the New Zealand broadcasting funding body, NZ On Air, releases quarterly CDs, *Kiwi Hit Discs*, of songs they find for airplay, and in 1998 began releasing an *Iwi Hit Disc*,[25] featuring Maori-language songs. But Maori-language MCs like Te Kupu remain few and far between.) In 'doin' damage in his native language,' Dean Hapeta and the Upper Hutt Posse use the rhetoric and idioms and declamatory styles of hip hop to express Maori resistance and sovereignty, and further indigenize rap and hip hop in the process. Rap becomes subservient to an expression of Maori philosophy and militant Maori dreams, and is absorbed into the wider project of Maori sovereignty.

As the above examples demonstrate, the vastly diverse linguistic, political and social dynamics which have developed in the hip hop scenes from Zimbabwe to Greenland to Aotearoa/New Zealand have developed illustrate that the rhizomic globalization of rap music has involved modalities of indigenization and syncretism which go far beyond any simple appropriations of a US or African-American musical and cultural idiom. The global indigenization of rap and hip hop has involved appropriations of a musical idiom which has become a highly adaptable and malleable vehicle for the expression of indigenous resistance vernaculars and their local politics and 'moral geographies' in many different parts of the world. However, the 'minor languages' (Maori and Italian dialects, the use of *verlan* and *veul* in French, for example, and the languages of other ethnic minorities within dominant languages such as French and English) pay a price for their status as 'resistance vernaculars'. While they can be regarded as deliberate strategies to combat the colonial hegemony of the English language in both the global popular music industry in general and in hip hop in particular (with its African-American linguistic variants, which nonetheless still represent a dominant, rather than a 'minor' language in global terms), their limited accessibility in both linguistic and marketing terms largely condemns them to a heavily circumscribed local context of reception. In contrast, the Swedish hip hop crew Looptroop prefers to reflect the predominant and continuing American-ization of hip hop and other forms of global popular culture, and express an alarming sense of Anglophonic homogenization of Europe:

> We've all had English in school since we were 10 years old and there's a lot of sitcoms and films on TV that are English/American. The whole of Europe is becoming more and more like America basically. I guess we're fascinated with the language. By the way rap in Swedish sounds a little bit corny and I think it's great that people as far away as Australia can understand us. I think that's the main reason why we rhyme in English.[26]

What Looptroop's embrace of the US homogenization of Europe risks, of course, is the erasure of any distinctively local, or even national features in their rapping and breakbeats. While their album *Modern Day City Symphony* reveals a highly proficient DJ Embe, the faux-US accents assumed by MCs Promoe, Cosm.i.c and Supreme to express what one of them refers to as 'my Swedish history's exclamation' means that the group simply ends up sounding like any number of anonymous aspiring US rappers. (And it is arguable that their US accents, in comparison with most US hip hop groups, sound decidedly 'corny'.) The city in question, in which they make their 'symphony', is identified as Stockholm, but there is little on the album either vocally or musically that distinguishes it from any copycat US city. Similarly, only five of the 24 tracks featured on the 1998 double CD compilation of Swedish hip hop, *Sidewalk Headliners*, which includes Looptroop along with Adl, Petter, Feven, Profilen, and others, are in Swedish (and even they sound American-accented) and there is little to identify them as Swedish apart from the language. The English liner notes to *Sidewalk Headliners* also suggest that Swedish hip hop seems primarily concerned with projecting itself 'outernationally' – for understandable commercial reasons – although it is notable that Swedish hip hop protagonists from ethnic minorities, such as Feven, the most prominent woman rapper in Sweden, who is of Ethiopian origin, went on to produce very distinctive and feisty recordings entirely in vernacular-slang Swedish, as have the decidedly rhythmic ragga-rappers the Latin Kings, who consist of MCs Salla and Rodde.

The bland, homogenized Americanisms of crews such as Looptroop demonstrate that it is rare for an MC who is a non-native speaker of English to produce raps which are competitive with counterparts from the USA or even the UK. The exception that proves the rule is Finnish MC Paleface, whose 2001 album *The Pale Ontologist* matches the wit and verbal dexterity embodied in his choice of name and title and surpasses most English-language hip hop releases. In the predominantly Finnish-language 'Suomi hip hop' scene, which underwent a post-Bomfunk MCs 'severe rapquake' in 2001, and which Petri Silas has described as 'very homogenous',[27] Paleface, otherwise known as Karri Miettinen, an English student at Tampere University, stands out for his sharply critical, cynical and rapid-flowing wordplay in tracks such as 'Maximize the Prophet' and 'The Iconoclast', his mellifluous baritone, the lush orchestral backing, and his clear, punchy and close-rhyming delivery. His scathing demolition of the bankruptcy of formerly pedagogic US hip hop and its current shibboleths and orthodoxies in 'Emcees Say the Darndest Things' (which contains an opening 'Listening Comprehension section' especially for English students) is well worth quoting:

> *Is an MC far-sighted, far-off*
> *Far-fetched or far-reaching?*
> *Stop spitting that self-possessed shit*
> *And start teaching*
> *It's never too late to turn the car around*
> *Screeching tyres speak of pious liars*
> *preaching bias*
> *it's time to count your blessings*
> *and calculate your trials*
>   ...
> American foreign politics have moved
> From cultural imperialism to Globalization
> Hundreds of millions of lost souls turn to
> Me hopin' I saves 'em

But Why bother using my Mic time wisely?
Why be Gil-Scott Heron when I can be Ron Isley?[28]

The *Pale Ontologist*, with its apparent parody of Eminem, was in my opinion the best global hip hop release of 2001, but as it was released on BMG Finland its circle of distribution was somewhat limited, demonstrating that even MCs who adopt English as a means of gaining a wider listenership than the geographic and diasporic reach of their national language tend to be stymied by the unequal power distribution of a US-dominated global music industry. As Silas notes, strategies such as Paleface's are developed because 'the language barrier would soon make sure that Finnish rap music stays hidden in Finland for all eternity',[29] but his chances of being appreciated on a global scale are hindered by distribution obstacles; unlike those of his equally eccentric techno and electronica countryman Jimi Tenor, who can benefit from the borderless homogeneity of the non-language-based international techno scene. In contrast, the extraordinary global reach of major label US hip hop ensures that it continues to be sold and consumed in the remotest corners of the world.

The global dominance of the US hip hop mainstream, which has become increasingly bankrupt and mediocre, angers many indigenous rappers who are producing work that is highly distinctive on a local scale, and addressing the cultural roots and dilemmas of local indigenous youth. Maori rapper Danny Haimona of Dam Native sees the popularity of US gangsta rap and R&B amongst young Maori and Pacific Islanders in Aotearoa/New Zealand as the biggest threat to their appreciation of their own culture. This culture is being expressed in local indigenous hip hop, which is struggling to compete:

> There's such an influx of American stuff, and we need to quell it, and we need to give these kids some knowledge on what's really up ... Kids don't want to be preached to, so what I'm trying to do is put it on their level, and take all the good influences from hip hop, and bring it close to home. There is a good vibe out there for New Zealand hip hop, but it's being poisoned by the Americanisms – the Tupacs and the Snoop Doggy Doggs. You have to have a balance, and Dam Native are trying to help kids work out that they have their own culture, they don't have to adopt Americanisms.[30]

In this context, the choice of local indigenous 'resistance vernaculars' becomes an important act of cultural resistance and preservation of ethnic autonomy which operates as a vital strategy for the survival of the local.

Notes

1. Russell A. Potter (1995), *Spectacular Vernaculars: Hip-Hop and the Politics of Postmodernism*, New York: SUNY, pp. 66–68.

2.   Roland Robertson (1995), 'Glocalization: Time-Space and Homogeneity-Heterogeneity', in Featherstone, Lash and Robertson (eds), *Global Modernities*, London: Sage, pp. 25–44.
3.   Lily Kong (1999), 'The Politics of Music: From Moral Panics to Moral Guardians', paper given at the International Association of Geographers' Conference, University of Sydney.
4.   For example, see Tricia Rose (1994), *Black Noise: Rap Music and Black Culture in Contemporary America*. Hanover: Wesleyan University Press.
5.   K. Maurice Jones. (1994), *The Story of Rap Music*, Brookfield: The Millbrook Press, p. 111.
6.   Cited in ibid., 106.
7.   www.cistron.nl/zimbabwe.ht
8.   Trans. from the Spanish by the author.
9.   Jake Barnes (1997), Review of Nuuk Posse, *Kaataq*. *The Wire*, **158**, April, 65. The Nuuk Posse's track 'Uteqqippugut' ('Back in business') is included on *The Best of International Hip-Hop* (see discography), an album which also includes rare material from Argentina, Algeria, Switzerland, Israel, Romania, Greece, Austria, France, Japan, Croatia, Australia, Portugal and South Africa. Only the last three tracks are in English.
10. André Prévos (2002), 'Post-colonial Popular Music in France: Rap Music and hip hop culture in the 1980s and 1990s', in Tony Mitchell (ed.) *Global Noise: Rap and Hip hop outside the USA*, Middletown, CT: Wesleyan University Press, pp. 39–56.
11. Steve Cannon (1997), 'Paname City Rapping: B-boys in the *Banlieues* and Beyond', in Hargreaves, A. and McKinney, M. (eds), *Post-Colonial Cultures in France*, London: Routledge, pp. 164, 155.
12. Susan Bell (1999), 'Talk of town irks academie', *The Australian*, 20 January (reprinted from *The Times* of London).
13. André Prévos (1998), 'The Rapper's Tongue: Linguistic Inventions and Innovations in French Rap Lyrics', paper given at the American Anthropological Association Meetings, Philadelphia.
14. Cited in Pierfrancesco Pacoda (ed.) (1996), *Potere alla parola: Antologia del rap italiano*, Milan: Feltrinelli, p. 118 (trans. from the Italian by the author).
15. Felice Liperi (1993), 'L'Italia s'è desta. Tecno-splatter e posse in rivolta', in Canevacci, Massimo *et al* (eds), *Ragazzi senza tempo: immagini, musica, conflitti delle culture giovanili*, Genoa: Costa & Nolan, 201 (trans. from the Italian by the author).
16. Suoni Mudù, *Mica casuale sarà*, Bari: Drum&Bass, 1996 (trans. from the Barese by the author).
17. Goffredo Plastino (1996), *Mappa delle voci: rap, raggamuffin e tradizione in Italia*, Rome: Meltemi, p. 100 (trans. from the Italian by the author).
18. Cited in Pacoda (1996), *Potere alla parola*, p. 42 (trans. from the Italian by the author).
19. Ibid., 42 (trans. from the Italian by the author).
20. Plastino (1996), *Mappa delle voci*, p. 98 (trans. from the Italian by the author).
21. South Posse (n.d.), *1990–1994*, Rome: CSOA Forte Prenestino (translation by the author).
22. Plastino (1996), *Mappa delle voci*, p. 100 (trans. from the Italian by the author).
23. Cited in Otis Frizzell (1994), 'Hip Hop Hype,' *Pavement* (NZ), 8, December, 48, 50.
24. Upper Hutt Posse (1996), *Movement in Demand*, Auckland: Tangata Records (trans. from the Maori by Dean Hapeta).
25. *Iwi* is Maori for tribe.

26. Cited in Duncan McDuie (1999), 'A Looped Nordic Sample', *Revolver* (Sydney), 1 November, 31.
27. Petri Silas (2002), 'The Mad Year of Finnish Hip Hop', *Finnish Music Quarterly*, **3**, 46, 49.
28. Paleface (2001), *The Pale Ontologist*, BMG Finland.
29. Silas (2002), 'The Mad Year', p. 49.
30. Cited in John Russell (1997), 'Rhymes and Real Grooves: Dam Native', *Rip It Up* (NZ), **240**, August, 18.

Discography

Dam Native, *Kaupapa Driven Rhymes Uplifted*, BMG/Tangata Records, 1997.
Feven, *Hela vägen ut*, Stockholm: BMG/Banan Republiken, 2000.
The Latin Kings, *Välkommen till förorten*, Warner Music Sweden/East West, 1994.
Looptroop, *Modern Day City Symphony*, Stockholm: Burning Heart Records, 2000.
Baaba Maal, *Firin' in Fouta*, Island Records/Mango, 1994.
Menti Criminali, *Provincia di piombo*, Rome: X Records, n.d.
Paleface, *The Pale Ontologist*, BMG Finland, 2001.
Positive Black Soul, *Salaam*, London: Island Records, 1996.
Silent Majority, *La majorité silencieuse*, Lausanne: Unik Records, 1994.
Suoni Mudù, *Mica casuale sarà*, Bari: Drum&Bass, 1996.
South Posse, *1990–1994*, Rome: CSOA Forte Prenestino, n.d.
Te Kupu, *Ko Te Matakahi Kupu*, Kia Kaha/Universal, 2000.
Upper Hutt Posse, *Movement in Demand*, Auckland: Tangata Records, 1996.
Upper Hutt Posse, *Ma te Wa*, Kia Kaha, 2000.
Upper Hutt Posse, *Te Reo Maori Remixes*, Kia Kaha, 2002.
Various, *The Best of International Hip-Hop*, Universal, 2001.
Various, *Da Hop: Le son de Dakar*, Virgin France/Jokoli, Delabel, 2000.
Various, *Italian Rap Attack*, Bologna: Irma Records, 1992.
Various, *Sidewalk Headliners*, Stockholm: EMI Svenska/Street Level Records, 1998.
Zimbabwe Legit, *Zimbabwe Legit*, Burbank, CA: Hollywood Basic, 1992.

Chapter 7

Rapp'in' the Cape: style and memory, power in community[1]

Lee Watkins

Introduction

Hip hop in Cape Town emerged mainly as a platform for articulating resistance to the apartheid regime. Presently, hip hop is still in the forefront of raising the concerns of those who feel excluded from various domains of power. The focus in this chapter is on hip hop and rap music among coloured youths in Cape Town,[2] for it is in this population group, and in this part of South Africa, that hip hop first emerged, more than 20 years ago. Furthermore, despite all the changes in South Africa, these hip hoppers have neither abdicated nor compromised their role. Instead, by using the ideological and performative aspects of hip hop, they constantly strive towards creating a community in which the whole is deemed as important as the individual. My argument is that rap music, break-dance, and spray-painting are the means by which the hip hop community is achieved and maintained, albeit within the locus of the movement, and on the fringes of society.

You can't get these brothers down

Since the early 1980s, youths in the margins of Cape Town have been using rap music and other aspects of hip hop culture as a form of political strategy and pleasure.[3] Rap music and hip hop were initially associated with resistance politics and male coloured youths. These days, rappers increasingly embrace issues that are of importance to the post-apartheid generation, such as nation-building, the cars they drive, or the persons they fancy. Hip hop is also becoming far more profligate, as it is spreading from its stronghold in the coloured community. Hip-hop was first associated with coloured youths and the politics of resistance, then coloured youths and political transformations. Now, in post-apartheid South Africa, hip hop is becoming more visible in the black townships of Cape Town. Inter-racial contact is stimulated by the ability of hip hop to move in many directions.

Around the globe, hip hop inhabits spaces on the periphery of urban centres. The common thread running through these scattered localities is that hip-hoppers use the music, break-dancing, spray-painting, and the effects of technology as a source of strength in their struggle for social recognition. The use of technology is largely determinist, as it is integral to the structure of the rap song, and in the way in which the hip hop community finds coherence. Having a strong command of technological applications is crucial to the act of composition. In the rap song, technology is fused with the delivery of words, leading to a form of orality identified by Rose as secondary (1994). The rap song is mediated as a technologically determined hybrid form.[4] Technological competence in song and performance negates perceptions of powerlessness experienced outside the hip hop community. This kind of competence may also be deemed an affirmation of manhood.

For the hip-hoppers in Cape Town, performance is an aspect of their everyday lives and a form of behaviour in which they are able to have some effect on their immediate environment. Hence, hip-hoppers are agents who participate in the movement because they have a desire to change the way they feel about themselves and the world in which they live. Through symbolic behaviour (performance), hip-hoppers are transformed from victims to victors. The process in which agency is displayed so profoundly is cyclical, reflexive, and space-bound.

The Cape Crusaders

The experiences of three crews and a number of individuals who have been involved in hip hop since its inception are recorded and reflected upon below. Prophets of Da City, better known as POC, have a long and colourful history. POC members interviewed were Deon, also known as DJ Ready D or Akil, and Shaheen. Black Noise have dedicated themselves to youth and community development. They conduct workshops regularly and perform more frequently and more widely than any other hip hop crew. Emile is the spokesperson for this crew. I also include the members of Grave Diggers Productions (GDP), John and Raoul, in the narrative.

Up close and very personal

As an anti-apartheid activist on the Cape Flats, it was imperative that I establish links with all social and cultural organizations whose sole purpose was geared towards social and political freedom. To this end, my interest in hip hop and rap was, and still is, motivated by the close association it had with the struggle against apartheid and, after 1994, with community development. Rap (and the consumption of overseas reggae) represented a vital part of the struggle against apartheid, and many activists identified with the movement. Not only were its sounds appealing, but so too was its strategy. Rappers mobilized and informed the oppressed, and their songs reflected immediate concerns such as corrupt housing authorities and the failing education system. Other songs were a direct challenge to the apartheid government.

I remember rappers at political rallies dancing on the streets and spraying every available wall with popular demands. At schools where I taught, learners often chose to display their rapping, break-dancing, and beat-boxing skills during open days, or 'American Day', a popular euphemism used by schools on the Cape Flats. Groups of learners would walk around school beat-boxing, and create spaces in the classroom where they could rehearse their break-dances for the talent show.

Until fairly recently, learners at schools went as far as imitating the East Coast and West Coast conflict among gangsta-rappers in the USA. Youths on the Cape Flats associate the violence of the conflict among gangsta-rappers in the USA with their immediate circumstances. This cross-reference is manifested in their behaviour. For instance, if a hand sign from an opposing faction were used, learners would often physically attack one another.

Through their sounds and gestures, hip-hoppers have contributed as much to the liberation struggle as oppressed young people in other organizations. In their capacity as social activists, or 'Cape Crusaders', as Prophets of Da City would have it, rappers and hip-hoppers continue to play an instrumental role in the development of young people. I concede that I admire their selflessness, and their capacity to spread the empowering potential of hip hop, particularly with young people in impoverished areas.

Review

Although hip hop in Cape Town has been the subject of numerous newspaper articles and inserts on television entertainment programmes for young adults, there is, to my knowledge, only one brief academic account that investigates its social importance (Haupt, 1995). This and Layne's study (1995) of dance bands and jazz in Cape Town, in the period after the Second World War are two of the main contributions to the study of popular music in Cape Town in recent years. In my research I have expanded upon the range of popular music studies in southern Africa. At the same time, I address the imbalances between research conducted in the centre, that is, along the Kwa Zulu Natal–Gauteng axis, and the periphery – the Western Cape – and between black and coloured musical experiences.[5]

Generally, the volume of research on popular music in the Western Cape fails to do justice to the wide variety of music scenes that are available for research. The main reason is that until about ten years ago, tertiary institutions (of which there are three) in the south-western region of South Africa focused entirely on the study of Western art music. This is because most music departments at tertiary institutions in South Africa had perpetuated a Euro-centric curriculum, in accordance with the dictates of apartheid and the preservation of white hegemony. Based on the constraints described above, I have had to use research paradigms applied in music studies in other parts of South Africa, and abroad.

Erlmann observes that in the study of performance, South African ethno-musicologists had not readily taken heed of the changes that had emerged from colonial conquest, dispossession, and industrialization (1991, 2). The experiences of transformation and post-apartheid South Africa may be added to the list. Until now, few scholars have taken up Erlmann's challenge. Ethnomusicological studies of recent times in which music and performance are described and interpreted are Coplan (1994), Erlmann (1996), James (2000), and Meintjes (1997). These scholars examine the relationship between social structure and musical behaviour. The emphasis is on how the oppressed under apartheid were able to affirm their identities, and transform themselves from victims to victors, through music making. Since hip hop in Cape Town emerged largely as a response to social injustices, the paradigm invoked by these scholars in the course of their research has assisted me considerably.

Others who examine the social context of rap music are Danaher and Blackwelder (1994), and Dimitriadis (1996). All of the more important studies on rap music and hip hop are from the USA. Exceptions in this regard are those of Elflien (1998) and Mitchell (1995), among others. Mitchell's description of rap music style and hip hop culture among Italian youths is an investigation of its specificity, and Elflien's is a brief discussion on rap music in Germany after the collapse of the wall in Berlin.

In this chapter I begin to map out a framework for the analysis of rap music in Cape Town. The analysis that I propose here is broad and as inclusive as possible of the various effects that I am able to discern. Until recently the discussion around rap music style has mainly been concerned with its abstractions and lyrics, rather than its actual sound properties. In this regard I am particularly drawn to the analyses offered by Keyes (1996) and Walser (1995), as these scholars analyse rap sounds within the context of place and displacement. Their interpretations allude to the sound history of the African-American. Further, one of the more remarkable studies of rap music at this time is that of Krims (2000). He introduces a model with a carefully devised form of notation in his analysis of Ice Cube's 'The Nigga You Love to Hate'.

Given the magnitude of the research that I had initiated, and various other constraints, I am unable to include everything about hip hop in Cape Town in this chapter, nor could I do so in my dissertation. Thus future research endeavours and publications should focus on the issues of hip hop in relation to gender, the black diaspora, globalization, the music industry in South Africa, socio-linguistics, the influence of gangsta-rap from the USA on young adults on the Cape Flats, and, with greater seriousness, its music style.

The place and its people

Cape Town is in the south-western corner of the Western Cape Province of South Africa. Until the early 1990s, most of the people in Cape Town were either white or coloured. Black people had largely resided in the eastern and central parts of

South Africa. There were, however, a few black townships in Cape Town, established in the early 1900s. Larger numbers of black people migrated to Cape Town, particularly in the 1980s, but since the few and small townships could not accommodate the volume of migrants, they were forced to create homes in sprawling informal settlements with poor infra-structures. Many of these settlements were regularly torn down in the middle of freezing winter nights by bulldozers. If caught without residence permits, black people were also imprisoned and repeatedly shunted back to the bantustans.[6] Their numbers at that time can therefore not be confirmed with accurate figures. Cape Town in the early twenty-first century has a far more equitable representation of all the population groups in Southern Africa. Further to this, the number of black people has increased substantially, a process due in part to the influx of refugees from the wars raging in central Africa.

Most of the hip-hoppers live on the Cape Flats, a desolate area situated far from the city centre. This area is notorious for its extremely high incidence of violent crimes, and is home to the impoverished and unemployed masses of Cape Town. Racial politics, with its origin in European colonialism, is fundamental to an understanding of life on the Cape Flats. A brief history of the construction of places in South Africa provides some context for the adoption of rap music and other aspects of hip hop.

Under apartheid, legislative procedures such as the Group Areas Act of 1950, the Separate Representation of Voters Act of 1951, and the Separate Amenities Act of 1953, enforced white residential racial exclusivity. These laws resulted in the shifting of especially black people from one place to another. Further, other pieces of legislation, such as the Influx Control and Pass Laws of 1952, were designed to restrict black urbanization.[7] These laws also secured an adequate supply of cheap black labour to the nascent white capitalist class.

The Cape Flats emerged in the 1960s as a dumping ground for coloured people who had been evicted from their homes in the southern suburbs, the city bowl, and District Six. Many coloured families refused to move to what people generally refer to as 'The Flats', and emigrated instead to countries like Australia and Canada. POC's song, poignantly evokes the joy of living in District Six:

I remember the days in District Six
The laughter of adults and little kids
Hanover Street and the markets with fish
Where the music was always the heartbeat
I remember the days of District Six
The sound of the snoekhorn [fish-horn] and the ouens [guys] used
To break with a lekker [groovy] song.

POC, 'The Roof is on Fire', *Ghetto Code*

Through sound and gesture, coloured hip-hoppers vigorously attacked the white minority government and strategically associated themselves with black people.

Although economic class is one of the platforms from which they move, colour consciousness ultimately directs the course that hip-hoppers pursue, hence the strong identification they have with black people in the diaspora and Latinos in the USA.[8] The identification with oppressed minorities in the USA, through hip hop, is to a large extent related to the experiences of black people in apartheid South Africa. This identification can be attributed to the demographic history of the Western Cape, the racial policies instituted under British colonialism, and apartheid. American imperialism, assisted by the onslaught of its media and entertainment industries, has in no small measure facilitated the process of racial identification.

Rapping and breaking in Cape Town

Many scholars have described the effects of culture flow and contact, and the impenetrable power of the media, on musical and cultural behaviour, within and across boundaries (Bamyeh, 1993; Breen, 1995; Erlmann, 1993; Garofalo, 1993; Monson, 1999).[9] In this regard, hip hop provides a model for understanding how these processes are manifested in the relationship that exists between those who dominate the cultural highways of the contemporary world, and their recipients. It is significant that the recipients of cultural artefacts from countries who dominate these highways do not accept them piecemeal. Rather, by adapting forms to suit local conditions, mere imitation emerges as something that paradoxically advances the notion of assimilation and resistance. In contemporary popular culture, rap music style is one of the primary means by which this phenomenon finds meaning (Mitchell, 1995). Furthermore, the presence of hip hop in Cape Town reveals that cultural dominance is not simply imposed from above. Rather, dominance is established across the shifting fields of relations that constitute a shared 'consensus' (Chambers, 1990, 44). For, like their peers in the rest of the world, hip-hoppers in the southern part of Africa have metamorphosed into global consumers. Hence in hip hop, consensus is continually negotiated and produced, for participation inside the different spheres of public space and social life.

The extremely accessible video film, for example, had a role in facilitating the propagation of cultural messages from the north. And here the similarity with the emergence of hip hop in Germany is striking: films like *Beat Street* (1984) and *Wild Style* (1982) introduced hip hop to youths in Cape Town as well (Elflein 1998). Through exposure to films on hip hop, rappers quickly realized the potential for hip hop to effect solidarity among all of the oppressed in South Africa. The performative aspects of hip hop were an added attraction. The relationship with the outside, and the adoption of musical effects from abroad, can be considered as gestures that are not new to people in Cape Town. Visits by minstrel troupes from the USA in 1862, for instance, and the emergence of music cinema at a later stage, instilled among coloured people a desire to adopt cultural influences from the West. In keeping with the tradition of incorporating musical influences from outside, oppressed young people embraced the aesthetic qualities and creative energy of hip hop, its radicalness notwithstanding.

Hip hop first became visible in 1982, when groups such as Ballistic Rockers, Hot Rods, Lightning Kid, Qtonians, and Pop Glide Crew appeared in a break-dance competition at a club called Route 66, in Mitchell's Plain.[10] With the growing popularity of break-dancing, clubs increasingly staged competitions on a regular basis. This in turn helped to improve break-dancing standards as crews were prepared for battle at any time. Most of these battles took place in parks, at Strandfontein Pavilion, on beaches, at Cape Town station, Club T-Zers, and Body Rock, in Athlone. Break-dancers took to performing in the streets of the city centre, and performances were received with enthusiasm. This situation changed as more and more break-dancers joined the scene.

During the early 1980s, acts of political resistance and protests were intensifying. As a last resort, the government declared a state of emergency in 1985. This heralded a new stage in resistance politics as the government introduced regulations aimed at crushing black resistance. The apartheid government regarded any gathering of black people in public as a threat to state security. Townships became war zones where residents were engaged in running battles with army troops. Curfews were enforced in all townships and groups of more than five were not allowed to congregate in public places. In Cape Town, state and city council officials banned all public performances of break-dancing, especially in the city centre, with the result that hip hop meetings and workshops had to be conducted in secret. These meetings served the purpose of educating new recruits about black history and political struggle. In addition, break-dancing and rapping techniques could be taught, refined, and staged.

Since its inception, hip-hoppers in Cape Town had used organizations in the USA related to hip hop as models for organizing themselves. These included the Universal Zulu Hip-hop Nation (UZHHN), and the Nation of Islam, so motivating those hip-hoppers who had already forged alliances within the black consciousness movement of South Africa. The South African chapter of the UZHHN was called 'The African Hip-Hop Movement' and King Jamo became the leader of the Hip-hop Movement. A club in Shortmarket Street, called The Base, hosted the first official hip hop club in Cape Town. The other organization in the USA with which affinity is expressed is the Nation of Islam. Many hip-hoppers in Cape Town were Muslim anyway, while others appeared to have converted, changing their names in the process. Deon, or Ready D, is now also known as Akil. By converting to Islam, hip-hoppers followed the trend established by jazz musicians in Cape Town, such as Abdullah Ebrahim and Hotep Galeta.[11]

Given their involvement with resistance politics, and their growing popularity, prominent hip-hoppers were harassed by the police, and their homes were searched on suspicion they were spreading anti-government propaganda. Despite the threat to their safety, graffiti artists continued painting their pieces. Members of the movement had to operate clandestinely while other forms of resistance in the community continued and intensified. In the mid-1980s, townships became increasingly more militarized as all community-based structures associated with the apartheid government became targets for sabotage. A strong military presence and police brutality awakened most people to the effects of apartheid and militarization. This consciousness motivated young children to join resistance campaigns.

When schools gathered for mass protest rallies, Emile's crew, Black Noise, and break-dancers from other crews would entertain the people by break-dancing, and competing with one another. However, they were subjected to ridicule since break-dancing and other aspects of hip hop culture were not considered relevant to protest. In their defence, hip-hoppers argued that dancing was a physical vent for the frustrations built up by trying to fight military equipment with stones. They considered their presence at these events as proof of their dedication to the struggle against apartheid.

By the late 1980s, rap music on the other side of the Atlantic Ocean had become a billion-dollar industry.[12] Black- and Latino-owned independent record labels merged with major record companies as distributors. In contrast, hip hop in Cape Town received attention of another kind, as those who were involved with the movement had to contend with increasing harassment from the state and its agencies. Emile recalls concerts that Black Noise shared with POC on Greenmarket Square, and on the Central Parade, in the city, where the police shut down the power supply due to the content of their songs. The police would also stop them in the road, demanding break-dance demonstrations, to prove that they were dancers and not activists. Despite all the political pressure, rapping steadily gained a higher profile in the community. The crumbling apartheid government was unable to stem the tide of resistance, and oppressed people generally became more vocal and demonstrative. Clubs were promoting rap competitions and more rappers entered the public domain, with rappers rhyming about any topic they desired. Soloists eventually formed crews, as the potential for making a living from rapping became more viable.

Among the first rappers were Marley, Dean, Emile and Worro, who formed the Chill Convention. The crew later changed the name while working with producer Mike Hattingh, and called themselves Black Noise. At the same time, Shaheen joined Deon, Ramone and Jazmo to form Prophets of Da City. Along with rapping another aspect of hip hop, turn-tabling, gained more popularity. Turn-tabling is one of the pillars of hip hop and is an essential component of rap music performances, but in South Africa music equipment is expensive. Currently, attempts are made to encourage all new recruits to learn the finer art of turn-tabling, but at that time turn-tabling involved only a small group of individuals. Rozanno X and Ready D were among the first turn-tablists.

In June 1990, the first major hip hop concert took place at the Baxter Theatre in Cape Town. This event followed the heightened visibility of the movement in

South Africa and in other parts of the world. At the concert, POC launched their careers with the release of the first South African rap album, *Our World*, which performed well in the market. Following the success of this event, the music industry recognized the economic potential in rap and became more involved. Black Noise released an album and became the second group in Cape Town to sign a record deal with a major local record producer, One World Records, owned by Tusk, a South African company. Meanwhile, POC started travelling extensively throughout Europe and the UK. These groups, however, were not marketed properly and, in the face of censorship and harassment by the police, were left floundering as their recording companies deserted them. Rappers felt betrayed by the industry.

Rappers desired more freedom of expression because recording companies in South Africa, who had previously supported the machinations of the apartheid government, had become increasingly prescriptive. Emile sees the need to sever ties with the industry as a direct consequence of being exposed to the strategies of such rap groups as Public Enemy, and other hard-core rappers in the USA. Rather than compromising, many of the crews in Cape Town terminated their recording contracts and funded their own releases.

Rappers did not have much recourse to legal and copyright protection, or the financial resources for the promotion of their music. Rather, they depended heavily on social networks, community radio stations such as Bush Radio, and the regional commercial station, Radio Good Hope (RGH), for publicity. Again, problems emerged. The relationship with RGH was one of frustration and anger, as this station broadcast rap music mainly from the USA, despite its claim to be 'the station for Cape Town's hip-hop nation'. Commercial radio stations had also played a significant role in the maintenance of apartheid. When censors banned a song, for instance, orders were followed without questions.

During apartheid the music industry and commercial radio stations vigorously excluded the musical expressions of those who challenged the system. In addition, commercial radio stations had largely excluded South African popular music, even non-political music, from their playlists. The situation is slowly changing, ever since the Independent Broadcast Authority rightfully insisted that more local content be included in their playlists.[13] At the dawn of the twenty-first century, the relationship between rap, the music industry, and commercial radio stations appears to be undergoing transformation. While transformation in the music industry may be imminent, hip-hoppers remain vigilant. For, as Deon observes, the industry will only support them once they realize rap music's lucrative potential.

There are a number of independent record companies, some of which have been taken over by larger multinationals such as Polygram, now Universal, while others continue to break even on their own. The latest releases by POC, Black Noise, and BVK were all produced by companies such as Universal and Making Music Productions. The latter is an independent producer in Cape Town. The artists themselves no longer distribute these albums. One of the country's oldest distributors, Musica, is selling Cape Town's rap music in a corner of its shop dedicated to South African music. On RGH as well, more local rap music is being broadcast. Rap sensation of the late 1990s, Brasse Vannie Kaap (BVK, 'Brothers of the Cape'), is enjoying unprecedented fame and popularity, and its contribution to the Afrikaans language, through song, is profound. Their latest album, *Yskoud* ('*Ice Cold*'), was released in Belgium and the Netherlands late in 2000, before its release in South Africa. Their songs capture the life experiences of youths on the Cape Flats. RGH features their music far more frequently than the music of any other local hip hop group. In December 1998, RGH chose Black Noise's latest release as album of the week. Songs from the album were played every night for a week, albeit after peak listening time.

The commitment that rappers displayed in the political arena has not waned. Their relationship with the apartheid government was one of resistance. In the period after apartheid, they remain critical of the ANC-led government. Now criticism is raised with a view to reconstructing South African society and, as such, criticism is no longer part of any full-on resistance campaign. When hip-hoppers have a problem with government policy they make it known, despite their continued participation in government projects. In fact, Cape Town's hip-hoppers are engaged in the struggle between resistance and co-optation. For instance, in 1990, POC and Black Noise performed on the Central Parade, a shopping and parking square in central Cape Town, to celebrate the release of former president Nelson Mandela from prison. Black Noise spearheads campaigns, called 'Heal the Hood', in which the focus is on the AIDS epidemic, crime, and unemployment. These campaigns are endorsed by civic leaders, and sponsored by a wide range of governmental and non-governmental organisations. Both POC and Black Noise participated in the government's drive for potential voters to participate in the elections of 1994 and 1999. In 1999 and 2000, POC and BVK also performed at the annually held Oppikoppi music festival in the Northwest Province. Rapping has also spread to other parts of South Africa. The rapper, Mizchif and the crew, Reck My Life, are active in Johannesburg, for instance.

Since Shaheen's departure from POC in 1999, and the crew's subsequent collapse, Deon has joined BVK, and he regularly participates in international turn-tabling. He is recognized as one of the best turn-tablists South Africa has yet seen. These developments in hip hop signal the beginning of a new relationship with the outside, one of greater visibility and, for BVK, accessibility especially to white Afrikaner audiences.

There are more positive developments in hip hop. At the end of 1997 and 1998, Cape Town rappers organized hip hop festivals. These festivals were designed as spaces for boasting, the exchange of dance styles, and dialogue among hip-hoppers. The festivals of 1999 and 2000 were somewhat erratic, due to the restrictions of Ramadan.[14] It is hoped that these festivals will become a permanent fixture. It is significant to note that visitors from overseas here both attended and participated in the proceedings. Workshops and competitions are held on the Cape Flats and in surrounding towns such as Paarl and Stellenbosch, and the festivals culminate in a major event where rappers and break-dancers from all over the Cape Peninsula and surrounding towns congregate to compete in the final battle. Dancers who excel are identified for the international dancing competitions held in Germany each year. In 1998 the festival was taken to the black townships of Langa and Gugulethu for the first time. After each festival a workshop is held to assess the successes and failures of the past year, and to map out the challenges to be met in the following year.

An observation I have made regarding hip hop in Cape Town is the near absence of women. All the hip-hoppers I interviewed stressed that they were not sexist and that they would welcome women on stage. Some informants observe that women are encouraged not to participate in what is essentially a street culture. I did, however, see two black women rappers in the previously designated black townships of Langa and Gugulethu. They were rapping in Xhosa, the African language spoken mainly by black people in Cape Town.

There are many new crews who are actively recruiting and performing in the community, and more crews are being published through independent labels. I suspect that this increase in hip hop activity is related to both to the euphoria of now having had a taste of freedom, and to the publicity in Cape Town's media about the east- and west-coast conflict among rappers in the USA. On the Cape Flats many young adults who are not hip-hoppers wear T-shirts that honour the murdered American gangsta-rappers, Tupac Shakur and Notorious BIG. However, hip-hoppers discourage the association with gangsta-rap, due to the violence on the Cape Flats. They regard it as an American problem, and they believe that this association potentially inflames the already violent atmosphere on the Cape Flats.

During apartheid most of the oppressed had visions and dreams that could be realized only through music and in performance. For many oppressed youths on the Cape Flats, hip hop and rap music provided an alternative space in which they could develop their own strength, with a view to reclaiming their human dignity. This space is still marginal, but through performance it became significant and powerful. Through the visions they share for a democratic South Africa, and in the enthusiasm they have for hip hop, hip-hoppers render this space meaningful.

A community of sound

How does a discussion of rap style begin to address the relationship between Africa and hip hop? In the body of discussions around rap music style, particularly those in which the musical properties of rap music are attributed, by routes and roots, to Africa, there are exceptions that have helped pave the way for a more serious consideration of rap music style. Scholars such as Keyes (1996) and

Walser (1995) deserve mention in this regard. They offer analyses that are rooted in musical images of Africa, and in musical practices among African-Americans. Together, the scope of their analyses presents a body of interpretation that is important not only to the study of rap music, but also to musicology itself. However, while their interpretations of rap style are inspiring, as a voice from southern Africa I find them problematic in that they are drawn to those features that can safely be attributed to traditional African music. The implication here is that, for a number of reasons, there is an underlying hope to see Africa the way it was, as in the period before colonization, and not the way it is at present. More specifically, while many things remain unchanged, the inevitability of change has embedded itself with far greater veracity than we dare to admit, particularly in former colonies. Thus while there may be a number of musical features that can be deemed traditional, and to be commonly shared among many of Africa's peoples, the experiences of those living in the southern part of Africa have been markedly different to those further north. Not least, the people in the south have to contend with the after-effects of both colonialism and apartheid.

My interpretation of rap music in Cape Town strikes a not entirely different route as I incorporate some of the ideas advanced by Keyes and Walser. Even so, these are modified by the fact that my premiss has to do with interpreting rap music as a diasporic genre, at home, in Africa. Such an interpretation has to take into account that social life in Africa has largely surrendered itself to the effects of globalization, and in this process many of the musical effects that are deemed to be African have increasingly been subjected to re-contextualization. Further, given its vitality, insufficient attention has been paid to the distinctly local, rather than trans-local, character of rap music (Krims, 2000). This shortcoming is especially critical as far as scholarship on rap music in Africa is concerned. Thus while rap music style in Cape Town does have features in common with rap music elsewhere in the world, and I will reflect on these in passing, my discussion will be limited largely to those features that are unique to rap music in Cape Town.

I begin by situating the analysis within the context of the black person in Africa. It is argued that the presence of hip hop in Cape Town provides a specific opportunity for further developing a critique of rap music that has little to do with its origins in the USA, and a great deal more with how it is produced within the local arena. Through such an approach, I also dispel the notion of Africa as unchanging, since the analysis of rap music style in Cape Town goes a long way towards a rediscovery of what it means to be African. If anything, the situation in Cape Town shows that any description of Africa in our time has to view the new African as someone who is both African and global. More specifically, a description has to show the African body as a global body, for through the African body can be traced a wide range of influences that are inspired by memory and trans-local exchange. The experiences of memory and trans-local exchange are inscribed in the African body's musical expressions and musical behaviour. These experiences vary from downright abuse to celebration.

Before any further discussion relating to style, consider the following, particularly as they pertain to the situation in South Africa. In the early twenty-first century, the South African story is an epic saga with multiple personalities in various stages of undress. The situation is both challenging and chaotic, yet it provides the tools through which rappers interrogate notions of aesthetics and style. To this effect, a more sustainable interpretation of contemporary Africanity can further develop an understanding of this interrogation.

The question of where rap music fits into the musical scene of Cape Town can be answered by a review of the musical history of the city. Musical influences in Cape Town are a result of the long established tradition of cultural exchange, between the Dutch and British colonial rulers, their slaves from the orient, and indigenous peoples such as the Khoi and San. Traditional and popular music in Cape Town reflect diverse musical interests culminating from this experience. Rappers borrow from this musical capital in their midst, they blend it with electronically generated sounds, and with music from elsewhere on the continent and from overseas. The appropriations and the contrasting sounds are figured into an aesthetic of difference, and dramatic contrasts. The end product is then a hybrid. Hybridity is present throughout the song. Musical fragments that appear to be incongruous are combined in a community of sound, in which the overall structure is as important as the individual sound bites.

Those who have written the music are, of course, in a far better position to tender a description of their influences. Referring to the style of their music, Shaheen (of POC) says that while growing up at school they used to tease each other with little rhymes, that Cape Town is known for its unique form of humour and linguistic codes, and that all of these are combined in rap music. He also points to the importance of imitation, not least among young children, who memorize the words and tunes of their favourite songs. While this can inhibit the development of a personal style, rappers do not want to sound like clones. In particular, it is considered that the music must have value, as hip hop both raises and answers questions (interview, October 1997). Raoul (of GDP) observes that rap is not about conformity, that it is like jazz, 'you try to define it, but you can never, because it is always evolving' (interview, October 1997). John (also of GDP) believes that rap music is mainly about originality, in using other pieces of music and making it your own, and that you are using other people's languages to express your emotions and feelings (interview, October 1997). It is considered that these developments represent a challenge for the style police.

At this stage I would like to draw attention to the language used by hip-hoppers in Cape Town, as this assists in understanding how social experiences can be expressed through music. In particular, it should be noted that hip-hoppers are not only structured in and through language but that acculturation in language, initiated a few hundred years ago, has resulted in and continues to generate a sense of the past meeting the present, and of the inside in dialogue with the outside.

The language popular in certain parts of Cape Town is a blend of Afrikaans with other codes such as prison and gangster languages, and is rendered erotic by an intonation that is street-wise and masculine. Modern Cape Afrikaans is traceable to the creole Dutch formerly spoken widely in the Western Cape, but as people from all parts of the world settled in Cape Town, they brought their languages with them. Contact between settlers and indigenous people such as the Khoi and San provided the grounds for linguistic exchange. Communication was facilitated by hybridizing languages, and in this context, Afrikaans emerged as a language with influences from the west, the east, and Africa. Today, Afrikaans is a language with rich nuances inspired by location and social status. The lyrics in one of POC's songs clearly demonstrate a sense of hybridity:

> Early in the morning I put breakfast on your table, and make sure that
> your pap [porridge] and coffee is there.
> *Ek sê dinges, smaak djy vir my, want ek smaak vir jou,*
> *Is djy waarvan ek hou.*
> [I say lovie, do you fancy me, because I fancy you,
> it's you I like.]
>
> POC, 'Net 'n bietjie liefde' ['Just a Little Love']

The language hip-hoppers use in their songs and in performance is a social code, and a hybridized language, much like officially recognized Afrikaans. It is a code with multiple forms of representations, and it is at times difficult for the outsider, even some Afrikaans speakers, to understand, especially when combined with ebonics, the ghetto-inspired hip hop language from the USA. In this regard, the code-switching and hybridity in the language, and in rap music itself, is an organized system for bringing different representations into contact with one another, a system having as its goal the illumination of one representation by means of another (Morris, 1994, 118). Thus like the language, rap music is ideologically loaded because its representational nature legitimates certain forms of knowledge and certain kinds of power.

Improvisation in rap music, especially during performance, is a creative gesture that challenges the sanctity of literacy and decorum in western art music, for instance. If there is improvisation, then the implication is that there has to be a theme. In this case, the theme has to do with using other people's music and making it your own. Through improvisation rappers configure their style to make allusions to the vast pool of sources they have at hand. At the same time it allows them to explore the potentialities of the form, to enter a place where no other rapper has gone before, so that the genre cannot really be locked into any definitive space. Improvisation in rap often results in the choice of fragmented slices of music from many different places, combined in a single song, and in this sense the song is contingent upon the creative impulse, leading to what is understood as hybridity. This feature of rap is global and it is what makes rap distinctive. However, the form this improvisation assumes depends mainly on the musical consciousness of the crew.

Example 7.1 is a sample from Black Noise's song, 'Awhoowha'. The song is concerned with the predilection among rappers for American rather than South African accents, and the support this behaviour inadvertently lends to the American music industry. The sample belongs to an Afrikaans song by Sonja Herholdt, 'Waterblommetjies in die Boland' ('Waterflowers in the Boland') and is

Ex. 7.1   Black Noise: sample from 'Awhoowha'

inserted in the middle of the song. The original song itself has an easily memorized melody and a simple harmonic structure and refers to an edible flower that grows in dams in a region outside Cape Town, so providing a nostalgic reference to the Afrikaner's attachment to the African soil. In the original version of the song the melody is sung with over-affected melancholy. The sample in 'Awhoowha' is a combination of the rappers' own voices with strings, and here the over-affected tone is exaggerated, to hint at the intonation that is dear to many Afrikaner performers.

I asked Shaheen and John to explain how and why they used samples. According to Shaheen, POC use mostly samples in their music, and they never use a drum machine. They appropriate sounds from old records and sample a snare or a groove. Unlike many other rappers, POC prefer not to use loops because it limits their creativity. Instead they prefer hooks, with snare, hi-hat, and a kick. If the hook is programmed in any order it is still considered part of the same kick. Sometimes the kick is from one source, and the hi-hat from another. This may sound weird to outsiders but the technique can be successful. Sometimes a sound is split across the keyboard, and then played around with. There have been instances where they would use three- or four-bar samples because it feels right. This might be in the introduction to a song. Later, other sounds are layered over the initial sound, one by one. Shaheen can also feel the direction the music is taking. He will 'mess around' with the chord structures and ask his father to help as well (his father was a member of one of the more popular funk groups in South Africa, Pacific Express). Sometimes they play tunes on the keyboard over the samples. POC also avoid using a set formula, because this results in stagnation. Experimentation and creativity are key principles in the way they compose their music (October 1997). John believes that sampling and technology allow rappers who have no musical training, to compose music (October 1997). Through the application of technology, a new form of music literacy has evolved.

Rap music in Cape Town stands apart from rap music in other countries for rappers here have sources that are unique to Cape Town: the humour, language, and traditional music of the place. Rappers integrate these elements into their music and everyday interaction. Moreover, it is partly through improvisation and sampling that rappers are able to construct a style that is in accordance with the *Infinity Lessons* of the Zulu Nation. The *Infinity Lessons* is the policy document of the UZHHN. It states that there can be no clear definition of music, that it encompasses many things, but it does not specify what is excluded, and perhaps rap music's power lies in this creative licence. Shaheen explained that in their music POC used their own language codes, and that they were not afraid to combine this with South African music. They turned to South African musicians such as Abdullah Ebrahim, and used 'slices' of traditional music, such as *mbaqanga*, *goema*, and *marabi*. The excerpts below reflect on the relationship with African traditional and popular music. Example 7.2 is the vocable, *helele*, in POC's 'Roots Resurrected'. I have heard this vocable in traditional music from many parts of Africa:

Ex. 7.2   POC: *helele* in 'Roots Resurrected'

He   le   le   ha   la   la   ha   la   la   he   le   le

Example 7.3 is a tune very similar to the riffs in *mbaqanga* music. It is from Black Noise's 'El Bale Lakhe'.

Ex. 7.3   Black Noise: 'El Bale Lakhe'

Example 7.4 is from a Black Noise song called 'African Sunshine'. It starts with a scratchy jig played on what sounds like a home-made stringed instrument. The tune is alienated from a precise pitch schedule. This is a form of musical behaviour that can be equated socially to alienation from domains of political and economic power, as experienced by many young adults in Cape Town and elsewhere in South Africa. In almost similar fashion I find my attempt at transcription below to be alienated from the actual sound, as it does not capture the scratchy grain of the instrument:

Ex. 7.4   Black Noise: opening jig from 'African Sunshine'

From here, this opening jig leads into a figure that is repeated for the next few bars. The music is played haltingly but somehow it stays within a beat. There is a slight accent on the first of every three notes to suggest a light dance, such as the *Vastrap*. The *Vastrap* is a folk dance popular among rurally based Afrikaners and mixed race peasants, who migrate around inhospitable areas in the western Cape in search of seasonal work. This dance (example 7.5) is usually performed outdoors.

Ex. 7.5   Black Noise: folk dance tune from 'African Sunshine'

In Cape Town, the history of borrowing and bricolage is as old as the city itself, especially among Malay choirs and Cape minstrels. With their style based on Arabic vocal traditions, Malay choral traditions have had a deep influence on the music that is referred to as 'Cape Jazz'. This style of jazz combines Malay choral traditions with the complex harmonies found in the religious choral music of black South Africans. Abdullah Ebrahim is one of the leading exponents of this type of music. Example 7.6 is a sample in POC's 'Roots Resurrected', played on the saxophone. It captures the Arabic flavour in Cape Jazz, and is combined with the *helele* above:

Ex. 7.6   POC: sample from 'Roots Resurrected'

Cape minstrels, who had emerged as a result of visits by minstrels from the USA, are inclined to use the outside as inspiration. More often their appropriations are blended into a style that is a caricature of the original song. Melodies from popular songs, particularly from the USA and the UK, are given lyrics in the local patois, a rhythmic kick, and fused with tinny banjos, guitars, and even cellos. With the assistance of technology, rappers have taken this manner of cutting and pasting their songs to a new level, one which conforms simultaneously to music traditions in Cape Town and black music styles in the diaspora.

I would like to advance the idea that in these musical forms a double hybridity emerges, as the hybridity in the language blends with, and stands apart from, the hybridity in the music. The two hybridities combine to form a whole and they are placed into an arena in which difference is central to the success of the structure of the song. This is a trope in hip hop that speaks to the relationship between the margin and the mainstream, and between the local and the trans-local. The aesthetic of double hybridity therefore reflects a consciousness of large-scale processes, and it is shared among a number of music genres in Cape Town, including rap.

A literary device such as parody assists the double hybridity in rap. Through parody, rappers in Cape Town add a local flavour and meaning to a global genre and the insertion both incorporates and challenges that which it parodies. For Black Noise, the sample from Herholdt's song in 'Awhoowha' is an object that can be used to mock Afrikaner nationalism. A few years ago Herholdt made it clear that black people need not attend her concerts, as her earnings from white people are more than enough. While many rappers regard the practice of sampling as paying homage towards other musicians, and of keeping their music alive, I believe that the use of samples is, in this case also a sign of trivializing the outside. The outside is made familiar and its authority reduced.

In a process that can be construed as a symbolic call and response, parody can also provoke those who rule into action. Call and response is of course a strong feature of traditional African music. During the sensitive negotiations between the ruling National Party and liberation organizations in the early 1990s, the South African Broadcast Corporation swiftly banned the POC song, 'Ons Stem' ('Our Call') from the airwaves. The song articulated the demands of the oppressed and mocked the apartheid government. Its title, 'Ons Stem', is a blunt twist on the title of the apartheid anthem, 'Die Stem' ('The Call') and demonstrates the way in which parody can bring about a direct confrontation between musical style and a world of significance external to itself.

In effect, rap music is a discursive genre that is open to multiple interpretations. The 'neither here nor there' definition of music in the *Infinity Lessons* makes provision for multiple interpretations, and through forms of representation, such as in the song 'Ons Stem', hip-hoppers accept cultural relativism as well as recognizing a lack of equivalence. It is also suggested that rap music is reflexive, for it illustrates that no experience exists in isolation. In contemporary society, culture contact is highly accelerated and it exposes us to musical experiences of 'the other' in an instant. This, in turn, allows for hip hop expressions to cement the relationships between disparate groups. In performance, especially, it creates a collective excitement and brings about a sense of solidarity and social consciousness, regardless of geographical boundaries (Frith, 1981, 217). It is thus apparent that the vitality of hip hop and rap style is dependent upon constant exchange with the outside. The musical style expresses a degree of commitment to hip hop, and it indicates membership of a specific movement which, by its very appearance, disregards or attacks dominant values (Breen, 1995, 11).

The double hybridity in Cape Town's rap music reflects the overarching social conditions that characterize contemporary South African society. This condition is the perpetuation of an experience that is always cumulative and in process. In modern times the original source of hybridity is to be found in the advent of colonialism. In South Africa cultures of the colonizers and the colonized came into contact, often violently, giving rise to numerous cultural figurations. Hence within rap music the double hybridity that engages the artists is more than simply an exchange or meeting of codes. This feature in rap music is a *collision*, which speaks as much of resistance and memory, as it does of the simple narration of the day-to-day experience of living in dysfunctional societies.

One of the paradoxes in hip hop, for example, is that the alienation hip-hoppers experience in the townships is translated into a style where boundaries seem to be of little consequence. At the same time their style shows that the notion of what a boundary is supposed to be is subject to dispute and re-negotiation. On the one hand boundaries are celebrated, yet they appear to be no longer sacrosanct. In this spirit, Cape Town's rappers blend the rich musical sources of South Africa and the rest of the world into a style that is an expression of their time and place in society. It is a style in which all sounds are deemed equal, and this is why I consider the rap song as *a community of sounds,* a sonic community in which sounds are different in both texture and meaning and yet have equal value. Its structure coincides with the notion of 'unity in diversity', a popular catch phrase in the South African lexicon, which is used to describe how vastly different cultures should be able to co-exist in post-apartheid South Africa. In South African rap songs, the effect of combining rhythms and vocal sounds from many sources, in addition to intensifying the vibrating effect of the song carries a double allusion: on the one hand to African art, in which bold colours and patterns exist simultaneously within the same cultural moment, and on the other hand to traditional African music, which combines many time lines (whereas many other forms of music emphasize one rhythm only).

In another dimension rap music embraces multi-layered textures that consist of rhythms and vocal sounds, combined within the same musical moment. Here it reflects its integration with another aspect of hip hop, spray-painting. Right at the beginning of my fieldwork hip-hoppers advised that if I were to study rap music, I would have to look at their paintings as well. Both rap music and spray-painting symbolically represent an African aesthetic or sensibility. In spray-paintings several dominant colours are used, and the immanent energy that prevails can be compared with the visual elements of traditional African artistic designs. The vividly painted geometric designs on the walls of Ndebele dwellings come to mind. The process of spray-painting begins with a neatly planned sketch and its designs are not dissimilar to the musical structure of the rap song. As with the sounds in the rap song, the bright colours in the spray-paintings seem to compete with each other. Sharply competing colours in spray-paintings, and competing sounds in rap songs, may not appear to be harmonious compositions to outsiders. They are, however, accepted by insiders who have the ability to deal with more than one dominant cultural element at the same time. Following their advice I have learnt that hip-hoppers are able to cross from spray-painting to rapping with ease, and this is because they understand the interconnectedness between the two.

Another concern rappers express is that of 'authenticity'.[15] The struggle to keep hip hop 'real', or authentic, adds pressure to the relationship hip-hoppers have with the outside. I would contend that in the case of rap music the double hybridity is a benchmark for what is deemed authentic. Black Noise interprets authenticity as an aesthetic in which their music articulates the style, intonation, and struggles of the local hip hop community. These hip-hoppers are reluctant to sell out to the industry, which demands formula and consensus above everything else. They are under pressure, for while having the outside constantly present, most hip-hoppers are still trying to hold onto the idea that they can retain the authenticity of the genre. Moreover, financial considerations, particularly for rappers from the 'old school', are foremost in their interactions these days, as age plays a role in determining exactly how far one can resist co-optation:

> I'm going kinda crazy, hip-hoppers nowadays are so damned lazy
> Posturing, wannabes, sound like you come from America
> Nobody wanting to represent Azania[16]
> Tell me what the hell is happening here
> Oh no, never will you support the local
> Americanise the vocal, but you're a local too
> So what you're gonna do
> When no one buys from you . . .
> Am I getting through, what the hell is real
> Is it real to have an accent not from here . . . hell no
> Is it real to spend money on those who abuse you . . . hell no
> Because we can have our own hip-hop community
> If you show some unity
>
> > Black Noise, 'Awhoowha', *Hiphop Won't Stop*

The drive to develop and sustain a South African identity in rap music adds a dynamic adjunct to conventional musical aesthetics in Cape Town. The main obstacle is that artists try not to imitate anyone else, and yet the sound pool is shrinking rapidly, so you cannot, according to Raoul, sound too different from anything that is out there already (October 1997).

The struggle kontinues

This chapter describes performance and music style, as spaces within a space (hip hop), within a space (Cape Town), the particular focus being on the dialogue between performance and place. All individuals have the capacity to bring about significant change and meaning to their lives, and in hip hop this process of transformation is enacted through performance and music style. Feelings of marginalization and alienation are reconfigured into behaviour that is positive. In most of the interviews the word 'positive' crept in repeatedly. More broadly, the dialogue is further enhanced by what Erlmann describes as 'globally connected performance practices' (1996, 12), and the emphasis on universal black emancipation. Hip hop's ability to strengthen underclass solidarity, within and across racial boundaries, is proven by the fact that it has, by now, acquired trans-racial popularity. Through its creative zeal and commitment to social development, hip hop in Cape Town can be deemed African, especially in idealist visions of the continent.

The struggle against apartheid, and the troubled transition of present-day South Africa, motivated young people to realize their creative potential. Participation in hip hop provides a platform for this potential and it seems that rap music and hip hop will, for some time yet, continue to fill the enormous chasm in their lives. In the passage from apartheid to the post-apartheid era, the concept of a hip hop community is repeatedly invoked through performance and in their musical expressions. The character of hip hop in Cape Town may well be transformed, as many new rappers are increasingly drawn to imitating US rap stars. However, by continuing the focus on themes of hope, strength and survival, in their songs and behaviour, hip-hoppers are able to move away from feeling dis-empowered, and this is part of a bigger strategy, as

> The struggle kontinues, cause fake MC's suck still they tend to
> Juggle the menues and jock all the trends u
> Can get and bit and chewed their naked lunches
> Crews are taking punches, hallucinating some just
> Never learn, cause they be just flavourless
> Forever burn, in the dangerous gray abyss
> Of your plagiaristic, major twisted concepts
> Are you afraid to risk it, or is it in your record company contracts
> To be a follower instead of a leader
> Now you're a borrower and you need to feed ya
> Conscience with consciousness
> I drop the bomb since nonsense just
> Floods the market
> But the prophet
> Resent the reps and rhymes of those who represent with techs and nines
> And sex and mindless texts and I'm just vexed and find this
> Frustrating plus stating
> It's a tug of war a struggle for
> The real deal
>
> POC, 'The struggle kontinues', *Ghetto Code*

Notes

1. This chapter is based on sections of my dissertation, submitted at the University of Natal, in Durban, South Africa. During the course of my research I was assisted financially by the National Research Foundation and the Mellon Foundation. I am

indebted to these institutions and the hip-hoppers in Cape Town, as well as Angela Impey, my former instructor, and Veit Erlmann, for their helpful comments on this piece.

2.   I use the terms 'black', 'coloured', and 'white', not to perpetuate racism, but to locate rap socially, and to pursue the notion of relativity among groups of people. On occasion, I use the term 'black' to describe all those who are not white.

3.   Informants reminded me that a true hip-hopper is one who is equally skilled in all aspects of hip hop. Rapping, or emceeing, is therefore an integral part of establishing overall competence. For this reason I prefer to use the term 'hip-hopper'. However, on occasion I vacillate between the two terms, at instances where the one is distinct from the other.

4.   I take issue with the term 'hybrid' as it cannot be considered to be a quality of music. However, I believe that the word 'hybridity' captures the essence of those linguistic and musical forms that emerge from the tensions seeping in from racial domination and resistance to it, and assimilation, as during apartheid and colonial South Africa.

5.   Byerly (1998) observes that the emphasis on white and black musical activities in ethnomusicological research has resulted in the alienation of groups like the South Africans of Indian descent, and particularly the 'mixed race community registered as "coloureds" under apartheid' (p. 39).

6.   Bantustans are the 'homelands' created for black people by the apartheid government. The purpose was to divide the black population along language and other cultural differences, with a view to fragmenting resistance to apartheid.

7.   During the last phase of British colonialism and before the advent of apartheid, the Cape Town City Council had already controlled the movements of black people into the city through a system of service contracts. Maylam (1995) observes that Cape Town was a pioneer in the implementation of influx control (p. 33).

8.   See Watkins (2001), '*Simunye*'.

9.   Emile of Black Noise wrote, and is distributing, a photocopied booklet called *What is Hip Hop?* One of the sections in the booklet is a history of hip hop in Cape Town. With his permission I have selected and included parts of his outline in this section.

10. Among the other crews at this time were Street Freaks, G Force, Prolites, Hawaiian Breakers, Cape Town City Breakers, Sisters in Command, and Supreme Rockers. The first spray painters were Gogga, Picasso, Da Vinci, and Baby.

11. Other members of the UZHHN included Shai, Gee, Muff, Paz, Ice, and Falco One. Falco One is still active at the start of the twenty-first century.

12. For example, Russell Simmons' Def Jam label is distributed by Universal.

13. The Independent Broadcast Authority (IBA) was launched soon after the first democratic elections of 1994. Its purpose is to develop and regulate the industry in South Africa. In 1995, it recommended that by the year 2000 all radio stations include a local content of 20 per cent in their playlists, since listeners had been fed a diet of mainly Anglo-American music in the past. Efforts to monitor the implementation of this protocol are inconsistent.

14. Ramadan is a holy month in the Islamic calandar. Following Christianity, Islam is the second most important religion in Cape Town.

15. I use the term 'authenticity' in the context proposed by Gilroy (1991). He interprets 'authenticity' as an evaluation of music that expresses the 'absolute essence of the group that produces it' (p. 114).

16. In ancient times, Arab traders referred to the south-eastern part of Africa as Azania. During apartheid, many liberation organizations proposed the name Azania, as an alternative to the name 'South Africa'.

Discography

Black Noise, *Hiphop Won't Stop*. Cape Town: Making Music Publications, 1998. CD.
Prophets Of Da City, *Ghetto Code*. Johannesburg: Polygram, 1998. CD.

PART 3

Musical Production and the Politics of Desire

Chapter 8

Positioning the producer: gender divisions in creative labour and value

Emma Mayhew

Introduction

In reading the music press for research into the representational issues surrounding popular women performers of the 1990s it became obvious, at least to me as I analysed various reviews and profiles, that production credits have become significant to the discourse of contemporary musical criticisms. Discussions of the overall sound of a track or album often include identifying the producer(s) as an authorial presence within the recorded text. Although the producer can be defined in very general terms as 'making the key decisions about how specific material should be recorded in a studio and supervising the sessions',[1] in the music press he/she can be positioned in various ways in relation to notions of creative work. At one extreme they may be taken to task for their interference in the artist's work. At another they may be lauded as artistic geniuses in their own right, controlling and creating the musical sound of an album. As the studio has become more significant in the creation of musics, the producer has likewise become central to the views of both fans and critics of recorded musical texts. However, feminists studying popular culture would point out that the producer's role has remained a male domain. Certainly at the top end of the recording industry women are significant by their absence as record producers (although, paradoxically, globally successful female performers are more likely to take up this role when they have reached a certain commercial longevity).[2]

This chapter explores the way this taken-for-granted male creative role is represented in music press articles, reviews and fan discussions in relation to the recorded performances of successful female performers. The discussion will begin with an outline of the concept of creativity, the dichotomy of the feminine/masculine, and the discourse of romanticism. This overview will help to set the scene for exploring the embedded patriarchal assumptions within the music critic's evaluations of the authorial status of the producer as well as how fans make sense of this role.

Valuing musicality

Before we can understand the authorial status of the producer in the representations of musical recordings in the popular press we also need to understand the history of women in contemporary popular musics and their role as performers. Although the recording process has been important in popular music since the 1940s, women have on the whole been able to access this space only as singers, or to a lesser extent as instrumentalists. Women, who have dominated the position of pop singer, have often been devalued through a construction of femininity as an unskilled, and/or a 'natural' musical position. Part of this creative distinction between men and women has a history not only within music (both classical and popular), but within the visual arts and literature. In western art, from at least the medieval period, men dominated the areas distinguished as art forms. During the Renaissance there was a clear separation made between craft and fine art in the visual arts, with professional painters and sculptors being patronized by the gentry and royal courts, so that the fine arts became institutionalized and legitimized as absolute art forms rather than merely decorative or practical. This process was not just one of class distinction but also of gender segregation in terms of artistic work and value.[3] In the musical as well as the visual arts the emergence of high and low forms, as well as gendered exclusion from musical roles such as the composer, was also apparent (see Citron 1993).

The eighteenth and nineteenth century saw the solidification of the creative subject as male. In fact the historical and ideological effects of romanticism as an artistic and aesthetic movement are important in understanding the kinds of aesthetic values which continue to have discursive legitimacy in the world of popular music criticism. Authenticity and its definition as 'the full development and expression of individuality'[4] has significant roots within romanticism and constructs the individual as central to artistic work. This can be seen in the subject position of the genius, embodying literally the individual pinnacle of artistic achievement. Through deploying essentialism, patriarchy continues to deny females access to artistic practices as well as ignoring and devaluing creativity practised outside legitimate artistic institutions. Feminists like Battersby have chronicled the development of the creative subject through patriarchal discourses:

> The genius's instinct, emotion, sensibility, intuition, imagination – even his madness – were different from those of ordinary mortals. The psychology of woman was used as a foil to genius: to show what merely apes genius. Biological femaleness mimics the psychological femininity of the true genius. Romanticism, which started out by opening a window of opportunity for creative women, developed a phraseology of cultural apartheid ... with women amongst the categories counted as not-fully human. The genius was a male – full of 'virile' energy – who *transcended* his biology: if the male genius was 'feminine' this merely proved his cultural superiority. Creativity was displaced *male* procreativity: male sexuality made sublime.[5]

These romantic ideals of the male intellect as central to the 'pure' and transcendental creative process have had an impact on the development of popular music criticism and discourses of rock authenticity. The distinctions made between genre exemplify romanticism as a continuing influence on musical value judgements:

> Developed as a set of ideas primarily in literature and philosophy, romantic thought saw the individual artist's ability to convey emotion as the goal of artistic creativity, and art itself as a central component of human life. Applied to commercial popular music in a late twentieth-century context, it provided a powerful means for a clear division between, on one hand, rock and soul ... and, on the other, pop and various despised genres such as country ... This schema is still a powerful means of organizing the way people think about music around the world.[6]

Other writers have noted the compatibility in values promoted by both rock and romanticism: 'The artistic virtues of rock and romanticism are originality, primal order, energy, honesty, and integrity.'[7] Similarly, Will Greckel suggests that the musical eras of romanticism and rock have very similar characteristics underlying their apparent musical differences. These parallel characteristics include, for example, the expression of intense emotion, the expression of rebellion against traditional social and moral constraints, technological advances in musical instruments, and the use of drugs.[8] More importantly, he points to the way in which musicians, in both periods, have become the individual centres of attention in the form of the 'star':

> The heroic figure common to both musical worlds of Rock and Romanticism is the star performer-composer. There are compelling similarities between the Mick Jagger of the Rock Era and the Franz Liszt of the Romantic Era. Both represent in their own way the virtuoso performer-composer ... the great showman on stage; the sex-symbol-lady-killer thronged with hysterical, idolizing women grasping for a personal souvenir ... the dashing figure with a sensational if not scandalous life-style; the archetype who personifies the characteristics of his particular era.[9]

Romanticism also exemplifies a hierarchical value of creativity which has been carried over into the pop/rock dichotomy and has helped continue to construct rock discourses. Rock and pop forms are negotiated through a hierarchical oppositional value of gender, although there are differences in the way rock as a discourse constructing musical identity is positioned against pop. One version emphasizes musical skill and classical notions of musicianship, while another places emphasis on rebellion, energy, immediacy, and originality. Yet, both tend to apply to male performers more than female. Although academics such as Grossberg (1992) have argued that there has been a loosening of universal claims to authentic performance, in reality there has been a significant continuation of conservative values within musical criticism that should not be ignored.[10]

Authorship and the record producer

In analysing the media press and music fan discussions, what becomes clear is that there is an obvious relationship between the role of the producer and the more abstract role of musical author or composer. For female performers their artistic status is often put under scrutiny in relation to the role of the producer and the issue of musical control. This is because artistic autonomy is most obviously recognized through the degree to which a performer is associated with the role of author. As the producer has become more and more associated with an authorial position (both taking writing credits and also being associated with a brand of sound), a female performer's positioning as a valued artist is tied up with her relationship to this role.

Roland Barthes, in his famous essay entitled 'The Death of the Author', explains the position of author as a historical construct, emerging from various European and English philosophical and social trends which have helped to construct authorship as a transparent position of creative intention embodied in the individual subject. Barthes explains: 'The author is a modern figure, a product of our society insofar as, emerging in the Middle Ages with English empiricism, French rationalism and the personal faith of the Reformation, it discovered the prestige of the individual, or, as it is more nobly put, the "human person".'[11]

Although Barthes goes on to deconstruct this figure through a structuralist theory of language, and thus problematizes this concept, in the everyday world of the music industry and commercial profit, authorship is normally defined with little reference to the problematic and contested nature of the role. Certainly, in the mainstream music press one of the authentic criteria articulated by critics is the role of the author or composer, where emphasis is placed on the ability of the performer to write her/his own musical material. Although cultural theory sees authorship as a contested concept, Richard Middleton points out that, even though academics may have taken up the postmodern turn in their approach to the issue of authorship, 'it is by no means clear that the popular music culture itself has followed suit'.[12] In order to be perceived as an authentic and thus a creative musician, a musical performer must show, to some extent, that they have had some hand in the writing of the material. Yet, the evaluation of what kinds of activities fit into the authorial role severely marginalizes the positive recognition of women's musical work. The male-dominated role of the record producer is now positioned as creating the overall sound of a recording (Jones, 1992). The case studies below focus on the issue of authorship and the way it positions individual female music performers as 'authentic artists', as well as undermining the creative subjectivity of others.

Interviews, album and concert reviews make it quite clear that the question of authorship is very much part of a mainstream critical discourse. Performers who take writing credits for songs usually stand a better chance of being evaluated more favourably in terms of their musical status. Many female artists who have become critically significant as leading musical forces have usually maintained a persona of singer/musician/songwriter. For example, P.J. Harvey, Björk, Tori Amos and Kate Bush have tended to preserve individual writing credit for most of the solo work they have recorded. Yet even these performers, as well as others, have collaborated with other writers, musicians and producers to produce multi-credited work.[13] This is because the recording process, by its very nature, is a collaborative phenomenon:

> The mediation of recorded music begins when the artist(s), producer, and engineer begin working. The compromises that occur between them constitute a large portion of the design of modern recordings. And, the artist's work is subject to modification by the producer, engineer, or anyone else having access to the master tape and recording facilities. Though a musician may gain control over sound by recording it, she also surrenders some control to the person who recorded it, the person who is responsible for the overall sound of the recording, the person paying for the recording, and so forth.[14]

Alanis Morissette

Although collaborative work is often accepted as a rock tradition, especially in regards to the rock band form of musical production, for female solo performers the collaborative approach is often constructed as creatively suspect. Patriarchal discourses mobilize individual authority in a very narrow and limited way, and often attempt to deny female performers authenticity as creative subjects. An obvious example of this is in an article entitled 'Behind Every Great Woman...' in the glossy British music magazine *Q*. The byline states, 'There's a male co-songwriter: horny-handed, Platonic tunesmen wearing at least one leg of the musical trousers'.[15] This one sentence frames a patriarchal discourse of male rationality and genius which figures throughout the article and which is often repeated in other representations. The male producer becomes the rational father figure to an infantilized undisciplined femininity. The piece in particular profiles Alanis Morissette's song-writing partner and producer Glen Ballard: '"I'm happy to be a silent partner," says Glen Ballard, de facto midwife to Alanis Morissette's 12-million-selling Jagged Little Pill ... Further, she says he guided her through moments when extreme confessional candour became frightening...'[16]

Here Ballard, paradoxically, is represented as a male genius who appropriates the feminine metaphor of midwife but who transcends this feminine association with biological creativity, represented by Morissette as the mother, by reproducing ideas rather than bodies. As Battersby has pointed out in her history of the genius figure in Western art culture, 'Creativity was displaced *male* procreativity: male sexuality made sublime.'[17] Thus Ballard is not positioned as creative through the mother metaphor but as the instrumental hand which guides Morissette's creativity and reinforces the criticisms elsewhere that Morissette's performance is an 'act' controlled by and formed by the patriarchal intellect of male rationality.

Ballard is also 'conceived' of as Morissette's metaphoric heterosexual partner who structures and moulds her musical texts into authentic ones, reflecting both her growth to adulthood as well as her submission to male expertise.[18]

This understanding of Morissette's position is repeated in many media narratives in the period after the release and global commercial success of her album *Jagged Little Pill*. For example her biographical write-up in the artist profiles on the *Rolling Stone* website similarly suggests the importance of Glen Ballard in creating a more authentic sound for her:

> After high school, Morissette moved to Los Angeles where she had the good fortune to hook up with songwriter/producer Glen Ballard, known for his work with Michael Jackson, Paula Abdul and Wilson Phillips. The creative chemistry between Ballard and Morissette was evident from the beginning. Ballard pushed Morissette to pursue darker, edgier themes in her music, venturing away from the cutesy teenager and towards the introspective young woman. (Cramer, n.d., online)

Morissette's history as a teenage pop star in Canada explains this patriarchal representation of Morissette and Ballard's creative relationship, Morissette becoming moulded and shaped by her superior skilled male counterpart. Also, because Ballard had already been associated with other pop chart successes (Wilson Phillips and Michael Jackson, for example) this relationship meant that although he was also suspect, at least he was seen as the successful 'pop savvy' part of the collaboration. However, much of the media reported on this narrative as coming from other critics, which they were simply re-telling rather than directly making such criticism. For example, *Rolling Stone* declared 'her critics suggest she's simply a contrived creation of the studio'[19] while a regular music writer for the Australian *Sun-Herald* wrote 'critics have accused Morissette and her record company of contrivance',[20] with such re-tellings laying Morissette's creative identity open to speculation.

Kylie Minogue

Efforts to gain credibility by taking up the position of lyricist or songwriter can often be seen as tokenistic attempts to attract an aura of musicality and acquire critical rather than commercial fame. Kylie Minogue, in her albums *Kylie* and *Impossible Princess,* tried for the first time in her career to engage in writing lyrics for many of the songs on the album. The response from the weekly *New Musical Express* was one of condescension: 'Kylie actually co-wrote only one of the songs on her new album. For all the talk of "expressing herself", she hasn't suddenly become Sinéad O'Connor.'[21] Here Minogue's musicality is devalued through comparing it with O'Connor, who represents an expressive 'real' performer compared with Minogue's audience-pleasing entertainment. Given O'Connor's extra-musical meanings of controversy and outspokenness, the juxtaposition between them is even more polarizing.

Creativity is clearly linked to a traditional notion of an author who is 'in control'; however, the above quotation shows that even when performers are given official song-writing credit there is often suspicion cast on their abilities in a collaborative forum. Collaboration with other (usually male) producers, writers, or performers often undermines a female performer's musical credibility in her own right. Media suspicion about the actual creative input of a female performer, in regards to co-authorship or writing collaborations, is intensified if there has been, or is, some kind of personal relationship between the female performer and the writer or producer, whether substantiated through media gossip or more official personal statements. For example, Courtney Love haters on the website alt.fan.courtney-love suggest that her husband, Kurt Cobain, covertly wrote the songs for her band Hole. Criticism of Love, and of Hole as a group, has further appeared through the collaboration and song-writing credits with Billy Corgan on the Hole album *Celebrity Skin*. His success and media persona as controlling music genius with his own band the Smashing Pumpkins created further doubt as to whether Love had to replace her husband's behind-the-scenes help with another male songwriter.[22]

As mentioned earlier, the importance of the recording studio in the compositional process of music-making makes the producer's role interchangeable with that of creative artist. The complex technology involved in the recording and performing process of pop music also plays a part in what is perceived as 'good' music. Both technology itself and the successful control of these tools are used as measures of good music. In Steve Jones's comprehensive analysis of popular music technology he states: 'The ideology of rock, and therefore its meaning, revolves around sound. Recording technology, as the means by which sound is manipulated and reproduced, is the site of control over sound, and therefore the site of musical and political power in popular music.'[23] If an artist is seen as having some input into the more technical roles of the recording process, even the decision-making process of hiring a producer, it can help maintain some musical credibility. The limited creative status of choosing producers well can be seen in the rather backhanded praise given to Kylie Minogue for the sound of her self-titled album:

> What *Kylie Minogue* proves is that if you're an artist of limited talent, the success of each project basically comes down to whose hands you put yourself in. The choice is everything. On this record, the singing budgie ... is packaged and presented by hot mixers Brothers In Rhythm, Terry Farley and M People, among others. Dance gods the Pet Shop Boys contribute a track as well ... there is more than enough talent twiddling the knobs to lend an air of credibility to proceedings.[24]

Kate Bush

Better still, if they can show that they are capable of producing their own music, female performers can gain significant music credibility. Kate Bush is one of only a few female, or male, performers who have fulfilled the role of composer and producer throughout most of her recording career. In general, the media accepts Bush's role as a creative musical subject. The praise of her ability to produce as well as write her own music is reflected in reviews of her most critically acclaimed album to date, *Hounds of Love*: 'Kate Bush produced *Hounds of Love* herself. It is an audacious effort, full of daring and danger. In lesser hands it would have been pretentious or precious. Instead, it is invigorating' (Tearson, 1986, online).

Her success in the role of producer is especially noted in music technology magazines such as *Digital Audio*, where the technical aspects of the sound recording are important criteria: 'The sound quality on this disc [*Hounds of Love*] is first-rate. Part of this may be attributed to Bush's sensitive approach to producing her own music, competent engineering, and digital mixdown …' (Hardy, 1986, online).

Her positions as both producer and musical technology expert are intertwined in representations such as 'Bush is a studio wizard and a master with synth-sequencing gadgetry' (Bradberry, 1990, online) and 'Bush is a reclusive studio obsessive' (*Washington Post*, 1989, online), which mix images of musical genius with images of romantic artistic creativity. The length of time which elapses between her albums is interpreted as a sign of the creative effort she puts into constructing her sound in the studio, 'The gap is not a surprise since the reclusive Bush is such an obsessive sound sculptor' (Kenny, 1993, online).

Bush's control over the recording process is positively valued because it is the measure of the 'truth' of her art. However, taking up the role of producer does not necessarily always mean positive affirmations of her records. In some cases Bush's use of the technologies of the studio are met with criticism within a traditional rock discourse. There is a dichotomy here: producing the over-calculated music that technology enables can result in the swamping of spontanous human expression. Claims that Bush is overly controlling in the studio run throughout her career, with Bush being represented as over-reaching her artistic role by not allowing for an 'objective' ear to edit her work: 'Kate Bush suffers from the deadliest of the seven sins: indulgence. There's nobody minding the shop, nobody who dares say: Hey Kate, these three songs are great, but these seven sound like something out of Suzanne Vega's nightmare.'[25]

Kate Bush's 'control' of the studio technology is presented through these two competing discourses, one which highlights her authentic skill as a 'real' creative subject, the other questioning Bush's creative 'objectivity' in statements such as, 'While previous outings harnessed studio technology to Kate's maverick whims, much of *Red Shoes* sounds imprisoned by it'.[26]

Fan Talk

The producer's role and influence is not just a preoccupation of the technophile rock critic. Fans also discuss the significance of this role in musical texts, and in constructing the artistic subject. Fan groups on the internet, for example, discuss in detail the significance of the producer to the musical text, both referring to offical critical discourse and adding their own comments. In discussing the need for outside producers, a Madonna fan states: 'I believe that true artists (such as M [Madonna] and Tori) put so much of themselves into their art that maintaining an objective POV [Point of view] becomes near to impossible' (Subject: Could M produce an album herself?, alt.fan.madonna, 27/2/96).

A dichotomy is articulated here between the emotional expression of the artist and the technical objectivity of the producer. Within this dichotomy of subjectivity/ objectivity those who use the musical technology intervene and shape the emotional artist into a meaningful product to sell, as well as one to be understood by an audience. Furthermore, the objective/subjective and producer/performer opposition is often easily read through an essentialized gendered subject, in which discourses of femininity and masculinity reinforce aesthetic values. Thus the producer is positioned as rational, lending technological expertise, instrumentality and structure to a feminine performance which lacks an ability to edit or transform emotional expression into a general communicative format. The positioning of the producer as objective artistic adviser is expressed by one fan's explanation for another fan's disappointment with the sound of Tori Amos's album *Boys for Pele*:

> ... maybe this is because Tori doesn't have someone to act as sounding board for her ideas, someone to say 'perhaps this is all too much, perhaps this isn't enough.' It does seem to me, after all, that Tori got real excited producing this on her own and released an album of 'noteworthy' length. So perhaps so much of the disappointment in this album is not so much the music, but the production. (Subject: Could it be the Production?, rec.music.tori-amos, 3/2/97)

Here we see how the sound of a recording is often referred to as separate from the music itself.[27] While the fan pinpoints the problem as Amos' inability to produce her own work, the criticism does not undermine Amos' music.

In general, both fans and critics talk about the accountability of the producer for the overall sound of the record, and their responsibility to enhance that artist's musical strengths. They also talk about the influence of the producer on the creation of the music itself. This is illustrated by the concern articulated by Sinéad O'Connor fans at the number of different producers involved in the production of her record *Faith and Courage*. The worry was that all these different influences would drown out an authentic O'Connor sound, as well as fragment and confuse the possibility of a unified and over-arching sound for the album. On the other hand, the diversity of influences and sounds was also seen as a possibility for O'Connor to find a larger audience, a possibility fans both hoped for and feared:

> In some ways I'm sad to see so many people interfering with Sinead's music (producers). She herself has stated that she likes working with John Reynolds because he allows her to do things her way and develop her own sound. Also, I love it when Sinead's songs are UNDERproduced (unplugged, stripped down, etc.),

because then the purity of her voice seems more raw and unadulterated (nobody does a capella like Sinead). BUT ... I also trust Sinead to assert herself with all these new producers. Also, I'm glad that she's experimenting with herself and her voice and allowing different people to become involved with her music. In that sense, this new album is very exciting, because it seems likely that we can expect some very new sounds. These producers are so lucky, getting to hear all Sinead's new songs! Oh another thing I like about so many producers is the potential for lots of singles with lots of b-sides. For some reason I have the feeling that this is going to be her most successful album, and I'm very excited about that. And my excitement is for selfish reasons: If her fame increases, she's more likely to keep making music and doing her tours and so on. (Subject: producers, jitr@posmodern.com, 9/2/2000)

The articulation of the imagined creative power relation between performer and producer was both an overt and covert concern in these fan discussions:

Well, I would hope that her producers try to get the best performance out of Sinead (though I would think that would take very little coaxing, no?). Hopefully the producers would inspire support, and encourage Sinead during the recording process. At least I thought that that was what they were to do. I suppose they make suggestions as well, but I would think Sinead would have the final say, no? Well, this is very exciting anyway I hope it works out and gives Sinead the world wide exposure she deserves (not that she doesn't already have it). (Subject Re: producers, jitr@posmodern.com, 10/2/2000)

The issue of creative control is a feature in most of these discussions, and is intensified by the knowledge that O'Connor produced much of her previous work. Her relinquishing of the production role is seen to be a creative act (wanting to collaborate with other musical ideas/subjects) as well as a possible commercial move. However, for both the above fans, art and commercial success are not mutually exclusive. Certainly the second fan quoted above hopes for commercial exposure of the record as a testament to his own aesthetic judgements (reflected in his position as Sinéad O'Connor fan).

With the development of recording technology the studio environment has changed from being simply a place to record finished compositions to a compositional tool. Male performers have had to do as much collaborative work in the studio environment as female performers. Yet in the representation of these musical relationships, the position of women is weakened through the assumptions already existing concerning the abilities and creative roles of women in the music industry. The fact that most producers are men makes it fairly easy for discourses of patriarchal control to creep into album reviews. This patriarchal representation of producers as creative power brokers is illustrated through the patronizing tone of many mainstream reviews. For example, although L7 are often praised for their rebellious performances and appropriation of the male rock form, the influence of their male producers can still be understood as central to their authentic sound:

Credit must be given to producers Rob Gavallo (Green Day) and Joe Barresi, who appears to have convinced the girls to let it all hang out and take the kind of chances that set them apart in the first place. *The Beauty Process: Triple Platinum* brings L7 back to their original raison d'être. (Gulla, 1999, online)

The authority of the male producers is obvious in their relationship to 'the girls' who make up the band. In the context of the narratives of rock history, this can be read as a more general understanding of women in rock as masterminded by male producers, managers, and writers.[28] While the producers are named, not all L7 members are mentioned individually. It also draws upon associations of girls being involved in popular music as members of the audience, rather than being the performers. Paradoxically, the designation of the L7 members as girls also resonates with the 'positive' rock discourses of youthful fun and rebellion. Since the formation of rock 'n' roll as a site of cultural practice it has been segregated from 'adult' culture. Even though the rock market has expanded to include all age groups, especially in terms of sales of re-issued old recordings, an ideology of youth as the authentic expression of alienation, and the core motivation of new popular music still remains. The recent re-appropriation of girlhood in the cultural texts and practices of the riot grrrl, of significance to the L7 audience, makes the patriarchal reading of the term 'girls' challengeable in this context. Yet the power relationship, represented by the media, between the male producer and female performer, is continually revisited in the language of album reviews.[29]

Ultimately, all female performers and performances, are subject to the historical and patriachal constructions of the artist, and more recently the authentic rock musician. This is because the authenticity of the musical subject has been modelled on a specific male subject, and thus the female musical subject is always lacking. Women, who step into the musical world for a long-term career, have to negotiate this construction in the media and in their working lives. Even performers like L7 who have appropriated the masculinity of rock, and the authenticity such a musical form entails, can be understood as creatively limited, in need of male rock expertise. Individual female performers, who are seen overwhelmingly as capable and creative musicians, at times attract criticisms and cynicism as to their 'true' role. A rather scathing profile of Björk claims that she uses the creative energies and ideas of her production collaborators, 'She does weird, waily pop diva. Her producers do the rest. Often they do even more than that. Which leaves her free to turn on the kooky gamine charm...'.[30]

Björk's pop diva position is contrasted to the 'real' musical talent of her producers. Björk provides the ornamentation and the entertainment, while the musical technicians provide the musical innovation. In the same article that clearly positions her as an opportunist, she articulates the double standard:

It happens to be that a lot of boys do beats, and a lot of girls tend to be more lyrical. If a boy does a record with beats, say someone like Tricky or Goldie, and they have several singers on it, that's cool, but if a singer does a record and gets several people to do beats, they're stealing.[31]

Björk's perceived role as the singer is a blessing and a curse, both inspiring praise for her skill but also casting doubt on her other creative input. However, Björk's continuing presence as a songwriter, and her producing credits, mean that her position as a unique and talented artist is secured. Her ability to reproduce her voice in live concerts is part of her authenticity, showing that she is clearly the author of her own voice. 'Catching Björk actually doing those bizarre vocal gymnastics live, with no studio assistance, is always something of a shock.'[32] Her more recent 'hands on' approach to production gives her a relatively stable creative identity, although negotiated through various degrees of eccentricity.

Conclusion

The problem of the patriarchal positioning of the producer as individual author is a significant one from a feminist analysis because the producer remains 'one of the most powerful areas of the music business'.[33] It is also exemplifies the tightly meshed relationship between institutional structures and discourse. Very few women, unless economically independent, have the chance to position themselves as producer. The masculinization of the role through the discourses of creativity, taken up in the music press, has also been the central mechanism excluding women. Certainly one criticism of female performers taking on the role of producer is that this can be a sign of over-indulgent control – she is seen as over-reaching her capacity as artist, paradoxically losing emotional and objective control of her own work by claiming such total authority. Kate Bush exemplifies the tension for women performers in claiming the production credits. On the one hand she gains critical acclaim and is celebrated for being bold enough, as well as having the talent to, take on a 'man's job'. Yet in many critiques of her more recent work her positioning as performer, composer and producer signals an over-indulgence in the creative role, an indulgence that ultimately mars her work: it becomes too personal, too narrow in scope for the listener to identify with. Bush in particular exemplifies the broader gender dichotomies of culture/nature being played out in the struggles over defining and valuing musical creativity. Certainly the position of producer, whatever role in reality he or she might play, is central to popular evaluations of musical texts and highlights the gender inequalities in the popular music industry as an economic and cultural structure of leisure and work.

Notes

1. Negus, K. (1992), *Producing Pop: Culture and Conflict in the Music Industry*, New York: Routledge, p. 82
2. Lucy O'Brien notes that while women like Janet Jackson are getting co-production credits there are still very few women producers working with all-male acts in the

rock end of popular music (O'Brien, L. (1995), *She Bop: The Definitive History of Women in Rock, Pop and Soul*, London: Penguin, p. 430).

3. Chadwick, W. (1990), *Women, Art and Society*, London: Thames & Hudson , p. 37.

4. Pratt, R. (1986), 'The Politics of Authenticity in Popular Music: The Case of the Blues', *Popular Music and Society*, **10** (3), p. 62.

5. Battersby, C. (1989), *Gender and Genius: Towards a Feminist Aesthetic*, London: Womens Press, p. 3.

6. Hesmondhalgh, D. (1996), 'Rethinking Popular Music After Rock and Soul', in Curran, J., Morley, D. and Walkerdine, V. (eds), *Cultural Studies and Communications*, London: Arnold, pp. 195–6.

7. Pattison, R (1998), *The Triumph of Vulgarity*, Oxford: Oxford University Press, p. 188.

8. Greckel, W. (1979) 'Rock and Nineteenth-Century Romanticism: Social and Cultural Parallels', *Journal of Musicology*, **3**, 177–8.

9. Ibid., pp. 199–200. Greckel does not comment on the quite obvious gender assumptions made in the above construction of the composer/performer as star. Yet the quotation reveals the common sense discourses which have placed the male rock performer as the norm of rock success and mastery.

10. Zanes, J.R.W. (1999), 'Too Much Mead? Under the Influence (of Participant-Observation)', in Dettmar, K.J.H. and Richey, W. (eds), *Reading Rock and Roll: Authenticity, Appropriation, Aesthetics*, New York: Columbia University Press, p. 67.

11. Barthes, R. (1977), *Image, Music, Text*, London: Collins, pp. 142–3.

12. Middleton, R. (1995), 'Authorship, Gender and the Construction of Meaning in the Eurythmics' Hit Recordings', *Cultural Studies*, **9** (3), 465.

13. For example, Annie Lennox has been most notably associated with Dave Stewart as writing partner, Madonna with Patrick Leonard and William Orbit, and Alanis Morissette with Glen Ballard.

14. Jones, S. (1992) *Rock Formation: Music, Technology and Mass Communication*, Newbury Park: Sage Publications, p. 188.

15. Sutcliffe, P. (1996), 'Behind Every Great Woman', *Q Magazine*, 119, August, 98.

16. Ibid., 98.

17. Battersby (1989), *Gender and Genius*, p. 3

18. Of course, what is missing from this representation is the acknowledgment that many male performers rely just as much on musicians, songwriters, producers, publicists, etc. to create their sound and image.

19. Wild, D. (1995), 'Alanis Morissette', *Rolling Stone*, 516, December, 54.

20. Thomas, B. (1996), 'Canadian Dry', *The Sun-Herald*, 3 March, 22.

21. Ridgers, D. (1994), 'A Wallaby Together', *New Musical Express*, 3 September, 13.

22. Almost all articles around the time of the release of *Celebrity Skin* repeated the narrative of controversy surrounding Corgan's actual influence on the sound of the record, a controversy which was made 'real' by these re-tellings. There seems to be no one original source which initiated suspicion about Love's plagiarism. Throughout her public career she has been romantically linked to many male musical stars, for example Michael Stipe and Trent Reznor, and this has fostered her representation as a devouring *femme fatale*.

23. Jones, S. (1992), *Rock Formations*, p. 72

24. Casimir, J. (1994), 'Kylie wins, if only by default', *Sydney Morning Herald* (The Guide Section), 14 October, 85.

25. Brearley, D. (1993), 'Kate Bush – The Red Shoes Review', *Australian*, 8 December, 12.

26. Dalton, S. (1993), 'Kate Bush – The Red Shoes Review', *Vox*, 38, November, 112.
27. See Jones, (1992), *Rock Formation*, pp. 51–2.
28. The rock history of all-female bands is often understood as one of male sexual exploitation, girls and women being used as a sexual novelty factor. The Runaways are the classic example of the use of such dismissive descriptions. Although the narrative of exploitation has obvious truths, it often is told at the expense of the recognition of the musical and fan legacy of such performers.
29. For example, male producers are seen as in control in the following review: 'Under the eagle eyes of knob twiddlers Tom Rothrock and Rob Schnapf (Beck, Foo Fighters), the original L.A. grunge goddesses take a different exit on their sixth outing' (Stovall, 1999, online). However, there is some ambiguity here as to the creative relationship: L7 are labelled as 'goddesses', giving them a powerful position as women in control; yet the description of the producers' position – above them, through the metaphor of their 'eagle eyes' – implies that the male producers are gods above these goddesses.
30. Elliott, P. (1997), 'Who the hell does Björk think she is', *Q Magazine*, 134, November, 5.
31. Björk, in ibid., 7
32. Gill, A. (1994), 'Björk: Video Review', *Q Magazine*, 95, August, 152.
33. O'Brien (1995), *She Bop: The Definitive History of Women in Rock, Pop and Soul*.

Chapter 9

'Believe': vocoders, digital female identity and camp[1]

Kay Dickinson

Introduction

In the two or so years since Cher's 'Believe' rather unexpectedly became the number one selling British single of 1998, the vocoder-effect – which arguably snagged the track such widespread popularity – grew into one of the safest, maybe laziest, means of guaranteeing chart success. Since then, vocoder-wielding tracks such as Eiffel 65's 'Blue (Da Ba Dee)' and Sonique's 'It Feels So Good' have held fast at the slippery British number one spot for longer than the now-standard one week, despite their artists' relative obscurity. Even chart mainstays such as Madonna ('Music'), Victoria Beckham ('Out of Your Mind', with the help of True Steppers and Dane Bowers), Steps ('Summer of Love') and Kylie Minogue (the back-ups in 'Spinning Around') turned to this strange, automated-sounding gimmick which also proved to be a favourite with the poppier UK garage outfits (you can hear it on hits such as Lonyo/Comme Ci Comme Ça's 'Summer of Love', for example).

In this chapter, I want to examine how and why the popularity of this timbral modifier ballooned in the subsequent years and to think through the new ideas it has bounced with it around the representational practices of the voice, of computer-made music, of femininity and of homosexuality. More specifically, I shall be homing in on the recent appropriation of the vocoder sound by female artists. I hope to demonstrate that, although it has traditionally been the preserve of certain more avant-garde male performers, from 1998 until the present, women working within the genre of pop have joined their throng, creating some fascinating and potentially empowering new meanings for the vocoder. However, before focusing on these more recent applications, it seems apt to cast around in the vocoder's more than 60-year history to see how it has been handled and what it has meant to its listeners.

The vocoder's history and meanings

The vocoder was invented in Germany in 1939 as a means of disguising military voice transmissions. Etymologically, the word is an abbreviation of 'voice coder' and so intentionally bears the connotations of 'coding' human expression, of delivering it in cyphers. Like so many military technologies, the vocoder eventually found its way into the music industry and has been manufactured and marketed by companies such as Korg, Roland, EMS and Moog.

At that time, it was a piece of analogue equipment which worked by super-imposing a ghost of a chosen – usually vocal – signal over an instrumental line, most often a keyboard or guitar track. A vocoder will divide the vocal source signal (called the 'modulator') into various frequency bands which can then be used to process a 'carrier' signal – the keyboard or guitar track – and render it more sonically complex. The result is an overlap where the instrument takes on the timbre and articulation of the vocals – including the coherence of the lyrics – whilst superimposing some of its own texture and a more emphatic sense of its tempered pitch, and thus its melodic priorities. The polyphonic capacities of the keyboard also allow the user to translate the modulator line into a chord, giving the impression of a chorus to a single voice. With the intervention into voice recording of the keyboard (and, on digital models, an on-screen keyboard), it becomes very easy to imprint 'real notes' onto vocal lines. As glissandi and more 'human', momentarily out-of-tune 'misses' are obscured, pitch changes become decidedly jolty and 'robotic' – perhaps the vocoder's most recognizable signature and signifier.

Unsurprisingly, then, early pop interest in the vocoder came from (mainly male) musicians with heavy investments in types of futurism, artists such as Kraftwerk, Stevie Wonder, Devo, Jean-Michel Jarre, Cabaret Voltaire and Laurie Anderson. Later, the vocoder became a stalwart technology of early electro and has, since then, infused contemporary hip hop and the work of more retro-tinged dance acts such as Daft Punk and Air.

Perhaps in response to this rising curiosity about a device that had, since the mid-1980s, seemed almost obsolete, on 26 September 1998 the Prosoniq Orange Vocoder plug-in for VST, a Cubase variant, was launched. Consequently, a real-time vocoder audio plug-in was available for the DAW (digital audio workstation) which has pretty much become the dance music industry standard because of its long-standing versatility and power. Patches included within the program offered such voices as 'rotating robot', a knowing nod towards the android analogies which have grown up around the vocoder. More than any other factor, the arrival of this particular piece of software at the end of 1998 helped open the floodgates for the slew of vocoder-laden tracks which followed in the wake of the mainstream success of 'Believe'. Simultaneously, the increased prominence of digital voice filters – developed to correct singers' pitches and sometimes subversively used to create a vocoder effect – added to the frequency with which this sound was heard in popular music.

However, the very noticeable vocoder-style vocal lurch to be found in 'Believe' emerged between these developments: in the digital era, but before the more easy-to-use vocoder software hit the market. Mark Taylor (the song's remixer) devised an interim mix'n'match solution after initially experimenting with a Korg VC10 vocoder. He describes the process:

> I played around with the vocals and realised that the vocoder effect could work, but not with the Korg; the results just weren't clear enough. So instead, I used a Digitech Talker, a reasonably new piece of kit that looks like an old guitar foot pedal, which I suspect is what it was originally designed for. You plug your mic straight into it, and it gives you a vocoder-like effect, but with clarity; it almost sounds like you've got the original voice coming out the other end. I used a tone from the Nord Rack as a carrier signal and sequenced the notes the Nord was playing from Cubase to follow Cher's vocal melody. That gave the vocals that 'stepped' quality that you can hear prominently throughout the track; but only when I shifted the Nord's notes back a bit. For some reason, if you track the vocal melody exactly, with the same notes and timing, you hardly get any audible vocoded effect. But I was messing about with the Nord melody sequence in Cubase and shifted all the notes back a fraction with respect to the vocal. Then you really started to hear it, although even then it was a bit hit-and-miss. I had to experiment with the timing of each of the notes in the Nord melody sequence to get the best effect. (An uncited quotation offered by Lynn Fuston of 3D Audio Inc in response to my chat-room plea)

This sucking of the human voice backwards into the less nuanced scale types of the computer's tone bank gives it a certain cyborg feel common to earlier vocoders. What happens, then, when these two concepts (human and android) overrun each other? What can it mean to mangle the specific ideas that each has come to stand for?

Sooner or later during these exercises, the manipulated human voice bangs into some deeply rooted beliefs about expressiveness within popular music, beliefs which so often grow out of how we constitute 'the human body' at any given time. The vocoder's thumbprint for the most part spans the zone of timbre, of vocal texture (the area of the guttural and the nasal, to give just two examples) where pop is arguably at its most corporeal. As it rubs up against all these other timbral indexes, the vocoder must necessarily negotiate its place within the 'palpable humanity' so central not only to pop's appeal, but also often to its worth/ worthiness. Through a semantic ripple effect, the vocoder's sound then carries along certain questions about music's position *vis-à-vis* technology and the bodily self, where one starts and the other stops, or whether distinctions of this order are, in fact, unhelpful.[2]

Technology, authenticity, the voice and corporeality

Evidently, there are conventions and conditions controlling what 'real' talent and 'real' music are at any given time. Leach identifies that the

> markers for authenticity in rock are the presence of a talented individual or small group formed organically from 'naturally' knowing one another, driven to write

songs as the only outlet for their (personal) emotions and (political) views, who forge the music and play it themselves, typically in the standard musical arrangement of two different guitars, lead and bass, with optional keyboard, obligatory drums and a vocalist who might be also a guitarist, and is usually the songwriter unless (as is possible) she is only a woman. The fundamental White masculinity of these groups is epitomized in their organic unity and the way the group channels its identity through one singer who forms the expression of a group-originated song. Such a band should progress naturally as artists (rather than being an industry confection and being told what to do) and would be able to perform live (rather than requiring the artifice of technology or the commercialisation of recording).[3]

These comforting and involving fantasies about value and meaningful expression have been and continue to be outrageously selective in their recourse to technology, labour and selfhood. Guitars and microphones – to pick the easiest examples – are somehow less intrusive in their mediation of artistic expression than other equipment, equipment such as the vocoder.[4] Evidently, the capacity for you to *be* the music (and for the music to be you) filters through these handpicked technologies. In turn, these are governed by certain dominant power groupings which lord it over the likes of genre division and access to equipment, and which are marshalled according to categories such as class, 'race', and, the two I want to concentrate on here, gender and sexuality. By the same token, one's sense of truth and truth to one's identity inevitably incorporate gender position and how life is experienced according to one's access to power.

The convention of loading the notion of artistic authenticity onto the human voice weighs heavily upon what the sound of the vocoder means.[5] For many listeners, specific musical practices (including a capitalization on certain timbres) can seem to make flesh the Romantic chimera of unfettered, pure expression. In particular, certain vocal conceits are cherished as exceptionally direct conduits to the core of the self, to some sort of emotive truth, with Bob Dylan's scratchiness or James Brown's grunts winning more of these types of prizes than the smooth, non-grating and physically less aligned vocal offerings of the likes of ABBA.

While the strategic manufacture and manipulation of these notions of authenticity have long been an upheld truth-claim within academia at the very least, and I do not wish to linger too long in so expertly colonized a scholarly zone, this philosophy cannot undermine these transmissions' ability to strike chords within their audiences by plucking certain accultured emotional strings. The expulsion of feeling through the voice, through visceral bodily vibrations, consequently bears the potential to trigger sentient responses within the listener too, responses which vary from elation to the threat of harm. The issue we need to focus on here is not the tactility *per se*, but how its meanings and consequences reverberate through equivocating networks of power. The involvement of the body – also a fluctuating cultural factor – means that all the attendant politics from which it is woven and which it attracts cannot be erased from the sphere of popular music and discourse. That notions of the body might simultaneously wander amidst debates over mechanization not only begs discussions of the 'standardization' of leisure and culture, but also of pain and harm, of inclusion and exclusion as they are translated by these political arenas into concepts of the self.

Evidently, vocoder tracks vividly highlight the inextricable bond between subjectivity and mechanization. They propose a dichotomy between the vocoded voice and the more 'organic' one which then crumbles under closer inspection, most obviously because both are presented as coming from the same human source-point. Cher's voice in 'Believe' does not strike us as coming totally from within; nor, though, should any recorded voice which has inevitably been minced through various pieces of machinery before we hear it, including those which turn it into and back out of zeros and ones, adding and subtracting along the way. And that is just the technological side of things. For the most part, however, non-professional discourses surrounding the recorded voice treat it as extremely close reproduction rather than rendition or a representation. Yet in vocoder tracks, the vitality and creativity inherent in the technologies in use stand centre stage, pontificating on questions of authenticity and immediacy. Almost incidentally this becomes an onslaught on a certain economically powerful, supposedly more 'real', yet often restrictive system of agency.[6] As McClary says of Laurie Anderson's vocoder work: 'The closer we get to the source, the more distant becomes the imagined ideal of unmediated presence and authenticity.'[7] The key question here is not: where is Laurie Anderson, but, if this is one Laurie Anderson, what can she mean?

That said, singularity and autonomy evidently loom large in performers' personae and in their selling power – to go against these certain accepted standards of truthful performance is to invite derision or worse. Many of the current vocoder tracks are shrugged off as meaningless gimmickry because they spring from that lowlier, more seemingly *ersatz* genre, pop (more of which later) – a reaction which shows some particularly destructive snobbery in action. Taking the issue of pop further, it also becomes difficult to by-pass entrenched systems of expertise and *work* as they reside within not only authenticity, but also artistic polish and effortlessness (or perhaps lack thereof) within respectable and respected music. The vocoder, after all, is often seen as a sparkly bauble which distracts us from a lack of talent hiding 'underneath'. The degree of individual star labour undertaken within pop is frequently considered to be lesser than that of, say, rock, especially if musicians do not write their own material, cannot cut it live, have to have their pitch digitally corrected, and so on. Although the vocoder outwardly fits this bill (it is read as being done to, rather than done by, the artist's voice), the flagrant embrace of technological opacity we hear in its mechanized obviousness opens up further, perhaps more fascinating, questions circling some tenuous notions of single-handed musical genius.

However, the issue here is not so much the need for an acceptance of mediation's place within creativity, but the urgency of discerning how power is thenceforth distributed to those seen performing with these technologies, those working with them – on stage and behind the scenes – and those consuming them.

What bodies are being represented sonically and visually? What work is being done by them or for them? What technologies are countenanced within the musical canons and the economies of the music industry? And how do political movements (such as those grouped as feminism) who are eager to shed particular types of subordination sit within these matrices? This last issue seems all the more current because, for the first time in its history, the vocoder is now much more readily conjoined with if not the female voice, then at least the 'feminized' one.[8] Apart from Laurie Anderson's experiments,[9] this marks a distinct shift in the device's application, and this must surely echo through what the vocoder, women's voices and men's rights to technology come to mean here. With this in mind, the role of recording technologies in the construction of female musical corporeality and feminist reactions to it cannot go unexplored.

As Downey, Dumit and Williams argue: 'In problematizing the body and foregrounding the politics and pleasures of sexualization, feminist studies have articulated just who and what is reproduced (and by what sorts of technologies) when a "human subject" is recognized.'[10] For these three (and many other theorists besides), the selection processes involved in the multiple technological ways and means of representation trail down from and up to specific conglomerations of power. Which types of technological mastery garner prestige and which do not (knowing one's way around Cubase ranking significantly higher than being able to work a 'domestic' or sweat-shop tool like a sewing machine) are telling here. Music technologies, then, also moonlight as systems of both control and empowerment; in the instance of the vocoder, this discursive formation constitutes women, as I am hoping to argue, in a peculiarly polysemic manner.

Women's musical participation, as Green (1997) points out, has traditionally short-circuited around core technology and this would include our decreased access to revered pop musical instruments like the guitar and certain computer software. Green argues that for many female music stars – many more than men – the *body* is their instrument, a condition which helps promote the age-old rooting of women in the 'natural' and the anti-technological. Yet the vocoder effect, however it is produced (and even by whom), impairs the 'naturalism' of the female voice not by ignoring it, but by creating the illusion of rummaging around inside it with an inorganic probe, confusing its listener as to its origin, its interior and its surface. At this point, oppositions of inside or outside, organic or inorganic, whole or dispersed haze over and their ability to hold court in so facile and divisive a manner wavers considerably.

These concerns have circled pop for an indefinitely lengthy period, although with a different flight pattern each time. Pop, maybe more than other genres, has seen many skirmishes over artifice's actual meaning and worth, but, although pop has economic clout here, its ideas often go unheard in the bustle cynically to cash in without admitting any actual faith in the genre's politics. It is not uncommon to hear sentiments along the lines of: 'It is only pop and the vocoder is just another means of pulling a wool spun of talentlessness over the eyes of the gullible.' What pop might have to say is less easily locked out, though, when its 'underhand' means of deflection are dabbled with by musicians of widely recognized singing ability, such as Sonique. When artists who are not currently seen to need to augment their skills so desperately and who cannot so easily be accused of hiding behind gimmicks turn to these self-proclamatory tools, they use their power to instigate a much prouder acknowledgement of computer co-enterprise.

Similarly, writers such as Celia Lury (1998) – here talking more broadly about prosthetics – are eager not to predict this as a disintegration of the self or even a loss of control and instead chart it as the growth of a more possessive individualism. This concept of the prosthesis undoubtedly has a lengthy string of historical precursors within our everyday lives and our means of expressiveness, being preceded by such accoutrements as guns, guitars, spectacles and tooth fillings. For Lury, 'through the adoption of prostheses, the previously naturally or socially fixed or determined aspects of self-identity are increasingly brought within the remit of choice or, better, selection.'[11] The use of prosthetics in this sense – and this would include women singing with vocoders – is maybe most profitably thought of not as a replacement for something lacking, but as a booster added on to enhance one's capabilities. This may be somewhat utopian given both the prices involved in choosing to purchase such implements, and the music industry's hold over its artists' creativity and its meanings in the first place. However, if things like vocoders are more actively thought of as tools rather than shields or parasites, women's attitudes towards them might prove distinctly less defensive. Speaking more broadly, perhaps the most salient point to remember here is that the fluctuation between performances of the self and technologies is of seismic proportions. With the ground shifting so dangerously, whole sections of society are at risk of being dragged into chasms from which it is enormously difficult to climb out. The extent to which pop cultural devices such as the vocoder might act as ropes for women in this plight is what I intend to investigate next.

Deliberately coupling with machines: female musicians and cyber identity

In edging towards a discussion of the positions for women within music technology, it might prove fruitful to head off into the realm of theory most commonly labelled cyber-feminism. Although often divergent in their thinking, key exponents such as Braidotti (n.d.), Haraway (1991), Wakeford and Squires (in Gray, 1995) and Plant (1997) are linked through their fascination with constructions of selfhood on boundary lines and with the potential for new technological interactions to effect female control and power. Whilst cyber-theorists rarely analyse music-making software, many of their observations about the wearing away of some of the harsher distinctions between the emotional/human and the mechanical/inorganic seem equally applicable to readings of the vocoder. Inevitably some of these writers' approaches are more hopeful than others (Plants, for example, delights in cyberspace as almost inherently empowering for women), and some are more perturbed by economic disability. Braidotti is perhaps the most cautious:

> while the computer technology seems to promise a world beyond gender differences, the gender gap grows wider. All the talk of a brand new telematic world masks the ever-increasing polarisation of resources and means, in which women are the main losers. There is strong indication therefore that the shifting of conventional boundaries between the sexes and the proliferation of all kinds of differences through the new technologies will not be nearly as liberating as the cyber-artists and internet addicts would want us to believe ... The alleged triumph of high-technologies is not matched by a leap of the human imagination to create new images and representations. Quite the contrary, what I notice is the repetition of very old themes and cliches, under the appearance of 'new' technological advances. (Braidotti, n.d.)

The question that now arises is whether certain uses of the vocoder sympathize with a reactionary or an empowering configuration of femininity. Before answering this, however, it seems more pressing to delineate the vocoder's specific cyber-potential.

The vocoder's popularity may well lie in the symbolic bridge it is seen to form between the vacillating perceptions of the human and the machine (or, more specifically, the digitizing, encoding machine). It can also be interpreted as a bond holding the two close when either concept becomes too flighty and abstract to be related to the other. Anything which draws attention to borderlines might also help elucidate old-guard distinctions which have been drawn up in the past. However, that said, simple dualisms do not sit well within the contemporary vocoder's timbral output and, although these circumstances might not necessarily inspire drastic renegotiation, it does formulate a very different relationship between the organic and the inorganic in comparison to the textures of other dance musics.

As elsewhere in the history of music, the (usually female) voice often serves as an emblem for pure human physicality within dance genres (this is particularly true of house and garage), while variations with more of an investment in stark automation (such as techno) purposefully eschew vocal lines. Returning to my key example, 'Believe', on the other hand, maintains many of the instrumental qualities of these genres, but plots out its vocal aesthetic differently. Its instrumental timbres, which have very little grounding in 'traditional' or non-computer-generated instrumentation, evoke the trancier end of techno. Shorter sci-fi stabs meet surging upward flourishes which also link 'Believe' stylistically to disco and Hi-NRG, associating the track with certain gay subcultural histories, a point which I want to discuss later. However, unlike most dance musics, 'Believe' is also very song-like with an alternating rather than a terraced structure. The vocals are uncharacteristically high in the mix – as they would be in a pop track – making 'Believe' an obviously presentable and popular hybrid of technologies and genres. In more than one sense, then, it dwells on borderlines.

Following dance music conventions (which often seep back and forth between other genres), Cher's vocals are frequently double-tracked or looped to create an echo effect. This evokes a sense of the multiplicity and incoherence of the self through the voice, but in ways which most pop fans are comfortable with. Interestingly, the vocoder effect only tinges the odd phrase during the verses and does not pervade the chorus at all until the fade-out, where it then colours everything Cher sings. Here Cher phases in and out of traditional notions of vocal 'reproduction' and deliberately obvious track manipulation. Unlike the use of the more sustained vocoder heard in, say, Kraftwerk's music, Cher's employment of it teeters between what is currently constituted as the organic and the inorganic, rather than heralding some bold and pure technological futurism.

Likewise, in the lyrics to 'Believe', Cher draws on love, strength and the pain of loss – supposedly visceral emotions – without pushing them away from her technological self. Here we return to the impossibility of distancing so-called manipulated artifice from the present understanding of pain. 'Do you believe in life after love?' encapsulates what are considered to be exclusively 'human' processes and concepts (most obviously 'believing' and 'loving'). In this sense, the song exemplifies the argument that damage and pleasure, although frequently shunted into the realms of the exclusively 'authentic' and corporeal, are necessarily technologically delineated – in music and elsewhere – but are not any less emotionally felt because of this.

Cher's assumed identity also encompasses many of these ideas about the body and technology and, as she cannot help but be illustrative of her gender, this becomes a feminist concern. It develops into an even more urgent one when the politics of her plastic surgery face up to the greater debates surrounding the representation, production and perception of women. The stakes are again raised because Cher's 'Believe', unlike more self-effacingly created dance tracks, follows the rules of pop stardom. The song is solidly 'Cher' and, although Cher is not solidly organic or singular as a site of production, she is still a star persona, a firm identity to which much of the song's meaning can be attributed, however speculatively. This 'Cher', though, now seems as much assembled as grown. She looks almost as though she has donned a smooth carapace with wrinkles and ambiguous edges airbrushed out. This sharp, surgically altered Cher, so different from the hair-flicking 1960s version resplendent in tactile, organic suede and sheepskin, assumes a much more droid-like set of signifiers. As a sideline, surely this could also be understood as a partial departure from the sadly more typical female rationale for having cosmetic surgery: to become more 'ordinary', to not stand out (Davis 1995). If this is the case, then it could be argued that Cher's more flagrant and odd transmogrifications may well deserve more sustained attention from feminist theorists because of their very flirtation with the *plastic* (rather than so rigidly and exclusively cosmetic) realms of non-essential surgery.

However, there are definitely less ambiguous or potentially destructive aspects of Cher to pin feminist dreams on. As I have suggested, within her contemporary, more visually and vocally machinic, incarnation she has not lost her coherence. She perpetuates a very firm sense of self and, whilst she mutates from time to time (as all good technology does), she is engineered according to principles which equate with notions of autonomous choice. This seems largely possible because of her position within the genre of pop (so often seen as a disempowering space). In pop's forms of stardom and fandom, the desire for iconic presences is practically inescapable, opening up certain fortuitously haphazard opportunities for assuming strength through solidity. Granted, there have been many attempts to shoot Cher's potency from under her by dismissing her as a freak. However, although the impetus behind this (most notably the cosmetic surgery) may make her anathema to many strains of feminism, it cannot dispel everything she means within representational politics: she is too popular and too much a part of discourse to ignore. That she is a woman and that she (however 'she' is constituted) raises questions not only about where machines and humans stop and start, but also how this inevitable conjunction might lessen or enhance female power is a worthwhile debate. This model of a woman's use of a vocoder strongly prompts us to think through some newer possibilities for women's profitable social mobility through music (and beyond) which might include a construction of a femininity which wields much more automated power within its conception of female selfhood.

Women, vocoders, power and agency

Admittedly, several men have featured on vocoder singles, most notably Gianfranco Randone of Eiffel 65 with 'Blue (Da Ba Dee)'. However, it is telling that the band's album is called *Europop* in reverence to a musical style not usually associated with heterosexual masculinity. During this post-'Believe' period, no long-standing male artists of the stature of Madonna (no Bryan Adamses or George Michaels) have used the device, nor even have the more 'feminized' male performers such as the contemporary boy bands. While a vocoder frequently pops up on the chartier UK garage tracks (featuring mainly on the female vocal sections), the femininity of that genre should also be taken into account. Garage has rapidly developed into a romance music,[12] a dance genre which appeals to women more than many other club musics. Garage clubs are often spaces where women appear fairly powerful (albeit in very traditionally feminine ways) and where machismo from men seems more out of place than at, say, drum and bass events. So, whilst men have maybe not left the arena altogether, they are definitely having to share this space that was once more exclusive, looking on as its geography is changed by the newly arrived immigrants.

   With women's increasing centrality within contemporary vocoder use established, it now remains to be seen whether this can actually benefit a feminist politics of representation. Certainly, as I have argued, women are usually held to be more instinctive and pre-technological, further away from harnessing the powers of machinery (musically and elsewhere) than men, so performers such as Cher can help by putting spanners in these works. Many people are not familiar with the word 'vocoder' but they know what it is and often refer to it in terms like 'that Cher noise'. This attributes mastery to a woman, even if she was not part of that particular production process, and here the benefits of solid pop stardom become evident. Even if the vocal manoeuvre was not negotiated by 'the real Cher', she does become a metaphor for what women could possibly achieve with more prestigious forms of technology.

There is also something potentially liberating, as I have suggested, about Cher pointing out the computer mediation of her voice. Cultural studies has long applauded women who engage in gender parody of a visual order – such as Madonna and Annie Lennox – but, in some ways, this can lessen the worth of the work they do within their careers as musicians. A vocoder intervenes at an unavoidable level of *musical* expression, it uses the medium as the message, encouraging the listener to think of these women as professionals within music practice. Interestingly, the voice is a sphere where many female artists with complex philosophies about masquerade maintain a particularly staid paradigm: that soul or hip hop stylizations are representative of a supposedly more honest form of communication, that African-American musical form is somehow more 'authentic' (Annie Lennox and Lil Kim, for example, work in these ways).

However it is carried out, though, a ludic attitude towards gender is not necessarily a feminist endeavour in its own right. In pointing out the performative side of femininity, a rationale should perhaps be delivered and women's political motivations often clash. By lending herself to workout videos and cosmetic surgery, Cher has toyed with what are enormously problematic issues for many feminists. Armed with much persuasive empirical data, writers such as Chapkis (1986), Bartky (1990) and Wolf (1991) have defined most cosmetic surgery as fragments of the larger web of capitalist, patriarchal oppression. There is definitely an amount of consternation surrounding Cher, asking whether she throws herself under the scalpel in a subversive or a reactionary manner, in ways which undo or reaffirm certain restrictive notions of female beauty. Certainly Bordo (who discusses Madonna, but with equal applicability to Cher) is enormously critical of most interpretations of body modification as 'postmodern play', arguing that there needs to a greater acknowledgement of how cosmetic surgery reinforces limiting and age-old ideas of beauty and otherness. She stresses that, 'This abstract, unsituated, disembodied freedom ... celebrates itself only through the effacement of the material praxis of people's lives, the normalizing power of cultural images, and the sadly continuing social realities of dominance and subordination.'[13] So, whilst Cher presents herself as a triumphantly active and sexual older woman, at what cost does she do so? She does not necessarily look good for her age – through some very expensive surgical decisions, she simply does not look her age at all. These are mixed messages indeed, and they may well have economically debilitating repercussions which both fall into and help maintain the standard and often insurmountable contradictions implicit in upholding femininity. Kathy Davis, in perhaps the most sensitive investigation of cosmetic surgery, offers an alternative analytical framework – one which is more forgiving of women's struggle for agency using the limited tools offered up by patriarchal structures:

> [the issue] is situated on the razor's edge between a feminist critique of the cosmetic surgery craze (along with the ideologies of feminine inferiority which sustain it) and an equally feminist desire to treat women as agents who negotiate their bodies and their lives within the cultural and structural constraints of a gendered social order . . . Cosmetic surgery [and here I would also wish to input vocoder use] can be an informed choice, but it is always made in a context of limited options and circumstances which are not of the individual's own making.[14]

Yet it may seem all too easy for someone as powerful as Cher to benefit from or subvert the rules which govern the choices women can make about their bodies. This insurgency is perhaps the beauty of the Cher persona, but also maybe its most frustratingly inaccessible quality from the point of view of ordinary women leading ordinary lives.

With all these arguments at the front of our minds, perhaps what Cher represents is a less muddling point of identification for a certain type of man than it is for women. This is something I shall be tackling later, but first I want to continue with an exploration of the extent to which Cher might come across, in certain instances, as male. One perhaps vital part of her track's inception marks this out: 'Believe' was produced by two men, Mark Taylor and Brian Rawling, and Cher did not write it either. Can this factor cut short the power I have already ascribed to vocoded female articulacy? Are Taylor and Rawling just other types of surgeon moulding Cher into something which cannot help but represent masculine dominance and the male resuscitation of a waning female singing career? Or is there still a lot to be said for the fact that pop's systems of stardom place the *female* Cher at the song's helm? As Bradby (1993b) points out, within dance music, the female vocalist is usually in a more transient position; she is often featured rather than a secure member of any outfit. Within these practices, and sampling in particular, it would not seem untoward to derive extremely disempowering readings from male producers chopping chunks out of women's performance.

But Cher is something different to that. As I have argued, Cher-as-not-man is the acknowledged presence here – as whole as any form of representation will allow. Her fetishization has encased her in a kind of armour – she has been 'technologized' as it were – and the end result works more in her favour. On the topic of fetishism, (heterosexual) male attraction to an android or digitized woman – from the robot in *Metropolis* to Lara Croft – need not simultaneously speak ill of feminism simply because it might pander to the tastes of an often drearily predictable type of straight man. Similarly, although male production and responsibility are a glaring issue here, they may well not be able to outshine what

Cher has to offer the renegotiation of women's musical presences. This is fundamentally a matter of deflecting attention away from the replicative and the productive and focusing instead on representation. Although not entirely omnipotent or emancipating, the fortunately misconceived citation of Cher as source point here does offer us food for thought and inspiration. This is a temporary fast track to the advantages of appearing technologically adept within music production, of assuming the implied ownership which accidentally springs from some of the systems of pop iconography. If this seems like playing dirty, then the rules by which the rest of the industry operate (particularly as regards the exploitation of female artists) need to be taken into account.

With these kinds of cards laid on the table, it is hardly surprising that female listeners might find this rather an uneasy alliance – one similarly sullied by Cher's position within the politics and economics of body modification. Having potentially cut myself off at the pass here, I now want to draw on extra troops who have been eager to accrue something beneficial from Cher's presence: gay men.[15] To do this, I need to search out, more specifically, the position of camp within cyber-theory.

Gay men, camp, cyber-theory and the politics of popular culture

For quite some time now, gender's relation to (digital) technology has occupied academics and, within this and of particular interest here, there have been various forays into the possible interplays between embodiment and disembodiment that they manifest. The favourite topic of discussion here, without a doubt, has been the chat room and how it might or might not confound standard strictures of gender or sexuality. However, the dynamics of chat rooms have much to do with one's limited access to any given subject's appearance or voice – quite the reverse of how the vocoder functions. As yet, there seems to be little work on what happens when the links between the audio-visually perceived body, gender and sexual identity are not eroded, when large portions of the product are passed off as non-digitally reproduced. The cyborg we see and hear, and how it relates to sexuality or, in this instance, to camp, has not really provoked much interest, despite definite parallels in each one's complication of the 'natural' and the 'normal'. Cher, a recognized icon within gay male culture, in some senses draws the two together, although she is preceded by a definite history of technologies manifesting certain homosexual sensibilities. While the camp markers of fussiness and snippy asides can be witnessed in the representation of automated entities (HAL in *2001: A Space Odyssey*, KIT in *Knight Rider* and *Star Wars'* C3PO, for example), these technologies are often thought not to be fluffy and gorgeous enough to be camp. There might also be an assumption that the sexless droid is automatically pumped out as heterosexual by default, or that sexuality is not an issue (although aesthetic alignment most certainly has to be). Camp, after all, is not a sexual practice.

To focus this argument, it would again be wise to home in on Cher's use of the vocoder as perhaps the first exception to a practice which was, at the time, still, for the most part, heterosexualized:[16] Laurie Anderson may question normative gendering but she is less interested in sexuality, and UK garage (unlike its American forerunner) does present a decidedly straight front. Unlike these musicians, Cher fits snugly into the diva role so beloved of various gay cultures. More specifically, she maintains the lone, rather monumental fronting of a dance track in the way that, say, Gloria Gaynor or Ultra Nate have done. Lyrically, 'Believe' also invokes a theme familiar to gay dance classics: the triumph and liberation of the downtrodden or unloved. This song is a bittersweet declaration of strength after a break-up and, by saying 'maybe I'm too good for you', Cher conjures up certain allusions to the vocabularies of gay pride.

One of camp's more pervasive projects is a certain delight in the inauthentic, in things which are obviously pretending to be what they are not and which might, to some degree, speak of the difficulties of existing within an ill-fitting public façade – something which evidently concerns 'Believe'. The track also volunteers a reliable amount of resolution: although it accords with contemporary notions of the *ersatz*, it is nonetheless touching and expressive and it achieves this without resorting wholly to certain restrictive concepts of authenticity which are implicitly grounded in straightness. Cher's affront to and dismissal of fraudulence's bad reputation shines forth from her position as an 'impostor' within a dance scene she is too mainstream and too old to be truly welcomed into. She is usurping a culture of pleasure which would ordinarily deny her access and her jubilance, despite not belonging, loops back into camp and certain strategies of queer everyday life.

Hand in hand with this enjoyment of the unconvincing comes a partiality for things which are maybe out of date, which have fallen by the wayside and this, again, shows support for the neglected underdog. This maps conveniently onto vocoder use once more: its timbre seems reedy and more a 1970s or 80s evocation of robotry than a newly contemporary effect. Like Cher herself, it has hardly been a recent 'latest thing', what all the kids are clamouring to associate themselves with. It is now a deliberately vintage sound and the fact that it was once the height of modernity lends it a certain charm.

Having given some indication of how 'Believe' rests upon camp, I now feel that finding out how camp might simultaneously offer a leg up to the song's female listeners (straight or otherwise) would be worthwhile. Firstly, as I have suggested, 'Believe' may have had to jostle particularly hard for political attention because it is a product of a more derided genre. Not so in the mainstream of queer musical aesthetics where pop, along with other genres which 'Believe' also looks to (such as disco, the torch song and US garage) is one of *the* most politicized musical forms. Essentially, camp disregards standard modes of readership and gives its objects subversive qualities without worrying about whether they are 'authentic', or written into them in the first place. Camp, then, might point out an even broader spectrum of strategies for all manner of (maybe even straight) people who are drawn to this music because they feel out of place within representation yet still have the need to forge their identities through these types of cultural produce all the same.

That said, this is a difficult operation and it is important not to aspire to kidnap camp from its valuable position within queer history – it must be observed *in situ* rather than stolen. As Andy Medhurst (1997) argues, camp has long been a shared pleasure within gay communities, a way of coping within a culture which marginalizes you, and a means of recognizing the like-minded within societies which, to one extent or another, outlaw homosexual practices. As such, it is not the most suitable bandwagon for straights to climb on just for the fun of it, not least because such an action would undermine a minority's sense of power through cultural ownership. Camp may seem to make light, but that does not mean it is to be taken lightly. Yet, having said this, camp has always basked in the limelight offered by (unfortunately) implicitly heterosexual institutions ranging from prime-time television scheduling to chart music. In many ways, this makes camp a shared cultural language – although some readers are habitually more fluent in it than others.

With these provisos heeded, camp can undoubtedly prove inspirational in its survivalist hints. It proposes an incredibly thoughtful model of how to consume a popular culture which does not necessarily purport to speak for certain marginalized social groups – and these might also include female musicians and female fans. As yet there are precious few other strategies for actually falling in love with the mainstream and keeping one's political convictions intact. By pushing current (largely straight male) standards of pop, perfection, fakery and behind-the-scenes mechanization in unusual directions, a vocoder, like other camp objects, might complicate staid notions of reality, the body, femininity and female capability. Even if all the other uses of vocoders have not been as knowingly camp as Cher's (not that intentionality has ever been a prerequisite), camp can motivate how they are listened to and how they might seem empowering to women. Although none of this reading 'too deeply' and warping of musical meaning is likely to break down all the repressive structures of the music industry, it can definitely contribute to more egalitarian hegemonic shifts within pop's role in identity construction. Camp has always been about making do within the mainstream, twisting it, adoring aspects of it regardless, wobbling its more restrictive given meanings – something which this reading of the vocoder undoubtedly does too. Most of all, camp is about appropriation and a *usage* of popular culture which might not accord with the masculinist *status quo*, despite any notion of 'original intent' or authorship. If everything is not as might be desired within music production, then a certain type of consumption provides solace and stimulus in the meantime.

These are greedy, opportunist readings both in the way they pick up on camp for further ulterior motives and in their possible lack of obviousness to the everyday listener. Surely, though, there is important work to be done in expanding the deliberately quasi-implausible, especially in areas of popular music where the manufacture of representations connives all too frequently to undermine the value of female performance. A control of meaning by way of rhetorical grasping and grabbing admittedly seems more precarious considering the inevitable sabotage to be expected from the various discouraging and destructive forces at work in music production and consumption. However, when theorizing the 'mere fripperies' of chart music culture it is surely still vital not to give up hope and to try and build something fortifying out of debris left by these male struggles for technological dominance. For the moment, then, strategies like camp seem not only profitable in the short term, but also more than capable of being adapted to accord with historical and technological change.

Notes

1. This chapter was first published in *Popular Music*, **20** (3), Cambridge University Press, 2001, 333–47.
2. Here a parallel arises with the case of Stephen Hawking whose now somewhat crude artificial speech device has become synonymous with him – in fact in many representational instances he might not be recognizable without it.
3. Leach, E. (2001), 'Vicars of *Wannabe:* Authenticity and the Spice Girls', *Popular Music*, **20** (2), 143–67.
4. Here it might be worth invoking the long-running feud between ELO and Queen over the use of synthesizers – another technology which frequently reeks of both inauthenticity and femininity. Queen's denigration of the synthesizer and love of the electric guitar might help explain the band's loyal heterosexual male fan base, despite the unabashedly camp antics of lead singer Freddie Mercury. Matrices of authenticity, gender and sexuality such as this will be discussed in detail this chapter.
5. My present emphasis on the role of production and recording in the cultural wrangles about authenticity is not intended to undermine the more popular academic topic of live performance and authenticity. I simply wish to help expand such debates into further spheres of music-making and listening.
6. This hegemonic position is continually and hotly debated, for example, when bands such as the Spice Girls are criticized for miming. The investment in this type of agency was enforced when Milli Vanilli were stripped of their Grammys for not singing their 'own' material.
7. McClary, S. (1991), *Feminine Endings: Music, Gender and Sexuality*, Minnesota: University of Minnesota Press, p. 137.
8. This becomes evident when referring back to the list of vocoder tracks and their artists with which I started this article.
9. Arguably, Anderson is less interested in the feminine potential of the vocoder. Although she is definitely using the device to start up a debate on gender, she uses it to deepen her voice through polyphony, to make herself sound more androgynous, as well as more android. Her work is perhaps more about the freedom to reject gender or to present an *unheimlich* grouping of simultaneous gender-scrambling musical selves.
10. Downey, G.M., Dumit, J. and Williams, S. (1995), 'Cyborg Anthropologies' in Gray, C. *et al*. (eds), *The Cyborg Handbook*, London: Routledge, p. 345.
11. Lury, C. (1998), *Prosthetic Culture: Photography, Memory and Identity*, London and New York: Routledge, p. 19.

12. Craig David's enormous success with a line of address which seems evocative almost of courtly love is representative of this.
13. Bordo, S. (1993), '"Material Girl": The effacements of postmodern culture' in Schwichtenberg, C. (ed), *The Madonna Connection*, Bolder CO: Westview Press, p. 289.
14. Davis, K. (1995), *Reshaping the Female Body: The Dilemma of Cosmetic Surgery*, London: Routledge, p. 5–13.
15. In talking about queerness, for the rest of this paper I wish to concentrate for the most part, on the interest in camp of gay men, rather than gay women. This is not to say that camp is exclusively the domain of gay men, but rather than there seems to be more of a tendency for lesbians to involve themselves in the music of other lesbians (or at least deliciously 'crypto' female performers) rather than dwell on the output of more evidently straight musicians such as Cher (Bradby, 1993a).
16. Since then Steps, Madonna, Victoria Beckham and Kylie Minogue (all of whom have substantial gay followings) have helped to 'queer' the vocoder.

Chapter 10

On performativity and production in Madonna's 'Music'

Stan Hawkins

Introduction

Madonna's songs offer up an expansive plane for debating the many issues implicated in perceptions of music production and recorded performance. In this chapter, the focus is directed at the signification of production and technology within the song 'Music', from the album *Music* released in September 2000. I want to argue that the relationship between musical production and Madonna's personal expression not only inscribes interesting advances in the mechanics of sound reproduction, but also shapes the nuances of performance via the performer as a fascinating constructed event. Undoubtedly, the strength of emotions elicited by Madonna's recorded performance concerns female representation through the technicalities of sound production. An exploration of the implications of these assertions now follows, in which I attempt to argue the issue of performative meaning in musical expression.

Inextricably wrapped up in how Madonna has marketed herself, her productions are clearly about how she wishes to enact her femininity, mediate her construction, and access her fans through fantasy. Not least, the technologies involved in her productions set up a range of expectations that relate to how and why we perceive her in specific ways. In a general sense, we might say that all pop recordings capture the audio dynamics of an ideal performance, where the focus falls on the star's intensity as performer as much as on the musical processes themselves. Because of this, the recording can harness stories that operate as implied cultural narratives, and thus transport the subjectivity of the singer or artist as central character.

The musical skills behind pop productions involve selecting both the subject matter and sounds to express an accumulation of ideas. In production terms, Madonna's recordings are derived from an appropriation of conventions linked to dance culture, electronica, and the erotics of gendered performance that inform the hedonistic body. In all her tracks, it is the technological modes of expression that become a focal point of the creative process and hence the enjoyment experience. Indeed, what characterizes her songs and videos is a narcissistic masquerading which exhibits a performativity that is both excessive and oppositional.[1] Of course, this raises the question of fantasy in pop expression.

Fantasy, as an experience, must be one of the crucial parts of enjoying pop music. John Fiske (1989) points out that the pleasure linked to fantasy in Madonna's case is also linked to notions of power, not least involving target groups such as teenage girls and women. Fiske has discussed how pop videos present us with a performative platform for pleasure. This form of pleasure, he insists, is 'based on the satisfaction of maintaining a sense of subcultural difference'.[2] If we apply this idea to the sound recording, the pop music that Madonna has always produced also discloses notions of community that have to do with the functional side of assumptions. This idea gains currency the more we explore the nature of performance and its overflow into pop erotica, desire, and sexuality.

On the implications of production in Madonna's recordings, a number of matters stand out for consideration. To start with, the idea of stylized production is a determining musical feature that ultimately convinces and wins over fans. For the present argument, I would suggest that it is in the affected nature of the production of 'Music' that the pop aesthetic is fully manifested. Within the production process there is a repertory of technical processes that are moulded into the full effect of the sound. This directly impinges on the function of technological innovation as a compositional ingredient of studio production. Each time we hear an amplified voice or instrument within the mix of 'Music', we react primarily to the technical dialects of audio signal processes; an important process I will return to later. As I have argued in earlier studies, studio production has possibly the most significant effect on the details of Madonna's sound, in a manner that lures us through time into the personal sphere of her identity (Hawkins, 1997; 2002). Engineered to ensure that the intended listener achieves a special association with the performer, Madonna's recordings are about controlling our sentiments. From this perspective, the power of her recordings inevitably lies in the production style she selects, which constitutes that imaginary circuit that depends entirely on listening; an activity of engagement that is performative in itself.

In all Madonna's songs to date, it is as if the detailed effects of technology are tied into the forceful mediation of her authorship as every sound becomes conditional on the fine balance between producer, engineer, artist, and, of course, the record company. Ever since the launch of her career in the early 1980s, Madonna's role in the studio has steadily evolved to a point where her input into the final product has been almost total.[3] Inherent in every one of her recordings one finds technical processes that not only reveal her collaborative relationships with teams of other musicians and producers (and the values entrusted to their work), but also the type of audience for which her music is marketed. Put differently, it is the audience that allows the communication of musical messages, and, thus, the extent to which production shapes the flavour of the song. If we consider, then, production as a strategic event, how do the technical procedures involved in the recording studio set the limits of what determines a specific response?[4]

The recording of 'Music' mediates a range of emotive states and moods as Madonna draws on her prior experiences to introduce her ideas to the listener/fan. While this track displays many of the structural forms found in Madonna's other songs, its overall production is significantly different. In no uncertain terms, this song charts the recent changes, trends, and developments in the pop industry. Most of all, 'Music' is shaped by the precise technical editing processes of the recording process. These processes function as an important reminder that there are ongoing changes in her mode of production. Laying down tracks in the studio is essentially a project that articulates Madonna's sonic trademark, and it is through the quality of her production work and her relationship with teams of engineers and producers that her albums and songs gain their popularity.[5]

We could say that Madonna's recordings are deconstructions of agency and desire[6] and that it is the studio conditions of her production that instate her performativity. As with her produced image, her musical productions deliberately push forward the bounds of production. Moreover, her music is realized in ways that not only highlight her femininity as a pleasurable and earnest entity, but also challenge and contest the context within which she works (McClary, 1991; Robertson, 1996; Whiteley, 2002). Surely, this is the central point: that our imaginative engagement with her music has everything to do with the way in which we are able to access her identity and our own social contexts through the idealized form of the recording.

Manipulating through production tricks

As I have already suggested, Madonna's sound productions are provokers of fantasy. Our associations with her voice in 'Music' are what primarily encode pleasure and fantasy in this song. What is presented to us from the outset is a splash of production tricks. Co-produced with the French producer Mirwais Ahmadzï, the title track 'Music' is charged with a spectacular array of editing techniques. As with the majority of Madonna's songs, the basic conception of the track is groove-based with the rhythmic and harmonic *ostinati* determining the directional flow and formal development.[7] All the way through, repetition controls the structural processes as much as the mobility of the song by supporting all the rhythmic development of material. Structurally, the song's form is couched in verses and choruses that are an accumulation of processes that disclose a wide variety of production techniques. On the whole, the sound processes embrace a spectrum of multiple effects that dominate all the musical parameters: harmony, melody, dynamic intensity, and instrumental choice. But most discernible is the produced effect in 'Music', which is constituted by the constant regulation of effects, sequencing, and edits.

In its excessive flavour, the production style of 'Music' also mediates an ironic sensibility that is not least quirky. Particularly, the handling of retro disco markers as strong signifiers make this explicit. As each bar builds up into groove patterns that stabilize the feel of the beat, every rhythmic impulse is teased out to the point of excess. Madonna elects to open the track with an affected, low register, sexy male voice, recorded close-up in a sleazy, American drawl: 'Hey Mr DJ, put a record on. I want to dance with my baby.' This phrase encapsulates the song's camp pop sentiment[8] and is tweaked to create an abundance of anticipation and tension. Following a reverse cymbal crescendo the groove revs up with a tightly quantized, funky syncopated figure dominated by a single monotonous pitch on a low voluptuous Hammond organ tone. The high-pitched vocoded vocals that follow on the words 'do you like to' – accompanied by disco string stabs, dry snares on the second and fourth beats, stereo panning of an intricately spliced-up guitar riff – provide the textural backdrop. These ideas in the introduction set the mood for the entire song.

Editing processes make their major impact on the shaping of Madonna's voice in 'Music'. The cyborg-induced vocoded strain, 'do you like to', surfs the all-insistent groove, and as Madonna enters the recording, taking over from the male voice that opens the song, the intricacies of her vocal processing become the most controlling feature in the production. A sub-bass accenting the two beats of the funk figure fills out the tightly edited groove pattern that carries the vocal phrases.

With the start of the first chorus, just under one minute into the song, the word 'music' is elegantly edited through a high degree of vocoding, which stretches out Madonna's voice with an urgency that is compelling. Instantly, this highlights a playfulness that is exaggerated through the sheer elasticity of her vocal phrasing, a gesture that alone discloses Madonna's camp quality.[9] In moments such as these, there is a feeling that the producers have gone out of their way to set up a horizontal plane of sonic attributes that are interrelated and carefully defined by their imaging in the mix. Significantly, all the artistic elements of musical coding, melody, rhythm, harmony, instrumentation, pitch, tonal inflection, dynamic usage, and phrase schemes are arranged in stark contrast to one another in a vividly mobile sonic image.

Amongst the many musical features that are profiled in the production is the variability of sound localization. By this I am referring to the specific control of audio mobility, which is regulated by frenetic digital edits that help propel the listener into a hyperreal soundscape. As if making this track an exercise alone in plotting her control through technical virtuosity, Madonna not only flirts with us, but also sets out to demonstrate her production skills in no uncertain terms. Musically, what this means is that the very simple melodic, rhythmic, timbral, and harmonic ideas are instilled within a range of virtuosic edits that are blended into the smooth consistency of the mix.

As I experience it, the pleasure in this track is based around a high degree of data control through the creative use of music software that proposes something both captivating and compulsive. In this respect, the production techniques create a notion of virtual sonic reality and sense of escapism. Importantly, the sensations induced by the recording are not just about loudness, degrees of delay, or levels of reverberation. There is always this sensation of being in the moment as we are escorted into a shimmering composite sound object that is controlled by timbral difference, dynamic contrast, and fluctuating levels of reverberation. Aesthetically, the sounds are located within the mix in a way that feels synthetic and mannered, while their timbral definition is profiled by a wealth of edits and mixes. Indeed, the full impact of the sound production suggests a compilation of ideas that enter and exit the mix at varying speeds. Constantly mobile, all the groove patterns are the result of a bag of production tricks; it is this that creates the pop fantasy.

Repeated hearings of this song reveal more and more how excessive the edits really are. For example, riffs and sampled sounds are pasted and dragged over one another at alarmingly high speeds, a technique often employed in the digital editing of dance styles. From this, it becomes obvious that all the sounds exist as computer information[10] and are edited in realtime through predetermined automation. By this I am referring to the detailed digital processes of panning, changes in equalization, alternating fader levels, and special effects, all of which form the precise edit points that determine the music's mobility. Often in pop tracks of this nature, it is the quest for polished style that is instigated by the intricate mechanics of recording technology, something that transpires only in a sophisticated audio environment, where displays of authorship occur in any number of guises. Given this, let us turn to how the audio image engenders musical relations in tandem with Madonna's performativity.

Pleasurable intimacy and distancing

Sensations of aural pleasure in pop music are often the result of well-calculated musical techniques. In Madonna's output, there is always a sense that her recordings constitute creative inquiries into representation and desire. In the verses of 'Music', Madonna's voice is profiled with relatively little studio treatment and confined to a pitch range of a perfect fifth, while her voice is positioned to the front of the mix. A minimal use of effects at this point creates a sonic intimacy that could be described as a constructed naturalness, a quality which is felt as erotic. Conversely, in the choruses, there is an exaggerated shift to an artificial sound with heavy effects programming as the melodic pitch interestingly shrinks to a minor third. In contrast to the verses, the choruses are characterized by an unprecedented boost in studio effects and vocoding. For example, with the onslaught of the first chorus the vocals are double-tracked and equalized in a way that heightens the effect of sonic contrast.

As if deliberately distancing herself from the intimacy of her verse sections, Madonna submits to a swirl of fancy vocal edits layered over enlarged beats in the chorus passages. These seem like larger-than-life moments of aural spectacle that serve to remind us that her sensuality is always captured by the physical connotations of groove-based dance music. Virtuoso editing and the subtleties and excesses of musical treatment reveal Madonna's desire for control as her over-processed vocal style guarantees a seductiveness that typifies her agency. In production terms, this is borne out by countless edits in the unfolding and treatment of the song's musical content. One case in point is the climactic build-up passage towards the end of the track that thrills and delights. Here, the thematic material culminates in a circular looping of two disparate melodic riffs, one instrumental, and one spoken. Pasted together like a puzzle for our ears, these two themes wrestle with one another to keep the momentum of the groove rhythmically and melodically vibrant in its final lap.

With a major-seventh leap to C♯, via an upper mordent slide (D2), there is a jarring clash in tonality that is quite unexpected. This then resolves through the pitches B♭2–C2 to the dominant pitch A2. Compelling in its melodic quirkiness, the dissonance of the C♯ deceives us into an unconventional harmonic minor shift, just before the melodic minor descending line ruins this illusion. Possibly the effect of this is to destabilize the tonal security of the song hitherto. In other words, the entry of the felicitous pitch C♯2, the sharpened seventh degree, rests outside the confines of the song's tonality, not least through its late introduction only within the last minute of the song (2:57). Significantly, the pretentiousness of this one altered tone creates something musically different and decisive by challenging the safety of the traditional tonal framework. Mixed to the fore of the track, this instrumental riff is taken up by a crass, analogue-type 1970s moog string synthesizer that blandly pelts out the incessant five-note angular melody to the song's eventual fade-out. Notwithstanding the high degree of excessive reiteration, this riff remains firm and controlled in its relation to the other main theme, 'do you like to?'. Initially, these two lines are reconciled through a simultaneous clash of C♯ and C♮. Quite subversive in mannerism, these contrapuntal phrases rapidly metamorphose into something alluringly beautiful that is quirky, vulgar and flamboyant at the same time. As one would expect in any Madonna production, such musical urgency is all about teasing through distancing and repetition. Let us now consider the implications of this.

Entities of embodiment: cybernetic delection of the flesh

Production techniques in 'Music' communicate an attitude of playfulness through Madonna's performativity. Indeed, the over-produced style of this track seems to parody the techno-geekiness of boy toyland. The aesthetic implications of this assumption are embedded in the riff described above. As I read it, the dialogue set up between the two melodic strands of this riff symbolizes a sense of internal struggle through parody. Technically, the two phrases battle it out to morph into one idea through their location in the mix. And, as if infected by one another, they shift elliptically from one pole to the next. Each fragment then radiates back to the site of its origin, as it invades a new sonic territory. It is in the very performative nature of such contrapuntal processing and digital editing – especially in terms of resistance and compliance – that an erotic sensibility emerges. In such moments, I would suggest that compositional inventiveness goes a long way in endorsing Madonna's political agency. To consider this point further, I would argue that throughout the production a degree of fetishism emanates from the affected quality of the vocal utterance, 'do you like to', which serves to enhance the experience of pop fantasy. Here, it is as if the voice parodies the fembot – Donna Haraway's term (1991) for the feminized machine that regurgitates the worst of all sexual stereotypes. We could read the hyperartificality of this gesture as a flamboyant bid to parody the autonomous agency of Madonna bent on extending pleasures of her femininity into computerized simulation and interior resistance.

Clearly, the production of 'Music' involves a meticulous processing of many musical details, which all lead to a state of extravagance on the one hand, and a simple set of melodic and rhythmic ideas on the other hand. The significance of this is borne out not only in terms of economic investment – this is a costly recording, and one hears this – but also through an attempt to do something different and digitally extraordinary. All in all, the editing precision reinvents the fun of disco and theatricalizes pop culture through sheer technical virtuosity, and exerts Madonna's performativity as sonic spectacle. In this sense, production as sonic experience becomes a powerful form of representing social relations and identities.

From this then, the aural spectacle of sound technology increases significantly in the mixing down of the final take. This is borne out by the gestures of digital editing which are ambitious and daring. To a point of exaggeration, the mix liberates all artistic expression from taking itself too seriously. I am referring here to the creative implant of familiar sounds and gestures into new contexts, something that emphasizes the constitutive process of postmodern pop. Indeed, the postmodern, automated, retro-electronic references have their roots in Europop, a genre that underlies a sensibility that Madonna has realized is a lot more than just ineffable. Self-mocking in their parody, it is as if all the electronic sounds in 'Music' disclose an attitude that, while disengaged on one level, is highly reflexive on another. Most of all, Madonna's incessant, affected vocoded whine, 'do you like to,' links the sensations of eroticism and automatism to compositional craftsmanship.

Positioned high in the mix, this sample is looped and phased through an Eventide H300 and then converted into an emulation of a phaser effect by use of filters and delay in the E6400. Mirwais has talked about this when discussing how he took editing techniques to their limits in 'Music' by experimenting extensively to acquire the desired effect. With a background firmly in Euro club music, he made his mark on the French dance scene in the 1970s. His contribution to this track is detectable through the strategies of sonic selection and manipulation that are prevalent in every moment of audio treatment through a unique utilization of music hardware and software. On the vocal tracks of 'Music' alone, he describes his approach to editing Madonna's voice: 'I put Auto-tune on individual syllables. Sometimes I use 40 tracks of audio just on one vocal track. Each has a different level and treatment, and then I do a composite. I couldn't do this with a normal analog studio setup' (Rideout, 2001). In the almost unrecognizable vocoded sample 'Boogie Woogie. Do you like to?', Mirwais decided to use an old EMS2000 vocoder on Madonna's voice, the effect of which would deliberately twist her natural voice into a cyborg-like character. Through vocoding, Madonna's voice was meticulously manipulated to provide what Mirwais has described as an effect of going 'in fits and starts'. Sonically, the impact of this technique was located in the manner with which the voice melts the natural voice into a series of surreal and disconnected loops as the pop diva skates between cyber fiction and social reality. Enacting the cyborg who is 'resolutely committed to partiality, irony, intimacy, and perversity',[11] Madonna's morphing of vocal embodiment through computerized manipulation (by Mirwais!) seems the ultimate cybernetic delection of the female flesh.

What could be more subversive than the manipulation of the human voice through fiction and fantasy? And, if Madonna signifies a denial of the natural voice through vocoding, does this constitute an act of political defiance? Indeed, the full significance of synthesis and artificiality in such a camp pop song as 'Music' rests in a number of contingent radical moments that seem to subscribe to a political agenda. What seems most explicit here is the dialogue between the cyborg and the natural human, something that suggests a mission well beyond the confines of the text into the imaginative domain of oppositionality. As I interpret it, the editing devices are more political than playful as they direct our attention towards an ideological space that is prised open by the reinvention and mutation of male-based technology and female representation. This would explain why production techniques in 'Music' are indeed strongly implicated in the intricate politics of pleasure and fantasy. In tracks such as 'Music' we cannot fail to acknowledge the artist's location within virtual sonic space as an entity of embodiment. Certainly, advances in audio technologies serve as much more than just an apparatus for entertainment – they form the crucial tools for sculpting changing social relations within countless communities. At any rate, the Madonna industry has come to symbolize a formalization of fluid cultural interactions that function to entice consumption through the mediation of music technology.

Performativity as ritual and dramatic purpose

In the track 'Music', the richly laced sonic tapestries in the final cyclical build-up bring to mind the intensity of Madonna's performativity. Signalling an important arrival point, her expression in the final minute of the song is robotic at the same time as it is elastic – a testament alone to the oppositionality of her playfulness. Complex multi-track editing nevertheless grants a listener-friendly accessibility that identifies Madonna's control over every milli-second of the mix, something that signifies a deeper set of political agendas. Expanding her musical palette across clever edits and tricky electronics, she forcibly stamps into her productions many points of musical and extramusical reference. In such moments, we are reminded of her remarkable passage into the male world of automatism, a voyage that has empowered her to date. Most of all, her vocal performances exploit a network of narrative excursions that transcend the lyrics she uses. The pleasures, then, in Madonna's texts are derived from overdubbing techniques that thrive on the piling up of a multitude of voices while still remaining distinctive. Under the rubric of polyphony (an ancient technique of composition stretching back 1000 years), she plunders all the traditions that fascinate us in musical expression, especially those elements of imitation, mimicry and allusion.

We might consider the potential of Madonna's musical transformations from one album to the next as her recourse to a performativity that functions as a tenuous cultural construction. Her vocal expression alone determines a form of theatrical enactment that contributes to the packaging of her as a desirable subject. Mostly, it is in her continual changes of vocal colouring that an ambiguity is sensed. Further, I would suggest that the self-reflexivity found in her vocal expression is never inconsequential; it is about a form of story-telling set within a fantasy that seeks to consolidate her identity. Perhaps the dominant feature of her aesthetic, then, is sounded out through the coming together of a wealth of musical elements that define her role. I am referring to a role in which authority becomes a dramatic function in itself, with the ushering in of a musical sensibility that always insists on imaginative response.

On a related issue, Sean Cubitt has explored the implications of recording techniques and production: 'The amplified voice is an ideal form, an image like a mirror image. It is like us yet bigger, more perfect, almost godlike; like Socrates' daemon, it is more coherent and more fully in control of its identity than we often feel ourselves to be.'[12] As with the fan, the analyst's active engagement with the voice grants access to a wealth of emotions. Turning to Lacan's mirror phase metaphor, Cubitt has insisted that the amplified voice connects us through an idealized image of our inner and exterior worlds. Certainly, all Madonna's vocalizations are processes of signification that produce the subject as an 'effect of language'.[13] Yet, this also signifies a lack and absence. Cubitt's point is that desire is only manifested through language, whose effect is something truly human. Signifying practices in music thus inhabit that area between our social worlds and desire where '(t)here is a deal of play between the conscious enjoyment of presence and the activity of the unconscious about absence, a play that underlies the pleasure of listening'.[14] Underlying the pleasures in listening then, the chasm between language and consciousness or being makes up the discursive field of struggles of exchange. So, if we accept that Madonna's recorded performances underwrite the determination of her purpose, this takes place through the structures of technological endeavour that mobilize all her musical aspirations.

To conclude, Madonna's performativity in 'Music' could be understood as a project of active communication, which is linked to the narcissistic, desiring subject. As desiring subject and empowered pop icon, I would suggest that Madonna skilfully recycles herself through music technology. Behind her productions there is a technical gloss that highlights the striking traits of her aural and visual spectacle. As Madonna records herself each time, she knows full well that she is a compelling subject of re-interpretation and desire. There is always a transient state of desire in her agency. This is rooted as much in musical style as performance design, and image sculpting, which Madonna knowingly offers up for her fans. Above all, her productions play the most crucial part in the transmission of her song's narratives as every song establishes its own special quality by means of its detailed construction. Time and time again, Madonna snaps up the trends in the market and rapidly reshapes them in a bid to entertain us. The result of all this is that her productions emerge with a controlled primacy where technical virtuosity forms an irresistible part of desire and fantasy in our reception and enjoyment of pop.

Notes

1. I would argue that it is different forms of conception that conflate musical evaluations and disclose humour as being present or not. As arguments centred on taste make clear, no form of response to music can be made in abstraction (Frith, 1996).
2. Fiske, J. (1989), *Reading the Popular*, London: Routledge, p. 118.
3. Not enough attention has been paid to Madonna's role in the production of her albums. I have argued this point in more detail elsewhere (Hawkins, 2002). Despite an increase in the profile of women composers and artists in the twentieth century, the issue of sexism in the music industry (in popular music and 'art' contemporary music) lingers on. That Madonna has co-produced most of her songs and written much of the material is seldom acknowledged (see also Cook, 1998, 107).
4. Note that I prefer the use of the term 'message' to 'product' in this instance, as 'message' implies that there are different ways by which to receive the music.
5. On this point, there are important implications, linked to her collaboration with predominantly male engineers and sound producers. This is a critical point that has its resonance in gender politics and the problematics of a male-driven music industry, a topic of more extensive debate in this section by Kay Dickinson, Emma Mayhew, and Jacqueline Warwick.
6. Here I am referring to the positioning of the female pop artist within a specific social and cultural setting. Madonna's *agency* is about her establishment of an individual relationship to systemic structures of both conformity and resistance. This also involves a special type of construction of femininity through drag display (Butler, 1993; 1999). She constantly invokes a range of desires and a strong sense of identity through challenging and accepting dominant paradigms that ultimately confirm her position in the record industry. In a well-thought-out theoretical framework for

addressing such interpretative analysis, musicologist Lori Burns has examined female agency and desire alongside the categories of Subject/Object perspective and Domination versus Subordination in a range of case-studies involving female artists. (See, for example, Burns and Lafrance, 2002, 55–61.)

7.   This type of compositional development typifies dance genres where the build-up of simple ideas is dependent more on studio effects and production techniques than traditional approaches to melodic, harmonic, and formal development. In an earlier article I have theorized the role of repetition in its shaping of dance aesthetics (Hawkins, 2001).

8.   Note that I employ the term 'camp pop' here to refer to pop music that is blatant in its celebration of artifice, commerciality, and immediate gratification. There is a queer interrelationship of these two terms, camp and pop, which acknowledges the surplus sensibility of a disposable culture that invokes signifiers of fun and pleasure that are oppositional. On the different uses of the terms camp, drag, and pop, Andrew Ross has problematized numerous pop styles, which include heavy metal, glam rock, punk, and rock. His use of the term 'Pop Camp' is mapped against a cultural and historical periodization of mass culture, with an important focus on the 1960s camp contradictory and layered cultured economy. In dealing with this concept, Ross emphasizes how camp was 'an antidote to Pop's contagion of obsolescence' (Ross, 1999, 321).

9.   For a full exploration of the construction of a camp aesthetic in this track, as well as an investigation of Madonna's use of drag, see my study of this, 'Dragging out Camp: Narrative Agendas in Madonna's Musical Production', in *Madonna's Drowned Worlds: New Approaches to her Cultural Transformations, 1983–2003*, ed. Santiago Fouz-Hernández and Freya Jarman-Ivens (2004), Aldershot: Ashgate, pp. 3–21.

10. Here I am referring to digital recording where specialized computers and software are used to edit the sound signals. The track 'Music' serves as a testament to state-of-the-art digital editing, in which degrees of creativity can be measured by the sheer magnitude of edit points. In editing, producers and engineers need to demonstrate a technical proficiency in an artistic manner in order for the music to convince.

11. Haraway, D. (1991), *Simians, Cyborgs and Women: The Reinvention of Labour*, London: Free Association Books, p. 151

12. Cubitt, S. (2000), '"Maybellene": Meaning and the Listening Subject', in Middleton, R. (ed.), *Reading Pop*, Oxford: Oxford University Press, p. 155

13. Ibid., p. 156

14. Ibid., p. 175

Chapter 11

'He's Got the Power': the politics of production in girl group music

Jacqueline Warwick

He makes me say things I don't want to say
He makes me do things I don't want to do
And even though I try to break away,
I can't stop doing things for him
Can't stop saying I adore him –
He's got the power, the power of love over me

The Exciters, 1963

The message and lyrics of this 1963 release by the Exciters seem to exemplify the nature of girl group music as most people understand it. When I tell people that I work on 1960s girl groups they often react with astonishment, and refer to songs like this to illustrate everything that's wrong with this music. How can I, a feminist, devote attention to a genre that promotes this kind of sexist model of passivity – shouldn't I be working on artists like Joni Mitchell or Janis Joplin as more positive examples of women in rock? People are also puzzled as to why someone with a formal education in music and a Ph.D. in musicology would waste their time on the girl group genre, where untrained singers perform simple songs written and produced by 'real' musicians – shouldn't I be working on Cathy Berberian or Thea Musgrave, who were virtuoso singers and collaborated with composers on their work?

I think that the girl group genre is significant to the development of feminism, the philosophies of the Civil Rights Movement, and the history of popular music. For one thing, the tremendous popularity of girl groups in the 1960s presents a rare instance of girls at the forefront of mainstream culture. The songs of the Shirelles, Ronettes, ShangriLas and other groups articulated the experiences and concerns of girls coming of age in a society that recognized 'teenager' as a new subject position. Girl group songs served as a forum for girls to discuss the topics of importance to them: boys, parents, social protocol and the challenges of entering womanhood. What is more, the professional system that produced the American girl group genre is an example of black and white musicians working together, a highly successful model of the integrationist policies espoused by figures like Martin Luther King. The girl group style was also an important influence on many of the most popular male artists of the period – bands like the Beatles and the Beach Boys performed girl group songs and carefully emulated the girl group style in their original compositions.[1]

In this article I want to respond to what is – in the world of music scholarship, anyway – the most common charge levelled against the girl group genre; namely, that girl group songs and lyrics were written by professional songwriters, that session musicians provided the instrumental tracks, and that adult male record producers controlled the whole operation, while the girl group singers themselves did nothing more than sing. It is true that girl group music offers a pre-fabricated girls' music to its listeners, and I want to suggest that the stageiness and artificiality of girl group songs can serve as a metaphor for the experience of girlhood.

I do want to comment on 'He's Got the Power' first. The song was written by the Brill Building team of Ellie Greenwich and Jeff Barry, one of several husband and wife teams successful in the 1960s, and the group the Exciters was an unusual girl group in that one of the members was male. The lyrics tell a story of straightforward domination by a lover who dictates 'his' girl's behaviour, but the potential for oppressiveness is undercut by the light-hearted buoyancy of the groove. Furthermore, lead singer Brenda Reid's full-throated rasp has a robust and self-assured vocal quality reminiscent of blues queens such as 'Big Mama' Thornton, lending the song a cheeky irony that is reinforced by the pointed use of solo kazoo throughout the song.

Music centered around female voices is often dismissed as derivative and 'fake'. This kind of assessment assumes that songwriting and playing instruments constitute more creative and important work than mere singing, and disallows the possibility of understanding the girl singer as an *auteur* of her music. But when songs exist in most listeners' ears only because of the highly individual vocal performances that brought them to life, should we attach too much importance to the roles of producers, songwriters, and recording engineers? And why have these issues been seen to devalue female pop stars but not artists like Elvis Presley, who exclusively performed material written by industry professionals?

Often, the producer of a record is considered the most powerful and important figure in the making of a record; 60s girl groups such as the Ronettes and the Supremes were famously controlled by the musical imaginings of Phil Spector and Berry Gordy. Within the environment of the session, the record producer generally determines which songs will be recorded, directs the sessions, and filters the resulting sounds through a mixing board in order to create the desired musical text. The producer's distance from actual music-making purportedly allows for a more sophisticated understanding of how best to prioritize sonic elements and fit the various parts together into a satisfying whole.

If we consider the politics of recording sessions from a singer's standpoint, however, the person occupying this role is far removed from the true production of music. An examination of the material conditions of recording determines that the musicians making the sounds documented in the recording process are the producers. Those running the equipment are in positions analogous to overseers in factories, or patriarchs whose wives' bodies are, in Nancy Hartsock's terms, 'instruments of production in pregnancy, giving birth or lactation'.[2] Feminist standpoint theory is a useful method for me because in the arena of music recording, the work of singers is most clearly a product of bodily effort, and it is commonly overlooked by instrumentalists and record producers who manipulate external apparatuses in order to make music. Ironically, mastery of an instrument becomes a badge of musical truth, while bringing music out from within the body itself is dismissed as facile and 'inauthentic'.

The discipline of popular music studies has been pioneered by members of the generation that came of age with bands such as the Beatles, Bob Dylan and Pink Floyd, artists who, in a shift away from previous practices, sang and played instruments in performing songs that they themselves had written. It is perhaps only natural that these scholars should uphold the values of the music that mattered most to them in their youth, and, in applying them to musics that operate according to a different paradigm, locate the creative power with those who control the technology. But the very sonic aesthetics and production values of girl group songs are in opposition to values both of the importance of technological control and of unmediated expression in music. While rock recording techniques – particularly those from the 1970s on – often aspire towards an invisible means of production, implying a concert performance that just happened to be captured on tape, girl group songs are clearly and unapologetically products of the recording studio. Many of the musical effects that characterize this music could not be created in the context of a concert; the crucial prominence of handclaps in a recording such as the Supremes' 1964 'Where Did Our Love Go?,' for example, could never carry in a live performance venue. Similarly, the hollow rattle that undergirds the Shirelles' hopeless devotion in 'Baby, It's You' (1962) would require a tambourine the size of a minivan to be heard on stage with a band, and the slithery metallic sound heard in Martha and the Vandellas' 1965 'Nowhere to Run' was famously created in the Motown studio by rattling the snow chains taken from someone's car.

In important ways, the production techniques of girl group songs mirror girls' experience in a culture that confines them to safe, domestic spaces and hands them ready-made and obviously pre-fabricated experiences to make their own. Consider the complex genealogy of the Shirelles' 1960 hit 'Will You Love Me Tomorrow?,' the first girl group song to earn the Number One position on the Billboard charts. The song is credited to the young (King was a mere eighteen) husband-and-wife songwriting team of Carole King and Gerry Goffin, and it explores the conflicting feelings of a girl struggling with one of the most momentous decisions in girl's experience: whether or not to trust her lover's promises and surrender her virginity. Incredibly, King and Goffin originally hoped to sell the piece to established recording artist Johnny Mathis.[3] Luther Dixon, a songwriter who had been closely involved with the Shirelles since they recorded his 'Dedicated to the One I Love' in 1959, happened to hear a recording of King doing a piano-vocal demo of 'Will You Love Me Tomorrow'. He was so struck with the song that he persuaded the publisher to let him take it to the Shirelles, who initially disliked it and felt it was too far away from the sound they had established. Journalist Alan Betrock reports that

> The Shirelles ... said it just wasn't right for them. Dixon felt otherwise and prevailed on the group to trust him, saying that when they heard his arrangement in the studio, it would be perfect for them. Dixon worked on the vocals with the group, and then had Carole [King] devise an intricate musical arrangement.[4]

Before embarking on an analysis of the song, I wish to unpack these statements and try to trace the genesis of the piece. 'Will You Love Me Tomorrow' is credited to Goffin and King, as are all the songs they worked on together, but Gerry Goffin seems conspicuously absent in the foregoing account. Furthermore, Dixon convinced the Shirelles that his arrangement of the objectionable song would induce them to like it, but then entrusted that arrangement to King. Nevertheless, with their coerced recording of 'Will You Love Me Tomorrow,' a song written by a teenage girl but intended for a man to sing, the Shirelles achieved the Number One position on the charts – a first for a girl group – and consequent superstar status.

Like most girl group songs, 'Will You Love Me Tomorrow' adheres to a strictly conventional structure of verse / chorus / verse / chorus / bridge / chorus / chorus and predictable harmonic language. It begins with a prominent C major chord on acoustic guitar over piano and a steady snare drum pattern that imitates a heartbeat. This heartbeat pattern characterizes so many girl group recordings that I have come to think of it as the 'girl group beat'. After its opening statement, the guitar retreats almost entirely for the rest of the song, and violins supply melodic contrast to the voices. Violins and string sections in general characterize many girl group recordings, hearkening back to Tin Pan Alley conventions and distinguishing these songs from the guitar-based rock of Chuck Berry and Elvis. Here, the closely-miked violins and snare have the cleanest, clearest sounds in the recording; Shirley Owens and the rest of the Shirelles seem to be much further away from the listener, and might literally have been further away from their microphones.

It would be easy to conclude that King and Dixon placed the mike far away from Owens because she had a weak, dull-sounding voice and tended to sing out of tune. Indeed, this kind of disparagement has typified much writing about girl groups. But to dismiss girl groups because their members are not technically skilful singers is to miss the point entirely. The girl group sound was predicated on the unpolished voices of girls like Shirley Owens, whose passion and earnestness prevent the musically conventional and formulaic songs from being empty and insipid. Of course, acknowledging the chain of events that brought Owens into the recording studio for this song raises the possibility that her performance might have been grudging and unenthusiastic; however, the sound of her voice on the record demonstrates that she was able to give a convincing and professional interpretation. Owens' ability to throw herself into the song illustrates the ways in which girls are adept at negotiating subject positions created for them.

Most girl group songs are best understood as representing a single – if often conflicted – subjectivity, wherein the interplay between lead singer and backing singers performs the struggle between different points of view that accompanies any individual's choice-making. In this song, there is no dialogue among the singers, as there is in songs by the ShangriLas, and the Shirelles as a group can represent a single point of view, with the violins providing the counterpoint. Thus, the lead vocal line, the heartbeat drum pattern, and the backing Shirelles, taken together all signify trepidation and nervousness; were these elements the whole text of the song, the listener would not doubt that the subject would end by spurning her lover's advances. But the violin line's dramatic range, soaring legato phrases and erratic fluttering figures – especially during the bridge section – counter this line of thinking and overwhelm it, if only by virtue of the violin's comparative loudness and closeness to the listener.

The rapturous violin voice, then, makes the outcome of the song indeterminate, and I contend that the ambiguity surrounding the singer's momentous decision is the key to the song's import. The seeming proximity of the strings contrasts with the way Owens' voice sounds submerged, and skilfully depicts the way passion threatens to overwhelm reason for this girl at this moment; placing the voice further forward in the mix would have produced an entirely different effect. What is more, the distance of the voice and the violins from the listener must be read as a deliberate artistic choice. Taken as a whole, the song creates a sense of an ordinary girl, heart pounding, who uses stock musical language to rehearse the questions she knows she ought to ask of her lover even as she is swept up by desires and feelings she doesn't yet have the words to articulate.

While the negotiations and compromises between King, Dixon and the Shirelles took place on an interpersonal sphere that was inaudible to listeners, the blurring of individual contributions to a song in order to present a pleasing homogeneous product is sonically characteristic of the records associated with Phil Spector. Working in the era of monophonic four-track recording, he created a distinctive style, his trademark 'wall of sound'. His studio techniques involved reducing (for example) four separately-recorded instrumental tracks to one track, then adding that to three other tracks that had been similarly mixed down, then mixing the four new tracks down to one, then layering that with vocal tracks which had been through the same process. This process necessarily caused some degree of deterioration in sound quality, an effect he liked because it made all the instrumental tracks blend together in a wash of sonority. Spector's grandiose aspirations led him to involve many more musicians in a recording session than was customary. He would record an extravagant forty to sixty instrumentalists on the rhythm track alone – in an era when most songs made use of ten to twelve instruments in total – and he also commanded a veritable army of session singers for backing tracks. His novel use of microphones was an equally important component of the wall of sound; he would place several of these throughout the recording studio, miking surfaces that might provide unusual sonorities. Finally, he and his recording engineers applied reverberation and echo effects generously to all tracks, so that the result is a distinctively opaque, shimmering sound in which individual contributions are difficult to discern.

Phil Spector's aesthetic vision is an apt metaphor for his worldview, in which individual will, distinct personality and any uniqueness of character were subsumed to the overall effect. His production style is so distinctive that we often tend to think of records that he produced as 'Phil Spector records', forgetting the names of groups who sang them and the songwriters who wrote them. In many cases, he deliberately obscured the identities of the singers he worked with, reasoning that invisible singers were interchangeable singers whose anonymity would never allow them to challenge his authority. Spector made sure that he owned outright the names of any groups he worked with, and of many groups that did not even exist, often shuffling studio singers from fictitious group to fictitious group, or using one group of singers on a record that he would then release under the name of a different group. For example, Darlene Love sang lead vocals on records that were released as singles by the Crystals and Bob B. Soxx and the Blue Jeans, while Cher recorded as Bonnie Jo Mason.

Phil Spector's most famous group was of course the Ronettes, those impossibly bad girls from Spanish Harlem, whose towering hairstyles, inch-thick eyeliner and dangerously high stiletto heels were matched by the sultry voices on their records. At the height of their fame, the Ronettes toured the United Kingdom with the Rolling Stones as their opening act, and made countless television appearances, but even they were subject to Spector's controlling whims. He often used only lead singer Ronnie Bennett (later Spector) on their records, bringing in session singers to perform the backing vocals, and in 1963 he sent the group on tour with Dick Clark with one of the girls' cousins filling in for Ronnie as lead singer. The fact that fans did not complain about this substitution (and in many cases might not have noticed) reinforces the fact that the Ronettes were above all a studio group, and that listeners interacted with them primarily through records and not live performances.

The Ronettes' first hit was 'Be My Baby' in 1963. This song presented listeners with a dramatically different kind of girl from the one who agonized over her boyfriend's advances in 'Will You Love Me Tomorrow'. Far from worrying about the dangers of sex, the girl in 'Be My Baby' is practically panting for it. The song opens with a striking drum phrase, the 'baion' beat that Phil Spector favoured on many records. In this song, the beat functions as a distinctive hook, and might conjure an uneven heart thumping followed by a gasp or sharply-indrawn breath – a depiction of the sensations of heart-stopping love at first sight. The dramatic range in timbre between the bass drum and the snare means that the sounds resonate through the listener's body in different spaces, insisting that this disorienting physical sensation be shared by all who hear the song.

Fans responded enthusiastically to the novel representation of a girl who seemed utterly self-assured in her desirability, acting with a great deal of aggression and using all the weapons in her sexual arsenal to conquer the boy she has chosen. Ronnie Spector's fluid movement between throaty growling and clear, sweet timbres is an important element of all Ronettes recordings, and effectively represents the dualities enacted by a sexy girl-woman. Her vocal quality, the sinuous, chromatic melody, the deep pounding of the bass drum, the high drama of the orchestration and production effects, and the predictability of the harmonic language combine to create a sense of inexorable will. The song has no middle eight or bridge section; in this musical articulation of a girl's desire and efforts at enticement, a move to a contrasting harmonic area might not only detract from the focus on her goal, but could also raise the possibility of different outcomes to the seduction. Instead of introducing this element of uncertainty, 'Be My Baby' insists that Ronnie Spector's feelings be returned.

This kind of sexual confidence could naturally be empowering for young girls experimenting with different kinds of adult personae, but at the same time it flouted conventional rules of behaviour and threatened a rigid social order. Middle-class, 'respectable' girls who 'tried on' the attitudes of the Ronettes may not have been instantly transformed into stiletto-heeled sexpots simply by listening to 'Be My Baby', but neither could they entirely return to the demure and prim stance of Patti Page or Doris Day. New possibilities had been raised; new ways of being a girl were visible and audible.

The bar for 'bad girls' was raised further with the marvels of melodrama created by the ShangriLas, a group of 'don't mess with me' Jewish teenagers from Queens. Unlike the demure-looking Shirelles, the ShangriLas projected an image of sullen street urchins, unsmilingly clad in skin-tight pants and high-heeled boots. Correspondingly, the subject matter of their songs was much darker, even frightening to some, than bouncy dance tunes like 'He's Got the Power'. A song like 1964's 'Leader of the Pack' means to be listened to, and its dramatic pauses, spoken voiceover, motorcycle sound effects and frequent changes of tempo discourage dancing, and could hardly be achieved outside the recording studio. The song's tragic tale is of a misunderstood teen rebel killed in a motorcycle accident after his girlfriend breaks up with him (though only at her parents' insistence), and this maudlin story provoked controversy and an official ban on the song in England.[5] The histrionics of the piece have made it ripe for spoofs and parodies, but the song can nevertheless be taken as an earnest and meaningful exploration of the heightened emotions of teenage girls. Ellie Greenwich, the songwriter, asserts that she and the ShangriLas took the piece seriously and found it moving,[6] and it obviously provided a site for exploring anguish and torment in a highly satisfying way for many listeners.

The song begins with spoken dialogue in unpolished Long Island accents between the twins Marge and Mary Ganser and lead singer Mary Weiss in some unspecified female space, probably the 'Ladies' Room' that is so often the site of important female conversations and girl talk. Over a clichéd melodramatic descent of stark octaves in the piano on C, then A, G, and F, and the girl group beat sounding portentously in the bass drum, Weiss hums to herself and adopts a nonchalant tone when the twins ask her about her mysterious and dangerous boyfriend, Jimmy, but then literally bursts into song as she describes how they met and what he represents to her. The baion beat undergirds this song adding to the drama, and the whiny quality of Weiss's voice, strained near the top of her vocal range, perfectly evokes the slightly smug girl who enjoys impressing her friends with the status her glamorous rebel boyfriend confers on her. The back-up singers respond, alternately begging for more information and retreating to wordless lines as she drifts into spoken reminiscence during a middle eight section in A minor.

Note that 'the Boy' in this song is constituted for us only through Weiss's description of him; she and the Gansers exist in a sort of girldom, where the only function of the hapless 'Jimmy' is to give them something to talk about. This procedure of constructing a shadowy male figure whose purpose is simply to heighten the drama between the more interesting female characters is a strategy common to soap opera writing. Drawing on Gayle Rubin's important work on the 'traffic in women', Patricia Juliana Smith describes this fetishized boyfriend as 'the Apparitional Boy, a simulacrum … the object of the female fantasy gaze, the token of exchange among girls.[7] 'Jimmy' is also a contested item between the protagonist and her parents, and thus symbolizes a girl's struggles to maintain parental approval and respectability and also participate in teen culture. Although the song is highly artificial, melodramatic and overblown, it nevertheless represents a sort of truth about the intense emotions of teenage girls grappling with the demands of generation and gender identity. Betty Weiss's tearful pouting and the Ganser twins' eager questions and awed backing vocables are crucial to the plausibility of the song.

It was precisely the untrained, often flawed but always impassioned characteristics of young female voices vacillating between childhood and womanhood that made the girl group sound. As much as producers such as Phil Spector liked to demonstrate that all voices were replaceable at a moment's notice, the characteristics of specific voices were integral to the success or failure of records. These voices and no others could perform the work of speaking to and for a generation of girls coming of age. The ideology of album-oriented rock, whereby a song must flow from the pen and the tongue of the same person in order to be 'true' and compelling, cannot be applied to girl group songs. Indeed, the songs revel in their artificiality and elude being pinned down to anything so tiresome as earnestness or authenticity.

This is not to say that the songs are insincere, though. On the contrary, the vocal performances I have discussed are heartfelt and enthusiastic; if they had not been, it is doubtful that these songs would have achieved the same level of commercial recognition. After all, the success of any song is predicated on the extent to which it rings true with its intended audience. The assessment of writers such as media studies scholar Susan Douglas suggests that many girls embraced these songs as primers for girlish behaviour and experience, so that in a way they became truths no matter how contrived their origins may have been (Douglas, 1994).

When we are burdened with rock's masculinist ideology of authentic, unfiltered expression of a single individual's feelings through music, it is difficult to see how this could be. But a system of valuing songs that insists on their honesty and an absence of mediation in the circumstances of their creation cannot apply to songs by and for girls, because girl culture and girl identity are invariably built on foundations laid by others. Accepting the roles and images offered to them and experimenting with pre-fabricated roles and identities are fundamental strategies for girls' self-fashioning, and should not be dismissed as submissive and derivative. Whether or not they consciously recognize it, girls are aware that so-called 'youth culture' is often actually 'boy culture', and that the onus is on girls to find ways of making cultural institutions and artefacts fit them. Entertainments and experiences created for children generally assume male experience as the norm, so that little girls watching a film such as Disney's *Toy Story* must perform a cross-gender identification in order to sympathize with the spaceman and cowboy. From an early age, girls become adept at this kind of flexible identification with role models, while boys are rarely presented with an opportunity to do so.

John Berger explores the divided identity that is naturally enacted by females:

> A woman must continually watch herself. She is almost continually accompanied by her own image of herself ... From earliest childhood she has been taught and persuaded to survey herself continually. And so she comes to consider the *surveyor* and the *surveyed* within her as two constituent yet always distinct elements of her identity as a woman.[8]

I want to argue that the experience of 'being split in two' and learning to identify across gender boundaries makes females more agile at self-invention than men, and quicker to adapt to circumstances requiring new kinds of behaviour. Perhaps accepting boy culture as youth culture and inventing ways to find themselves in it empowers girls, because it requires them to learn the language and ways of boys as well as their own, making them – in essence – bi-cultural.

Music is a particularly valuable site for making these kinds of translations and negotiations, because its ephemeral form does not tie it to a single meaning, but rather it takes on new meanings as it circulates. It is hardly surprising that girls should be willing to accept as their own music that makes no secret of its artificiality, or that young singers like the Shirelles could throw themselves into songs that did not originate from their own experiences. Dismissing girl groups on the grounds that they are like wind-up dolls whose material is forced upon them by other, more creative minds ignores the parallels between girl music and girl identity in its largest sense. The important question, then, is not *whether* girls imbibe experiences fabricated for them, but *how* they do it, and how they make meanings from doing it. Once we see that girl group music involved a hierarchy of professional musicians, some of whom were male and some of whom were adults, but that the music nevertheless functioned as a valuable medium for real girls to explore and articulate their actual experiences and ideas, we can begin to consider girl music and girl culture as more than a mere and less worthy offshoot of youth culture.

Notes

1. In fact, British beat bands did not scorn mainstream pop songs by professional songwriters as much as the nostalgic histories of rebelliousness and innovation would have us believe, and they worked with many of the songwriters and producers who developed the girl group sound and shaped youth culture in the mid-twentieth century. On their first two albums, furthermore, the Beatles covered more songs written for the Shirelles than songs by Chuck Berry. Bands like Manfred Mann, Herman's Hermits, and the Mindbenders also scored major hits with versions of girl group songs; the original version of 'Do-Wah-Diddy' was by the Exciters, 'I'm into Something Good' was a solo effort by Earl-Jean McCrea of the Cookies, and 'Groovy Kind of Love' was first recorded by Patti Labelle and the Bluebelles. Brian Wilson of the Beach Boys was a devoted fan of the Ronettes and other Phil Spector Girl Groups, and wrote 'Don't Worry Baby' with the hope of having the Ronettes record it. The Beach Boys also recorded the Crystals' 'Then He Kissed Me,' changing the pronouns and the roles of actor and acted upon to conform to conventional gender roles in 'Then I Kissed Her.' Erasing this aspect of 1960s music distorts our understanding of popular music and youth culture in that decade, a period generally considered a watershed moment in the evolution of the teenager. Misremembering the music of the 60s thus has significant consequences and affects the way that we understand youth culture in the present.
2. Hartsock, N. ([1983] 1987), 'The Feminist Standpoint: Developing the Ground for a Specifically Feminist Historical Materialism', reprinted in Harding, S. (ed.), *Feminism and Methodology*, Bloomington: Indiana University Press, p. 157.
3. Betrock, A. (1982), *Girl Groups: the Story of a Sound*, New York: Delilah Books, p. 14 The mind fairly boggles at the idea of Mathis, a barely closeted crooner with a largely young, female fan base, maintaining his dreamboat status with a song about the possibly dire consequences of submitting to a lover's entreaties. The conspiracy of blindness that enveloped men like Mathis, Little Richard and Liberace would surely have stirred in the face of such unabashed vulnerability and sexual insecurity. It is interesting to speculate about the extent to which the Women's Liberation Movement and the Gay Civil Rights Movement might have unfolded differently had Mathis's A&R man not turned the song down before Mathis heard it.
4. Ibid., p. 14.
5. Ibid., p. 102. In spite of – or perhaps partly because of – the ban, it reached No. 11 on the British charts.
6. Greig, C. (1989), *Will You Still Love Me Tomorrow? Girl Groups from the Fifties On*, London: Virago Press, p. 80.
7. Smith, P. (1999), '"Ask Any Girl: Compulsory Heterosexuality and Girl Group Culture', in Dettmar, K. and Richey, W. (eds), *Reading Rock 'n' roll: Authenticity, Appropriation, Aesthetics*, New York: Columbia University Press, p. 107.
8. Berger, J. (1972), *Ways of Seeing*, London: Penguin Books, p. 46.

Bibliography

Anderson, B. (1983), *Imagined Communities: Reflections on the Origin and Spread of Nationalism*, London and New York: Verso.

Appadurai, A. (1990), 'Disjuncture and Difference in the Global Cultural Economy', in Featherstone, M. (ed), *Global Culture: Nationalism, Globalisation and Modernity*, London: Sage (pub. also in *Public Culture*, 2 (2), 1990).

Ardener, E. (1989), *The Voice of Prophecy*, in Chapman, M. (ed), Oxford: Basil Blackwell.

Atherton, M. (2000), 'The Didjeridu in the Studio and the Dynamics of Collaboration', in Tony Mitchell *et al.* (eds), *Changing Sounds: New Directions and Configurations in Popular Music* (Proceedings of the IASPM International Conference 1999), Sydney: UTS: pp. 15–20.

Back, L. (1987), 'Coughing up fire: sound systems, music and cultural politics in S.E. London', *Journal of Caribbean Studies*, 6 (2), 203–18.

Bailey, J. (1994), 'The Role of Music in the Creation of an Afghan National Identity, 1923–73', in Stokes, M. (ed), *Ethnicity, Identity and Music: The Musical Construction of Place*, Oxford: Berg.

Baker, Houston A. Jr. (1991), 'Hybridity, the Rap Race, and Pedagogy for the 1990s', *Black Music Research Journal*, 11 (2), 217–28.

Bamyeh, Mohammed A. (1993), 'Culture', *Current Sociology*, 41 (3), 31–65.

Banerji, S, and Baumann, G. (1990), 'Bhangra 1984–8: Fusion and Professionalization in a Genre of South Asian Dance Music', in Oliver, P. (ed), *Black Music in Britain: Essays on the Afro-Asian Contribution to Popular Music*, Milton Keynes: Open University Press.

Barkan, E., and Shelton, M.D. (1998), *Borders, exiles, diasporas*, Stanford: Stanford University Press.

Barnes, Jake (1997), 'Nuuk Posse, *Kaataq*' (review), *The Wire*, 158, April, 65.

Barthes, R. (1977), *Image, Music, Text*, London: Collins.

Bartky, S. (1990), *Femininity and Domination: Studies in the Phenomenology of Oppression*, London: Routledge.

Battersby, C. (1989), *Gender and Genius: Towards a Feminist Aesthetic*, London: Women's Press.

Beck, U. (1992), *Risk Society: Towards a new modernity*, London: Sage.

Bell, Susan (1999), 'Talk of town irks academie', *The Australian*, 20 January (reprinted from *The Times* of London).

Bennett, A. (1997), 'Going down the pub: The pub rock scene as a resource for the consumption of popular music', *Popular Music*, 16 (1): 97–108.

——— (2000), *Popular Music and Youth Culture: Music, Identity and Place*, Basingstoke: Macmillan.

Berger, J. (1972), *Ways of Seeing*, London: Penguin Books.

Bernard, R. (1976), 'Introductory Remarks on the Ethnography of Islands: Kalymnos: the island of the sponge fishermen', in Dimen, M. and Friedl, E. (eds), *Regional Variation in Modern Greece and Cyprus: Towards an ethnography of Greece, Annals of the New York Academy of Sciences*, **268**.

Betrock, A. (1982), *Girl Groups: the Story of a Sound.* New York: Delilah Books.

Bierma, Paige (1996), 'Hip Hop Havana', *Vibe*, March, 94–98.

Bordo, S. (1993), '"Material Girl": The effacements of postmodern culture', in Schwichtenberg, C. (ed), *The Madonna Connection*, Boulder, CO: Westview Press.

Bourdieu, P. (1993), *The Field of Cultural Production*, London: Polity Press.

Boyden Southwood Associates (1992), 'A Cultural Strategy for Bristol', Boyden Southwood and Bristol City Council.

Bradberry, B., 'Kate Bush (1990) – The Sensual World: Review', *Option* [Online], Jan/Feb, available from Gaffaweb. http:gaffa.org/rev_tsw2.html/#musician (accessed 20 September 1998).

Bradby, B. (1993a), 'Lesbians and popular music: does it matter who is singing?', in Griffin, G. (ed), *Lesbianism and Popular Culture*, London: Pluto Press.

——— (1993b), 'Sampling sexuality: gender, technology and the body in dance music', *Popular Music*, **12** (2), 155–73.

Braidotti, R., 'Cyberfeminism with a Difference'. www.let.ruu.nl/womens_studies/rosi/cyberfem.htm.

Brearley, D. (1993), 'Kate Bush – The Red Shoes: Review', *The Australian*, 8 December, 12.

Breen, Marcus (1995), 'The End of the World as We Know it: Popular Music's Cultural Mobility', *Cultural Studies*, **9** (3), 486–504.

Burns, L. and Lafrance, M. (2002), *Disruptive Divas: Feminism, Identity and Popular Music*, London: Routledge.

Butler, J. (1993), *Bodies that Matter: On the Discursive Limits of 'Sex'*, London: Routledge.

——— (1999), *Gender Trouble: Feminism and the Subversion of Identity*, London: Routledge.

Byerly, Ingrid (1998), 'Mirror, Mediator, and Prophet: The Music Indaba of Late-Apartheid South Africa', *Ethnomusicology*, **42** (1), 1–45.

Cantor, J. (1999), 'Portrait of the Artist as a Communist Bureaucrat', *Miami New Times*, 24 June.

Cassirer, Ernst (1955), *The Philosophy of Symbolic Forms*, vols 1–3, New Haven: Yale University Press.

Chadwick, W. (1990), *Women, Art and Society*, London: Thames & Hudson.

Chambers, Iain, (1990), *Border Dialogues: Journeys in Postmodernity*, London: Routledge.

Chapkis, W. (1986), *Beauty Secrets*, London: The Women's Press.

Chude-Sokei, L. (1994), 'Post-nationalist geographies: rasta, ragga, and reinventing Africa', *African Arts*, **27** (4), 80–84.

Citron, M.J. (1993), *Gender and the Musical Canon*, Cambridge: Cambridge University Press.

Clarke, J., Hall, S., Jefferson, T. and Roberts, B. (1975/1997), 'Subcultures, Cultures and Class', in Gelder, K. and Thornton, S. (eds), *The Subcultures Reader*, London: Routledge. 100–113.

Clifford, J. (1992), 'Traveling Cultures', in Gossberg, L., Nelson, C. and Treicher, P. (eds), *Cultural Studies*, New York: Routledge.

—— (1997), *Routes. Travel and translation in the late 20th century*, Cambridge, MA: Harvard University Press.

Cohen, R. (1997), *Global Diasporas: An Introduction*, London: UCL Press.

Cohen, S. (1991), *Rock Culture in Liverpool: Popular Music in the Making*, Oxford: Clarendon Press.

—— (1993), 'Ethnography and Popular Music Studies', *Popular Music*, **12** (2), 123–37.

—— (1997), 'Men Making A Scene. Rock music and the production of gender', in Whiteley, S. (ed), *Sexing the Groove. Popular Music and Gender*, London: Routledge.

Connerton, P. (2000), 'Lieux de mémoire, lieux d'oubli', in Huglo, M.P. *et al.*, *Passions du passé: recyclages de la mémoire et usages de l'oubli*, Montreal: L'Harmattan, pp. 51–92.

Cook, N. (1998), *Music: A Very Short Introduction*, Oxford: Oxford University Press.

Coplan, D. (1985), *In Township Tonight! South Africa's Black City Music and Theatre*, Johannesburg: Ravan.

—— (1994), *In the Time of Cannibals: The Word Music of South Africa's Basotho Migrants*, Johannesburg: University of the Witwatersrand.

Cramer, C. (n.d.), 'Alanis Morisette Profile', *Rolling Stone* [online]. www.rollingstone.com/sections/artists/text/artistgen.asp?afl=&LookUpString=50 (accessed 26 July 1999).

Cross, Brian, (1993), *It's Not About a Salary: Rap, Race and Resistance in Los Angeles*, New York and London: Verso.

Crowdy, D. (2001), 'The Guitar Cultures of Papua New Guinea: Regional and Stylistic Diversity', in Bennett, A. and Dawe, K. (eds), *Guitar Cultures*, Oxford: Berg.

Cubitt, S. (2000), '"Maybellene": Meaning and the Listening Subject', in Middleton, R. (ed), *Reading Pop*, Oxford: Oxford University Press, pp. 141–60.

Dalton, S. (1993), 'Kate Bush – The Red Shoes: Review', *Vox*, 38, November, 112.

Danaher, William F. and Blackwelder, Stephen (1994), 'The Emergence of Blues and Rap: A Comparison and Assessment of the Context, Meaning and Message', *Popular Music and Society*, **17** (4), 1–12.

Davis, K. (1995), *Reshaping the Female Body: The Dilemma of Cosmetic Surgery*, London: Routledge.

Dawe, K. (1994), 'Performance and Entrepreneurialism: The Work of Professional Musicians in Crete', unpublished Ph.D. thesis, The Queen's University of Belfast.

—— (1996), 'The Engendered *Lyra:* Music, Poetry and Manhood in Crete', *The British Journal of Ethnomusicology*, **5**, 93–112.

—— (1998), 'Bandleaders in Crete: Musicians and Entrepreneurs in a Greek Island Economy', *British Journal of Ethnomusicology*, **7**, 23–44.

—— (1999), 'Minotaurs or Musonauts? Cretan Music and "World Music"', *Popular Music*, **18** (2), 209–25.

—— (2000), 'Roots Music in the Global Village: Cretan Ways of Dealing with the World at Large', *The World of Music*, **42** (2), 47–66.

—— (2002), 'Between East and West: Contemporary grooves in Greek popular music (c.1990–2000)' in Plastino, G. (ed), *Mediterranean Mosaic: Popular Music and Global Sounds*, New York: Routledge/Garland Publishing Inc.

—— (2003) 'Lyres and the Body Politic: Studying Musical Instruments in the Cretan Musical Landscape', *Popular Music and Society*, **26** (3).

Dawe, K. with Dawe, M. (2001), 'Handmade in Spain: The Culture of Guitar Making', in Bennett, A. and Dawe, K. (eds), *Guitar Cultures*, Oxford: Berg, pp. 63–87.

Daynes, S. (2001), *Le mouvement Rastafari: Mémoire, musique et religion*, thèse de Doctorat en Sociologie, Paris: Ecole des Hautes Etudes en Sciences Sociales.

Decker, J.L. (1994), 'The State of Rap: Time and Place in Hip-Hop Nationalism', in Ross, A. and Rose, T. (eds), *Microphone Fiends: Youth Music and Youth Culture*, London: Routledge, pp. 99–121.

DeNora, T. (2000) *Music in Everyday Life*. Cambridge: Cambridge University Press.

Desroche, H. (1960) 'Les messianismes et la catégorie de l'échec', *Cahiers Internationaux de Sociologie*, **XXXV** (1), 61–84.

—— (1973), *Sociologie de l'espérance*, Paris: Calmann-Lévy.

—— (1974), *Les religions de contrebande*, Paris: Mame.

Dilov-Junior, L. (2001), '21 vek, chalgata I mediite' [21st Century, Chalga and Media], *Media & Reklama*, January, p. 14.

Dimitriadis, G. (1996), 'Hip-Hop: From Live Performance to Mediated Narrative', *Popular Music*, **15** (2), 179–93.

Douglas, R. (1994), 'The Search for an Afrocentric Visual Aesthetic', in Welsh-Asante, Kariamu (ed), *The African Aesthetic: Keeper of the Traditions*, Westport, CT: Greenwood Press, pp. 159–73.

Douglas, S. (1994), *Where the Girls Are: Growing Up Female with the Mass Media*, New York: Random Press.

Downey, G.M., Dumit, J. and Williams, S. (1995), 'Cyborg Anthropologies', in Gray, C. *et al.* (eds), *The Cyborg Handbook*, London: Routledge, p. 345.

Dresser, M., Jordan, C. and Taylor, D. (1999), *Slave Trade Trail Around Central Bristol*, Bristol City Council.

Durrschmidt, J. (2000), *Everyday Lives in the Global City*, London: Routledge.

Easton, P. (1989), 'The Rock Music Community', in Riordan, J. (ed), *Soviet Youth Culture*, Bloomington and Indianapolis: Indiana University Press.

Edwards, G. (ed) (2000), 'Region in figures, South West', London: Office for National Statistics, Department of Environment, Transport and Regions.

Elflien, Dietmar (1998), 'From Krauts with attitudes to Turks with attitudes: some aspects of hip hop history in Germany', *Popular Music*, **17** (3), 255–65.

Elliot, P. (1997), 'Who the Hell Does Bjork Think She Is', *Q Magazine*, 134, November, 5–7.

Emile YX. (1997), *What is Hip-Hop?*, Cape Town: Independent.

Erlmann, V. (1991), *African Stars: Studies in Black South African Performance*, Chicago: University of Chicago.

—— (1993), 'The Politics and Aesthetics of Transnational Musics', *The World of Music*, **35** (2), 3–15.

—— (1996), *Nightsong: Performance, Power, and Practice in South Africa*, Chicago: University of Chicago.

Evans, D. (2001), 'The Guitar in the Blues Music of the Deep South', in Bennett, A. and Dawe, K. (eds), *Guitar Cultures*, Oxford: Berg.

Feld, S. (1990), *Sound and Sentiment: Birds, Weeping, Poetics and Song in Kaluli Expression*, 2nd edn, Philadelphia: Pennsylvania University Press.

Feld, S. and Basso, K.H. (eds), (1996), *Senses of Place*, Santa Fe: School of American Research Press.

Fernandez, J. (1986), *Persuasions and Performances: The Play of Tropes in Culture*, Bloomington: Indiana University.

Fernando, S. (1995), *The New Beats: Exploring the Music and Attitudes of Hip Hop*, Edinburgh: Payback Press.

Finnegan, R. (1989), *The Hidden Musicians: Music-Making in an English Town*, Cambridge: Cambridge University Press.

——— (1998), *Tales of the City: A Study of Narrative and Urban Life*, Cambridge: Cambridge University Press.

Fiske, J. (1989), *Reading the Popular*, London: Routledge.

Flores, Juan (1992–93), 'Puerto Rican and Proud, Boyee', *Centro: Bulletin of the Centro de Estudios Puertorriqueños*, Winter, 337–46.

Forman, M. (1994), 'Movin' Closer To An Independent Funk: Black Feminist Theory, Standpoint and Women in Rap', *Women's Studies*, **23** (1).

Frith, S. (1996), *Performing Rites: On the Value of Popular Music*, Oxford: Oxford University Press.

Frizzel, O. (1994), 'Hip Hop Hype', *Pavement* (NZ), 8, December, 48, 50.

de la Fuente, Alejandro (1998), 'Race, National Discourse and Politics in Cuba: An Overview,' *Latin American Perspectives*, **25** (3), 43–69.

Funk-Hennings, E. (1985) 'The Music Scene of the Skinheads in East- and West-Germany Before and After the Reunification', in Hautamaki, T. and Jarviluoma, H. (eds), *Music on Show: Issues of Performance*, Department of Folk Tradition, University of Tampere, Finland (proceedings of 8th International Conference of the IASPM, University of Strathclyde, Glasgow, UK, July 1995).

Garofalo, R. (1990), 'Crossing Over: 1939–1989', in Dates, Jannette L. and Barlow, W. (eds), *Split Image: African–Americans in the Mass Media*, Washington, DC: Howard University Press, pp. 57–121.

——— (1993), 'Whose World, What Beat? The Transnational Music Industry, Identity, and Cultural Imperialism', *World of Music*, **35** (2), 16–32.

——— (1997), *Rockin' Out: Popular Music in the US*, Boston: Allyn and Bacon.

Gates, H. (2000), 'A Reporter At Large: Black London', in Owusu, K. (ed), *Black British Culture and Society: A Text Reader*, London: Routledge.

Gaytandjiev, G. (1990), *Populjarnata muzika – pro? kontra?* [Popular Music – Pros and Cons], Sofia: Narodna Prosveta.

Giddens, A. (1991), *Modernity and Self-Identity: self and society in the late modern age*, Stanford, CA: Stanfford University Press.

Gilroy, P. (1991), 'Sounds Authentic: Black Music, Ethnicity, and the Challenge of a Changing Same', *Black Music Research Journal*, **11** (2), 111–36.

——— (1993), *The Black Atlantic: Modernity and Double Consciousness*, London: Verso; Cambridge MA: Harvard University Press.

Goffman, Erving (1971), *The presentation of self in everyday life*, Harmondsworth: Penguin.

Gordon, E.T. (1998), *Disparate diasporas. Identity and politics in an African-Nicaraguan community*, Austin: University of Texas Press.

Gray, C. (ed) (1995), *The Cyborg Handbook*, London: Routledge.

Greckel, W. (1979), 'Rock and Nineteenth-Century Romanticism: Social and Cultural Parallels', *Journal of Musicology*, **3**, 177–202.

Green, L. (1997), *Music, Gender, Education*, Cambridge: Cambridge University Press.

Greger, S. (1985), *Village on the Plateau*, Studley: Brewin Books.

Greig, C. (1989), *Will You Still Love Me Tomorrow?: Girl Groups from the Fifties On.* London: Virago Press.

Grossberg, L. (1992), *We Gotta Get Out Of This Place: Popular Conservatism and Postmodern Culture*, New York: Routledge.

Gulla, B. (1999), 'L7 – The Beauty Process Triple Platinum: Review' [online], available from: Wall of Sound. http://wallofsouond.go.com/archive/reviews/ (accessed 28 July 1999).

Hall, S. ([1973] 1980), 'Encoding/decoding', in Centre for Contemporary Cultural Studies (ed), *Culture, Media, Language: Working Papers in Cultural Studies, 1972–79*, London: Hutchinson, pp. 128–38.

————— (1995), 'Negotiating Caribbean Identities', *New Left Review*, 209, 3–14.

————— (ed) (1997), *Representation: Cultural Representations and Signifying Practice*, London: Sage.

Hardy, H. 'Kate Bush (1986) Hounds of Love: Review', *Digital Audio* [online], available from: Gaffaweb. http://gaffa.org/reaching/rev_hol.html#audio (accessed 20 September 1998).

Haraway, D. (1991), *Simians, Cyborgs and Women: The Reinvention of Labour*, London: Free Association Books.

Harris, K. (2000), '"Roots ?": The Relationship Between the Global and the Local Within the Extreme Metal Scene', *Popular Music*, **19** (1), 13–30.

Hartsock, N. ([1983] 1987), 'The Feminist Standpoint: Developing the Ground for a Specifically Feminist Historical Materialism', reprinted in Harding, S. (ed), *Feminism and Methodology*, Bloomington: Indiana University Press, pp. 157–80.

Haslam, D. (1999), *Manchester, England*, London: Fourth Estate.

Haupt, A. (1995), 'Rap and the Articulation of Resistance: An Exploration of Subversive Cultural Production during the early 1990s, with particular reference to Prophets of Da City', unpublished Masters mini-thesis, University of the Western Cape.

Hawkins, S. (1997), '"I'll Never Be An Angel": Stories of Deception in Madonna's Music', *Critical Musicology Journal*, online publication: University of Leeds.

————— (2001), 'Joy in repetition! Structures, idiolects, and concepts of repetition in Club music', *Studia Musicologica Norvegica*, **27**, Oslo: Universitetsforlaget.

————— (2002), *Settling the Pop Score: Pop Texts and Identity Politics*, Aldershot: Ashgate.

Hebdige, D. (1979), *Subculture: The Meaning of Style*, London: Routledge.

————— D. (1987), *Cut 'n' Mix. Culture, Identity and Caribbean Music*, London: Routledge.

Herzfeld, M. (1985), *The Poetics of Manhood: Contest and Identity in a Cretan Mountain Village*, Princeton: Princeton University Press.

————— (1991), *A Place in History: Social and Monumental Time in a Cretan Town.* New Jersey and Oxford: Princeton University Press.

Hesmondhalgh, D. (1996), 'Rethinking Popular Music After Rock and Soul', in Curran, J., Morley, D. and Walkerdine, V. (eds), *Cultural Studies and Communications*, London: Arnold.

Homiak, J. (1994), 'Rastafari voices reach Ethiopia: film review', *American Anthropologist*, **96**, 958–63.

Huq, R. (1999), 'Living in France: The Parallel Universe of Hexagonal Pop', in Blake, A. (ed), *Living Through Pop*, London: Routledge.

Hurbon, L. (1986), 'New religious movements in the Caribbean', in Beckford, G. (ed), *New religious movements and rapid social change*, London: Sage, pp. 146–76.

Ivanovas, S. (n.d.), *Where Zeus Became a Man with Cretan Shepherds*, Athens, Greece: Efstathiadis Group.

James, D. (2000), *Songs of Women Migrants: Performance and Identity in South Africa*, Johannesburg: University of the Witwatersrand.

Jenkins, R. (1997), *Rethinking ethnicity: Arguments and explorations*, London: Sage.

Johnson, P. (1996), *Massive Attack, Portishead, Tricky and the Roots of 'Trip-Hop'*: *Straight Outa Bristol*, London: Hodder and Stoughton.

Jones, P. and Youseph, R. (1998), 'The Black Population of Bristol in the 18th Century', Bristol Branch of the Historical Association, The University, Bristol.

Jones, S. (1992), *Rock Formation: Music, Technology and Mass Communication*, Newbury Park: Sage Publications.

Joshua, H. and Wallace, T. (1983), *To Ride the Storm: The 1980 Bristol Riot and the State*, London: Heinemann.

Kaufman, D. (1990), 'Ot vuzrojdemskata chalgija kum suvremennite svatbarskite orkestri' [From Nineteenth-Century *Chalgija* to Contemporary 'Wedding Bands'], *Bulgarski Folklore*, 3, 23–32.

Kenny, G. (1993), 'Red Shoes Don't Make It', *Newsday* [online], 21 November, available from: Electric Library Australasia. www.elibrary.com/s/edumarkau/search.cgi?id= 157203614x127y37255wO (accessed 20 February, 2000).

Keyes, C. (1996), 'At the Crossroads: Rap Music and Its African Nexus', *Ethnomusicology*, **40** (2), 223–48.

Kong, L. (1999), 'The Politics of Music: From Moral Panics to Moral Guardians', paper given at the International Association of Geographers' Conference, University of Sydney.

Krims, A. (2000), *Rap music and the poetics of identity*, Cambridge: Cambridge University Press.

Kuper, A. (1994) 'Culture, Identity and the Project of a Cosmopolitan Anthropology', *Man*, **29** (3), 537–54.

Kurkela, V. (1996), 'Producing "Oriental": A Perspective on the Aesthetics of Lower Arts in the Eastern Balkans', paper presented at the IASPM conference in Ljubljana.

Lash, S. and Urry, J. (1993), *Economies of Signs and Space*, London: Sage.

Layne, V. (1995), 'Popular Music and Cape Town: Contextualising the Social and Economic History of Dance Band and Jazz Culture in the Western Cape circa 1930–1970', unpublished Masters dissertation, University of Cape Town.

Leach, E. (2001), 'Vicars of *Wannabe*: Authenticity and the Spice Girls', *Popular Music*, **20** (2), 143–67.

Levy, C. (1993), 'Rok muzikata v Bulgaria: nachaloto' [Rock music in Bulgaria: the beginning], *Bulgarsko Muzikoznanie*, 3, 9–17

——— (1999), 'Musik in post-diktatorischen Zeiten: Der Gestus des Anspruchsfollen oder einfach Zensur?', in Pieper, W. *et al.* (eds), *Verfemt, verbannt, verboten: Musik und Zensur – weltweit*, Lohrbach: Der Grune Zweig, p. 206.

——— (2000a), 'Interpreting *Chalga*: Old Indigenous Sounds in New Configurations', in Mitchell, T. *et al.* (eds), *Changing Sounds: New Directions and Configurations in Popular Music* (proceedings of the IASPM International Conference 1999, Sydney: UTS, pp. 84–9.

——— (2000b), 'Produtsirane na poslanija v suvremennata "etnicheska" muzika' [Producing meanings in contemporary "ethnic" music], *Bulgarsko Muzikoznanie*, 3, 69–89.

Lewis, G.H. (1992), 'Who do you love ? : The dimensions of musical taste', in Lull, J. (ed), *Popular Music and Communication*, 2nd edn, London: Sage

Leyshon, A., Matless, D. and Revill, G. (eds) (1998), *The Place of Music,* New York and London: The Guildford Press.

Liperi, Felice (1993), 'L'Italia s'è desta. Tecno-splatter e posse in rivolta,' in Canevacci, Massimo *et al.* (eds), *Ragazzi senza tempo: immagini, musica, conflitti delle culture giovanili*, Genoa: Costa & Nolan, 201 (translation from the Italian by the author).

Lipsitz, George (1992–93), 'We know what time it is: youth culture in the 1990s', *Centro: Bulletin of the Centro de Estudios Puertorriqueños*, Winter, 297–307.

———— (1994), *Dangerous Crossroads: Popular Music, Postmodernism and the Poetics of Place*, London: Verso.

Lortat-Jacob, B. (1993), *Sardinian Chronicles*, Chicago: The University of Chicago Press.

Lury, C. (1998), *Prosthetic Culture: Photography, Memory and Identity*, London and New York: Routledge.

McBride, W.L. (2000), 'Cultural Differences and Cosmopolitan Ideals: A Philosophical Analysis', in *Globalization and Cultural Differences* (proceedings of the Fourth International Fulbright Conference, 19–21 May), Sofia: Fulbright, pp. 21–31.

McClary, S. (1991), *Feminine Endings: Music, Gender and Sexuality*, Minnesota: University of Minnesota Press.

Mcleay, C. (1994), 'The Dunedin Sound – New Zealand Rock and Cultural Geography', *Perfect Beat*, **2** (1), 38–50.

———— (1998), 'The Circuit of Popular Music', unpublished Ph.D. thesis, School of Earth Sciences, Macquarie University.

Mach, Z. (1994), 'National Anthems: The Case of Chopin as a National Composer', in Stokes, M. (ed), *Ethnicity, Identity and Music: The Musical Construction of Place*, Oxford: Berg.

Manuel, P (1998), *Popular Musics of the Non-Western World: An Introductory Survey*, New York: Oxford University Press.

———— (1995), 'Music as Symbol, Music as Simulacrum: Postmodern, Pre-Modern, and Modern Aesthetics in Subcultural Popular Music', *Popular Music*, **14** (2), 227–39.

Marcus, G. ([1989, 1993] 1998), *Lipstick Traces: A Secret History of the 20th Century*, Cambridge, MA: Harvard University Press.

Martin, D.-C. (1999), *Coon Carnival: New Year in Cape Town, Past and Present*, Cape Town: David Philip.

Martin, P. (1995), *Sounds and Society: Themes in the Sociology of Music*, Manchester: Manchester University Press.

Massey, D. (1993), 'Power-Geometry and a Progressive Sense of Place', in Bird, J., Curtis, B., Putnam, T., Robertson, G. and Tickner, L. (eds), *Mapping the Futures*, London: Routledge.

———— (2001), *Space, Place and Gender*, 3rd edn, Minneapolis: University of Minnesota Press.

Maurice Jones, K. (1994), *The Story of Rap Music*, Brookfield: The Millbrook Press.

Maylam, P. (1995), 'Explaining the Apartheid City: 20 Years of South African Urban Historiography', *Journal of Southern African Studies*, **21** (1), 19–38.

Medhurst, A. and Munt, S. (1997), *Lesbian and Gay Studies: A Critical Introduction*, London: Cassell.

Meillassoux, C. (1986), *Anthropologie de l'esclavage*, Paris: PUF.

Meintjes, L. (1997), 'Mediating Difference: Producing Mbqanga Music in a South African Studio', unpublished Ph.D. thesis, University of Texas.

Middleton, R. (1993), 'Popular Music Analysis and Musicology: Bridging the Gap', *Popular Music*, **12** (2), 177–90.

—— (1995), 'Authorship, Gender and the Construction of Meaning in the Eurythmics' Hit Recordings', *Cultural Studies*, **9** (3), 464–85.

—— (ed) (2000), *Reading Pop: Approaches to Textual Analysis in Popular Music*, Oxford: Oxford University Press.

Mitchell, T. (1995), 'Questions of Style: Notes on Italian Hip-Hop', *Popular Music*, **14** (3), 333–48.

—— (1996), *Popular Music and Local Identity: Rock, Pop and Rap in Europe and Oceania*, London: Leicester University Press.

—— (ed) (2002), *Global Noise: Rap and Hip hop outside the USA*, Middletown, CT: Wesleyan University Press.

Monson, I. (1999), 'Riffs, Repetition, and Theories of Globalization,' *Ethnomusicology*, **43** (1), 31–65.

Morgan, K. (1999), 'Edward Colston and Bristol', Bristol Branch of the Historical Association, The University, Bristol.

Morris, P. (ed) (1994), *The Bakhtin Reader*, London: Edward Arnold.

Negus, K. (1992), *Producing Pop: Culture and Conflict in the Music Industry*, New York: Routledge.

—— (1996), *Popular Music in Theory*, Hanover, NH and London: Wesleyan University Press.

O'Brien, L. (1995), *She Bop: The Definitive History of Women in Rock, Pop and Soul*, London: Penguin.

Pacini Hernandez, D. (1996), 'Sound Systems, world beat and diasporan identity in Cartagena, Colombia', *Diaspora: A Journal of Transnational Studies*, **5** (3), 429–66.

Pacoda, P. (ed) (1996), *Potere alla parola: Antologia del rap Italiano*, Milan: Feltrinelli.

Paleface (2001), The Pale Ontologist, BMG Finland.

Patterson, O. (1967), *The Sociology of Slavery: An Analysis of the Origins, Development and Structure of Negro Slave Society in Jamaica*, New York: McGibbon and Kee.

Pattison, R. (1987) *The Triumph of Vulgarity: Rock Music in the Mirror of Romanticism*. Oxford: Oxford University Press.

Pérez, L. (1992), 'US–Cuban Relations', paper delivered at the Thomas Center, Gainesville, Florida.

Peycheva, L. (1998), '"Tsigania" I bulgarska identichnost' ['The "Gypsy thing" and Bulgarian identity'], *Bulgarski Folkore*, **1–2**, 132–6.

Plant, S. (1997) *Zeros and Ones*, London: Fourth Estate.

Goffredo Plastino (1996), *Mappa delle voci: rap, raggamuffin e tradizione in Italia*, Rome: Meltemi.

Potter, R. (1995), *Spectacular Vernaculars: Hip-Hop and the Politics of Postmodernism*, New York: State University of New York.

Pratt, R. (1986), 'The Politics of Authenticity in Popular Music: The Case of the Blues', *Popular Music and Society*, **10** (3), 55–78.

Prévos, A. (1998), 'The Rapper's Tongue: Linguistic Inventions and Innovations in French Rap Lyrics', paper given at the American Anthropological Association Meeting, Philadelphia.

————— (2002), 'Post-colonial Popular Music in France: Rap Music and hip hop culture in the 1980s and 1990s', in Mitchell, T. (ed), *Global Noise: Rap and Hip Hop outside the USA*, Middletown, CT: Wesleyan University Press, pp. 39–56.

Regev, M. (1996), '*Musica mizrakhit*, Israeli rock and national culture in Israel', *Popular Music*, **15** (3), 275–84.

Reynolds, S. (1998), *Energy Flash*, London: Macmillan.

Reynolds, S. and Press, J. (1995), *The Sex Revolts: Gender, Rebellion and Rock 'n' Roll*. London: Serpent's Tail.

Rice, T. (1994), *May It Feel Your Soul: Experiencing Bulgarian Music*, Chicago and London: The University of Chicago Press.

Richmond, A.H., Lyon, M., Hale, S., and King, R. (1973), *Migration and Race Relations in an English City: A Study in Bristol*, Oxford: Oxford University Press.

Rideout, E. (2001), 'Mirwais on Music', *Keyboard and Music Player*, **57**.

Ridgers, D. (1994), 'A Wallaby Together', *New Musical Express*, 3 September, 12–13.

Ritzer, G. (2000), *The McDonaldization of Society* (New Century Edn), Thousand Oaks, CA: Pine Forge Press.

Rivera, Raquel (1996), 'Boricuas from the hip hop zone: notes on race and ethnic relations in New York City', *Centro: Bulletin of the Centro de Estudios Puertorriqueños,* Spring, 202–15.

————— (1997a), 'Festival de Rap Cubano: Son de la Moña', *The House in Your Face*, **2** (6), 36–7.

————— (1997b), 'Rap Cubano', *Stress*, December, 11–12.

Robertson, P. (1996), *Guilty Pleasures: Feminist Camp from Mae West to Madonna*, London: I.B.Tauris.

Robertson, R. (1995), 'Glocalization: Time-Space and Homogeneity-Heterogeneity', in Featherstone, M., Lash, S. and Robertson, R. (eds), *Global Modernities*, London: Sage, 25–44.

Rose, T. (1994), *Black Noise: Rap Music and Black Culture in Contemporary America*, Hanover, NH: Wesleyan University Press.

Ross, A. (1999), 'Use of Camp', in Cleto, F. (ed), *Camp: Queer Aesthetics and the Performing Subject: A Reader*, Ann Arbor, MI: The University of Michigan Press.

Russell, J. (1997), 'Rhymes and Real Grooves: Dam Native', *Rip It Up* (NZ), 240, August, 18.

Safran, W. (1991), 'Diasporas in modern societies: myths of homeland and return', *Diaspora*, **1** (1), 83–99.

Savage, J. (1992), *England's Dreaming. Sex Pistols and Punk Rock*, London: Faber and Faber.

Schade-Poulson, M. (1999), *Men and Popular Music in Algeria: The Social Significance of Rai*, Austin: University of Texas Press.

Scheler, Max (1980), *Problems of a Sociology of Knowledge*, London: Routledge and Kegan Paul.

Schumacher, T. (1995) 'This is a Sampling Sport: Digital Sampling, Rap Music and the Law in Cultural Production', *Media, Culture and Society*, **17** (2), 253–73.

Schutz, A. (1970a) *Reflections on the Problem of Relevance*, New Haven and London: Yale University Press.

————— (1970b), *On Phenomenology and Social Relations*, Chicago: University of Chicago Press.

Shank, B. (1994), *Dissonant Identities: The Rock 'n' Roll Scene in Austin, Texas*, London: Wesleyan University Press.

Shepherd, J. (1982), 'A Theoretical Model for the Sociomusical Analysis of Popular Musics', *Popular Music*, 2, 145–77.

Silas, P. (2002), 'The Mad Year of Finnish Hip Hop', *Finnish Music Quarterly*, 3, 46, 49.

Slobin, M. (1993), *Subcultural Sounds: Micromusics of the West*, London: Wesleyan University Press.

Smart, B. (1993), *Postmodernity*, London: Routledge.

Smith, P. (1999), '"Ask Any Girl": Compulsory Heterosexuality and Girl Group Culture', in Dettmar, K. and Richey, W. (eds), *Reading Rock'n'roll: Authenticity, Appropriation, Aesthetics*, New York: Columbia University Press, pp. 93–125.

Sokol, Bret (2000), 'Hip-Hop and Socialism: In Cuba the Revolution will be Rhymed', *Miami New Times*, 20 July, www.miaminewtimes.com/issues/2000-0720/kulchur.html/printable_page.

Sontag, S. ([1964]) 2001) 'Notes on Camp', in *Against Interpretation and other essays*, New York: Picador.

Stokes, M. (1994) (ed), *Ethnicity, Identity and Music: the Musical Construction of Place*, Oxford: Berg.

——— (2000), 'East, West, and Arabesk', in Boru, G. and Hesmondhalgh, D. (eds), *Western Music and Its Others: Difference, Representation, and Appropriation in Music*, Berkeley, Los Angeles and London: University of California Press, pp. 213–33.

Stolzoff, N.C. (2000), *Wake up the town and tell the people. Dancehall culture in Jamaica*, Durham, NC: Duke University Press.

Storey, J. (2001), *Cultural Theory and Popular Culture*, London: Prentice Hall.

Stovall, N. (1999), 'L7 – Slap Happy: Review', *Entertainment Weekly*, [online], 3 September, available from: Electric Library Australasia. http://library_O&dtype=0~0&dinst=O (accessed 15 July 2000).

Straw, W. (1983), 'Characterizing Rock Music Culture: The Case of Heavy Metal', in Frith, S. and Goodwin, A. (eds) (1990), *On Record: Rock, Pop and the Written Word*, London: Routledge.

——— (1991), 'Systems of Articulation, Logics of Change: Communities and Scenes in Popular Music', *Cultural Studies*, **5** (3), 368–88.

Suoni Mudu, *Mica casuale sarà*, Bari, Drum&Bass, 1996.

Sutcliffe, P. (1996), 'Behind Every Great Woman', *Q Magazine*, 119, August, 98–9.

Tagg, P. 'Popular Music Studies versus the "Other"'. www.theblackbook.net/acad/tagg/index/html.

Taha, Kofi (1999), 'Cuba's union rap', *The Source*, August, 52.

Tasker, Y. (1998), *Working Girls: Gender and Sexuality in Popular Cinema*, London: Routledge.

Taylor, P.D.M. (1990) 'Perspectives on history in Rastafari thought', *Studies in Religion*, **19** (2), 191–205.

Tearson, M (1986), 'Kate Bush – Hounds of Love: Review', *Audio* [online], available from Gaffaweb. http://gaffa.org/reaching/rev_hol.html#audio (accessed September 1998).

Thomas, B. (1996), 'Canadian Dry', *The Sun-Herald*, 3 March, p. 22.

Tolsi, N. (2000), 'Brothers and Sisters, Meet da Man', *Sunday Tribune* (Durban, South Africa), 10 September.

Todorova, M. (1997), *Imagining the Balkans*, Oxford: Oxford University Press.

Toop, D. (1991), *Rap Attack 2: African Rap to Global Hip Hop*, New York: Pluto.

Turino, Thomas (1995), Musical nationalism and professionalism in Zimbabwe', paper presented at the 40th annual meeting of the Society for Ethnomusicology, UCLA.

Tyler, S.A. (1997), 'Post-Modern Ethnography', in Gelder, K. and Thornton, S. (eds), *The Subcultures Reader*, London: Routledge.

Wade, P. (1999) 'Working culture: making cultural identities in Cali, Colombia', *Current Anthropology*, **40** (4), 449–62.

Wallis, R. and Malm, K. (1984), *Big Sounds from Small Peoples: The Music Industry in Small Countries*, London: Constable.

Walser, R. (1993), *Running with the Devil: Power, Gender and Madness in Heavy Metal Music*, London: Wesleyan University Press.

———— (1995), 'Rhythm, Rhyme, and Rhetoric in the Music of Public Enemy', *Ethnomusicology*, **39** (2), 193–217.

Warren, R.L. (1972), 'The Nazi Use of Music as an Instrument of Social Control', in Dennisoff, R.S. and Peterson, R.A. (eds), *The Sounds of Social Change*, Chicago: Rand McNally and Company.

Washington Post (1989), 'Kate Bush – The Sensual World: Review' [online], December, available from: Gaffaweb http://gaffa.org/reaching/rev_tsw2.html/#musician (accessed 20 September 1998).

Watkins, L. (2000), 'Tracking the Narrative: The Poetics of Identity in the Rap Music and Hip-hop Culture of Cape Town', unpublished Masters dissertation, Durban, South Africa.

———— (2001), '"Simunye, we are not one": Ethnicity, Difference, and the Hip-hoppers of Cape Town', *Race and Class*, **43** (1), 29–44.

Waxer, Lise (1998), 'Cali Pachanguero: A Social History of Salsa in a Colombian City', Ph.D. dissertation, University of Illinois at Urbana-Champaign.

Webb, P. (2002) 'Negotiating the Music Industry in Bristol', Ph.D. thesis, University of the West of England.

———— (2003), 'Bristol' entry, in *Encylopedia of Popular Music of the World – Locations Volume*, London and New York: Continuum Press.

Welsh-Asante, Kariamu (ed), (1994), *The African Aesthetic: Keeper of the Traditions*, Westport, CT: Praeger.

Wheeler, E.A. (1991). '"Most of My Heroes Don't Appear on No Stamps": The Dialogics of Rap Music', *Black Music Research Journal*, **11** (2), 193–216.

Whiteley, S. (ed) (1997), *Sexing the Groove. Popular Music and Gender*, London: Routledge.

———— (2000), *Women and Popular Music. Sexuality, Identity and Subjectivity*, London: Routledge.

Wild, D. (1995), 'Alanis Morisette', *Rolling Stone*, 516, December, 52–57, 95.

Willett, R. (1989), 'Hot Swing and the Dissolute Life: Style and Popular Music in Europe 1939–49', *Popular Music*, **8** (2), 157–63.

Wolf, N. (1991), *The Beauty Myth: How Images of Beauty are Used Against Women*, New York: William Morrow and Company Inc. www.harmony-central.com/software/Mac/Articles/Orange_Vocoder/

Zanes, J.R.W. (1999), 'Too Much Mead? Under the Influence (of Participant-Observation)', in Dettmar, K.J.H. and Richey, W. (eds), *Reading Rock and Roll: Authenticity, Appropriation, Aesthetics*, New York: Columbia University Press.

Index